Age and Ageing in Contemporary Speculative and Science Fiction

Bloomsbury Studies in the Humanities, Ageing and Later Life

Series Editor
Kate de Medeiros

Bloomsbury Studies in the Humanities, Aging and Later Life responds to the growing need for scholarship focused on age, identity and meaning in late life in a time of unprecedented longevity. For the first time in human history, there are more people in the world aged 60 years and over than under age five. In response, empirical gerontological research on how and why we age has seen exponential growth. An unintended consequence of this growth, however, has been an increasing chasm between the need to study age through generalizable data – the "objective" – and the importance of understanding the human experience of growing old.

Bloomsbury Studies in the Humanities, Aging and Later Life bridges this gap. The series creates a more intellectually diversified gerontology through the perspective of the humanities as well as other interpretive, non – empirical approaches that draw from humanities scholarship. Publishing monographs and edited collections, the series represents the most cutting edge research in the areas of humanistic gerontology and aging.

Series editorial board:
Andrew Achenbaum, University of Houston, USA
Thomas Cole, University of Texas Health Science Center, USA
Chris Gilleard, University College London, UK
Ros Jennings, University of Gloucestershire, UK
Ulla Kriebernegg, University of Graz, Austria
Roberta Maierhofer, University of Graz, Austria
Wendy Martin, Brunel University, London, UK

Titles in the series

Ageing Masculinities, Alzheimer's and Dementia Narratives, edited by Heike Hartung, Rüdiger Kunow and Matthew Sweney
Age and Ageing in Contemporary Speculative and Science Fiction, edited by Sarah Falcus and Maricel Oró-Piqueras

Forthcoming titles
Ageing and Embodied Time in Modern Literature and Thought, by Elizabeth Barry

Age and Ageing in Contemporary Speculative and Science Fiction

Edited by
Sarah Falcus and Maricel Oró-Piqueras

BLOOMSBURY ACADEMIC
LONDON • NEW YORK • OXFORD • NEW DELHI • SYDNEY

BLOOMSBURY ACADEMIC
Bloomsbury Publishing Plc
50 Bedford Square, London, WC1B 3DP, UK
1385 Broadway, New York, NY 10018, USA
29 Earlsfort Terrace, Dublin 2, Ireland

BLOOMSBURY, BLOOMSBURY ACADEMIC and the Diana logo are trademarks of Bloomsbury Publishing Plc

First published in Great Britain 2023
Paperback edition published 2024

Copyright © Sarah Falcus, Maricel Oró-Piqueras and contributors, 2023, 2024

The editors and contributors have asserted their right under the Copyright, Designs and Patents Act, 1988, to be identified as Authors of this work.

For legal purposes the Acknowledgements on p. xii constitutes an extension of this copyright page.

Series design by Rebecca Heselton
Cover image: Abstract Mixed-Light Pattern / Shadowmeld Photography/ Wikimedia Creative Commons

All rights reserved. No part of this publication may be reproduced or transmitted in any form or by any means, electronic or mechanical, including photocopying, recording, or any information storage or retrieval system, without prior permission in writing from the publishers.

Bloomsbury Publishing Plc does not have any control over, or responsibility for, any third-party websites referred to in this book. All internet addresses given in this book were correct at the time of going to press. The author and publisher regret any inconvenience caused if addresses have changed or sites have ceased to exist but can accept no responsibility for any such changes.

A catalogue record for this book is available from the British Library.

A catalog record for this book is available from the Library of Congress.

ISBN: HB: 978-1-3502-3066-8
PB: 978-1-3502-3070-5
ePDF: 978-1-3502-3067-5
eBook: 978-1-3502-3068-2

Series: Bloomsbury Studies in the Humanities, Ageing and Later Life

Typeset by Newgen KnowledgeWorks Pvt. Ltd., Chennai, India

To find out more about our authors and books, visit www.bloomsbury.com and sign up for our newsletters.

Contents

List of figures	vii
List of contributors	viii
Acknowledgements	xii

Introduction: Intersections between ageing studies and speculative and science fiction   1
Maricel Oró-Piqueras and Sarah Falcus

1. Remaking ourselves: Age, death and techno-bodies in the fiction of transhumanist immortality   9
Teresa Botelho

2. Ageing and youthing: Portrayals of progression and regression in science fiction film and TV   29
Peter Goggin and Ulla Kriebernegg

3. Ageing and generation in recent narratives of longevity   49
Sarah Falcus and Maricel Oró-Piqueras

4. Biological slaves: Discardable bodies in dystopia   71
Maria Aline Ferreira

5. Contemporary perspectives on ageing in European dystopian literature   93
Aleksandra Pogońska-Baranowska

6. Ageing and age-based extinction in twentieth- and early twenty-first-century speculative and science fiction: William F. Nolan and George Clayton Johnson's *Logan's Run* (1967) and Christopher Buckley's *Boomsday* (2007)   115
Stella Achilleos

7. 'Whatever comes after human progress': Transhumanism, antihumanism and the absence of queer ecology in Lidia Yuknavitch's *The Book of Joan*   135
Sean Seeger

8. A spectral future: Dementia and the nonhuman in *Marjorie Prime*   155
Michael S. D. Hooper

9   A cure for ageing: Digital cloning as utopian end-of-life care in the
    'San Junipero' episode of *Black Mirror*   173
    Eszter Ureczky
10 Ageing, anachronism and perception in dystopian narrative: The
    case of Margaret Atwood's 'Torching the Dusties'   195
    Susan Watkins
11 Playing with possibilities: Ursula Le Guin and speculations on the
    human condition: An anocritical approach   213
    Roberta Maierhofer

Index   227

Figures

10.1	Wilma using binoculars, 3.25 min	204
10.2	Frank hiding in the laundry hamper, 10.16 min	205
10.3	Close-up shot of Frank's eye, 00.28 min	206
10.4	Butler figure looking back at Frank, 5.20 min	207
10.5	Protesters in baby masks, 10.24 min	208

Contributors

Stella Achilleos is Associate Professor of Early Modern Studies at the Department of English Studies, University of Cyprus. She has published widely within her areas of expertise, which include the following: the intersections between early modern literature and political philosophy; ageing, old age and biopolitics; early modern utopian thought; and the discourses and practices of friendship in early modern literature and culture. She is co-editor of *Reading Texts on Sovereignty: Textual Moments in the History of Political Thought* (2021), and her current research projects include a book-length study on violence and utopia in the early modern period.

Teresa Botelho is Associate Professor of American Studies at the Faculty of Social Sciences and Humanities, NOVA University of Lisbon, Portugal. She is a member of the research group *Mapping Utopianisms* (CETAPS) and convener of the research strand *American Intersections* at CETAPS. She is also a member of the *Challenging Precarity Global Network* and of *Rihua: Red Iberoamericana de Humanidades Ambientale*. She has published extensively on African American and Asian American culture and literature, theatre and drama, science fiction and dystopian literature. Her current interests include the collaboration between science and literature, technological utopias/dystopias and the transhumanist and post-human philosophies, refugee literature and climate change fiction.

Sarah Falcus is Reader in Contemporary Literature at the University of Huddersfield, UK. She is the co-editor (with Katsura Sako) of *Contemporary Narratives of Ageing, Illness, Care* (2022) and the co-author (with Katsura Sako) of *Contemporary Narratives of Dementia: Ethics, Ageing, Politics* (2019). She co-edited a special issue of *International Research in Children's Literature* (with Alison Waller, 2021). She is the primary collaborator on the project Ageing and Illness in British and Japanese Children's Picturebooks, 1950–2000: Historical and Cross-Cultural Perspectives, funded by the Japan Society for the Promotion of Science. She is the co-director of the Dementia and Cultural Narrative Network.

Maria Aline Ferreira is Associate Professor at the University of Aveiro in Portugal, where she teaches English literature and cultural studies. She holds a PhD from the University of London (Birkbeck College) on D. H. Lawrence and E. M. Forster. Her main interests comprise the intersections between literature and science, bioethics, ageing studies, feminist utopias and women's studies. Her publications include *I Am the Other: Literary Negotiations of Human Cloning* (2005) as well as numerous articles in international journals. She is now finishing a book provisionally entitled *The Sexual Politics of the Artificial Womb: Fictional and Visual Representations*.

Peter Goggin is Associate Professor in Rhetoric (English), Senior Global Futures Scholar with the Julie Ann Wrigley Global Futures Lab and affiliate faculty with the School for the Future of Innovation in Society at Arizona State University, United States. His books and articles include research in such areas as literacy studies, academic serendipity, environmental rhetoric, feral animals, mermaids, science fiction and oceanic islands. In addition to Arizona, Peter has taught graduate and undergraduate courses and seminars in Romania, China, Bermuda, Boston, Pittsburgh and Austria.

Michael S. D. Hooper is an independent scholar and private tutor. He is the author of *Sexual Politics in the Work of Tennessee Williams: Desire over Protest* (2012) and several essays in the *Tennessee Williams Annual Review*, including 'Painting His Nudes: Tennessee Williams's Homoerotic Art' (2019). He has edited the Methuen Student Edition of *A Streetcar Named Desire* (2009), has written the Williams entry for the online *Routledge Encyclopedia of Modernism* (2016) and has contributed to *A Student Handbook to the Plays of Tennessee Williams*, edited by Katherine Weiss (2014). His essay 'Pedro Almodóvar's Homage to Tennessee Williams' appears in *Tennessee Williams in Europe: Intercultural Encounters, Transatlantic Exchanges*, edited by John S. Bak (2014).

Ulla Kriebernegg is director of the Center for Interdisciplinary Research on Aging and Care and Associate Professor of American Studies at the University of Graz, Austria. In her research and teaching, she focuses on North American literary and cultural studies, ageing and care studies, and health humanities. Her latest book, *Putting Age in Its Place* (forthcoming), deals with the spatiality of care in cultural representations of care homes. Ulla is chair of the Age and Care Research Group Graz and vice president of the European Network of Aging Studies (ENAS). She is Associate Editor of *The Gerontologist* and member of the Gerontological Society of America's Humanities, Arts and Cultural Gerontology Panel. Since 2020, she has been a Fellow of the Trent Centre for Aging and Society, Canada. Ulla has taught internationally (the United States, Trinidad and Tobago, Cuba and Uruguay) and has won several teaching and research awards.

Roberta Maierhofer is Professor of American Studies and Director of the Center for Inter-American Studies at the University of Graz, Austria. For three decades now, she has been serving the gerontological community as a present and past member of editorial boards, committees and forums, such as the *Journal of Aging, Humanities, and the Arts*; Aging and Ageism Caucus of the National Women's Studies Association; the Modern Language Association; Humanities and Arts Committee of the Gerontological Society of America; as well as dissertation boards and advisory councils. As a founding member of ENAS, she also supported the establishment of the North American Network in Aging Studies. In her publication, *Salty Old Women: Gender and Aging in American Culture* (2003), she developed a theoretical approach to gender and aging (Anocriticism).

Maricel Oró-Piqueras is Associate Professor at the Department of English and Linguistics at the Universitat de Lleida, Spain. She is also been a member of the research group Dedal-Lit since it started working on the representation of fictional images of ageing and old age in 2002. Her research interests include ageing and old age in contemporary fiction as well as representations of gender and ageing in film and TV series. She is co-editor of *Serializing Age: Ageing and Old Age in TV Series* (with Anita Wohlmann, 2016) and *Re-Discovering Age(ing): Narratives of Mentorship* (with Núria Casado-Gual and Emma Domínguez-Rué, 2019). She has also published her research in journals such as the *Journal of Aging Studies* and *The Gerontologist*.

Aleksandra Pogońska-Baranowska holds a master's degree in the field of foreign languages and cultural studies with a major in Italian, Spanish and English studies from the Faculty of Modern Languages, University of Warsaw, Poland. Her current research interests are focused on the evolution of the dystopian genre in the twentieth and the twenty-first centuries. She is the author of *Immaginare il futuro: le narrazioni distopiche nell'Italia del terzo millennio* (2019) and 'La vecchiaia è una tragedia? Soluzioni distopiche' in the volume *Il futuro della fine: rappresentazioni dell'Apocalisse nella letteratura italiana dal Novecento a oggi* (2020) and co-author of 'Al passo col tempo: Lidia Ravera dal 1968 al 2018' in the volume *Controculture all'italiana* (2019). She is also a translator and has translated numerous works in the field of literary studies.

Sean Seeger is Senior Lecturer in Literature at the Department of Literature, Film and Theatre Studies at the University of Essex, UK. His research and teaching focus on modernism, utopian studies, queer studies and speculative fiction. His other scholarly interests include modern cultural and intellectual history, literature and social theory, and cultural studies. In addition to numerous essays and articles, Sean is the author of *Nonlinear Temporality in Joyce and Walcott* (2017), the first dedicated comparative study of James Joyce and Derek Walcott. Since 2019, he has been collaborating with Dr Daniel Davison-Vecchione, a sociologist at the University of Cambridge, on a series of articles on speculative fiction and social theory. They are currently working on a book-length study of the topic.

Eszter Ureczky is Senior Lecturer at the Department of British Studies of the Institute of English and American Studies, University of Debrecen, Hungary. Her main teaching and research areas include contemporary Anglophone and Eastern European fiction and film. She has a theoretical background in biopolitics, the medical humanities, disability studies and ageing studies. She defended her doctoral dissertation entitled 'Cultures of Pollution: Epidemic Disease and the Biopolitics of Contagion in Contemporary Anglophone Fiction' in 2017 and she organized an online conference entitled Crises of Care: Pandemic Culture, Biopolitics and the Medical Humanities in 2021.

Susan Watkins is Professor of Women's Writing in the School of Cultural Studies at Leeds Beckett University, UK. She is the author of *Twentieth-Century Women Novelists: Feminist Theory into Practice* (2001), *Doris Lessing* (2010) and *Contemporary Women's Post-Apocalyptic Fiction* (2020). She is co-editor of *Scandalous Fictions: The Twentieth-Century Novel in the Public Sphere* (2006), *Doris Lessing: Border Crossings* (2009) and *The History of British Women's Writing, 1945–1975* (2017), and she has published articles on women's writing in the *Journal of Southern African Studies*, *Frontiers: A Journal of Women Studies*, *LIT: Literature Interpretation Theory* and *Feminist Review*. She co-edited the *Journal of Commonwealth Literature* from 2010 to 2015 and was Chair of the Contemporary Women's Writing Association from 2010 to 2014.

Acknowledgements

The editors would like to thank all of the contributors for their commitment to this project in the face of the disruption caused by Covid-19.

The third-party copyrighted material displayed in the pages of this book is done so on the basis of 'fair dealing for the purposes of criticism and review' or 'fair use for the purposes of teaching, criticism, scholarship or research' only in accordance with international copyright laws and is not intended to infringe upon the ownership rights of the original owners.

Introduction: Intersections between ageing studies and speculative and science fiction

Maricel Oró-Piqueras and Sarah Falcus

Speculative and science fiction, as genres intimately concerned with time, have always addressed questions of longevity/immortality, the impaired and rejuvenated (posthuman) body, the life course, demographic control and, more broadly, human and planetary futurity. In the process, they have alternately troubled and reassured their readers. They may be genres interested in the creation of future and other worlds, but as critics continually stress, they are genres that revise the past and address present concerns.

Teresa Mangum – in her analysis of what she calls 'rejuvenation narratives', those concerned with the prolongation of youth (2002: 70) – argues that these texts are engaged with 'larger concerns about time' (2002: 80). We could extend that argument to all science fiction (SF) and speculative modes: time, temporal ordering and the relationship between past, present and future are, and have always been, at the heart of these genres. It is not then a great step to suggest that central to science fiction and speculative writing is ageing itself, understood as the experience of a human life in time. Today, with narratives of crisis dominating media and often political responses to an ageing population in many countries of the world, SF and speculative fiction continue to engage with large-scale demographic change and its implications for social, economic and political organization. At the same time, as genres that push at the limits of the human and our relationships with others (understood very widely), they offer ways of thinking about and representing both the philosophical and experiential aspects of ageing and generation. SF and speculative modes, then, explore ageing at the level of the individual, the social and the species. In this, they offer vital and sometimes prescient explorations of the combination of fear and desire emerging from our own 'posthuman ageing' (see Andrews and Duff 2019).

In this volume, we bring SF and speculative fiction together with ageing studies. Scholarship in the latter field has proliferated in the past twenty to thirty years. As Leni Marshall states, just as women's and gender studies have worked to 'fill the gaps in awareness of how cultural constructions of gendered bodies affect individuals' and groups' experiences' (2015: 8), ageing studies intends to 'fill the gaps' in the knowledge of the experience of ageing, across the life course. Margaret Morganroth Gullette's argument that we are 'aged by culture' (2004) and that we live in a still-ageist society has been taken up by literary, film and theatre scholars, who have found in many representations of ageing and old age the dominance of narratives of either 'decline' or 'successful ageing' (Katz and Marshall 2004), the latter a discourse that locates the responsibility for a supposedly attainable 'agelessness' with the individual. Recognizing the importance of cultural narratives in the lived experience of ageing itself, ageing studies, more fundamentally, asserts the intimate relationship between narrative and progression along the life course. As Gullette states, 'Whatever happens in the body, and even if nothing happens in the body, ageing is a narrative' (2011: 5).

Despite the tendency for those working in ageing studies to prioritize realist narratives, the seemingly obvious connection between age, ageing and science and speculative fiction has drawn the attention of some scholars (e.g. Mangum 2002; Domingo 2008; Port 2012; Schotland 2013; Kriebernegg 2013, 2018; Brand 2016; Hartung 2017; Snaith 2017; Adiseshiah 2019; Falcus 2020). Addressing topics such as rejuvenation and immortality, generation, anti-ageing, posthuman ageing and the 'demodystopia', these studies have begun to establish the key concerns shared by ageing studies and SF/speculative studies and the value of adopting and aligning approaches from both fields in thinking about both human and non-human ageing. Ageing studies shares with SF and speculative scholars not only a central focus on time (at an individual, social and species level), identity and intersectionality (including the intersections of race, gender, age and sexuality) but also an interest in 'popular' forms and narratives, especially TV and film, with both fields paying attention not only to representation and genre but also to the relationship between popular narratives and their readers/viewers.

Given our liberal use of the terms so far, this is an apposite moment at which to speak to the thorny issue of genre and definition. Defining science, and to some extent speculative, fiction has been a long-standing goal, even obsession, of critics in the field. And these attempts to secure definition, or alternatively, to insist that it cannot be done, bring to the fore debates about – amongst other things – populism and literary value, subgenre, diversity, historicity and formalism. Though the term *science fiction* came into use only in the 1920s, definitions of SF seek to trace its history, tending to align it with the popular American tradition or establish it within a more 'literary' heritage (see Bould and Vint 2011; Luckhurst 2005; Roberts 2006). Others, notably Darko Suvin (1979), take a more formalist position, and his influential, if debated, notion of 'cognitive estrangement' echoes through some of the chapters in this volume. But science fiction is also, as P. L. Thomas (2006: 17) recognizes, something identified by readers themselves and intrinsically tied up with the close relationship between SF, readers and fandom. It is also, related to this, a convenient marketing category and inextricably linked to populism and the more pejorative use of the label 'genre fiction', undoubtedly a reason for the persistence of the trend for authors to deny that their works should be classified as SF (see the Atwood/Le Guin controversy [Thomas 2006: 7] and also Ian McEwan's recent comments on his novel *Machines Like Us* [see Księżopolska 2020]).

Further complicating any attempts to define SF is its close relationship with related and overlapping genres, such as fantasy, speculative writing, dystopia and utopia. Debates about the borderlines between these terms often fall foul of complex negotiations of literary value and literary history. Mark Bould and Sherryl Vint argue that 'there is no such thing as a "neutral" or "objective" definition of the genre because the very features of what is named as SF emerge in the process of pointing and naming' (2011: 5). Genre is central to this volume and to many of the chapters within it, but we recognize that genres are not stable categories; instead, 'genres create effects of reality and truth, authority and plausibility, which are central to the different ways the world is understood' (Frow 2006: 16). Texts themselves, then, 'do not "belong" to genres but are, rather, uses of them; they refer not to "a" genre but to a field or economy of genres, and their complexity derives from the complexity of that relation'. This then has implications for how we approach genre in this book since 'uses of texts ("readings") similarly refer, and similarly construct a position in relation to that economy' (Frow 2006: 16–17). The need both to situate texts in relation to genre and yet also to recognize the 'complexity of that relation' is made abundantly clear in the juxtaposition and combination of genre and subgenre in many of the chapters in this collection, from the 'dystopian science fiction' of Seeger's chapter to the 'speculative dystopian' of Falcus and Oró-Piqueras. The chapters in this collection both use genre categories and locate texts within these, whilst at the same time the collection as a whole adopts Bould and Vint's recognition that SF (and by extension speculative fiction) is a 'fuzzily-edged, multidimensional and constantly shifting discursive object' (2011: 5).

This collection builds on the emerging work at the meeting of ageing studies and SF, opening up the conversation around other-world fiction and what it is to live a human life in time. Bringing together scholars from both fields, the collection includes analyses of science and speculative novels, short stories and essays. Given the importance of the visual medium to SF/speculative writing, the volume includes chapters on visual texts, including film, TV and a play in performance. The contributions range from chapters that establish genre-based trends in the representation of age and ageing to very focused studies of particular texts and concerns. Despite the variation in approach and theoretical engagement within the collection, as a whole the contributors consistently probe the relationship between speculative fiction/SF and our understanding of what it is to be a human in time: the time of our own lives and the times of both the past and the future. In other words, as the different chapters in the volume will consistently argue, SF and speculative fiction offer fertile ground to explore conceptions related to age in increasingly ageing societies.

The collection analyses texts from Europe, North America and South Asia. The emphasis does tend to fall on Western, primarily anglophone, texts and the anglophone tradition of SF criticism. Though this is undoubtedly a reflection of the cultural and national locations and scholarship of the contributors, we recognize that this is a particular narrative of and approach to science and speculative fiction, one that does not account for the increasingly globally visible speculative and science fiction traditions in other parts of the world, notably South Asia and China (see Song and Huters 2018; Isaacson 2017; Suparno 2020). This collection does not aim to be comprehensive, and extending the work of this volume to contextually situated analyses of SF and speculative traditions from other parts of the globe will be key to future scholarship in the area.

The chapters that follow develop a number of key and overlapping concerns at the intersection of ageing and SF/speculative fiction: genre and progress/futurity, longevity and immortality, demographic change, biopower and 'discardable bodies', care and generationalism. Time and temporality are persistent concerns in the volume, expressed through explorations of genre, futurity, anachronism and generation. The centrality of rejuvenation, immortality and post/transhumanism in science and speculative fiction (see Clark 1995) is evidenced by the interest in these topics within the volume as a whole. The collection moves very broadly from chapters that address a range of texts to those that offer detailed case studies of a specific text or author.

The time of the human life course dominates the first part of the collection, where there is a persistent emphasis upon the significance of narratives of longevity. The collection begins with Teresa Botelho's analysis of rejuvenation in fictional representations of posthuman and transhuman immortality, considering how they both celebrate and critique technological utopianism. Peter Goggin and Ulla Kriebernegg then pursue this exploration of the plasticity of the life course and ageing in SF and speculative texts through a wide-ranging discussion of age 'progression and regression' in popular, contemporary anglophone science and speculative TV and film. Despite the potential TV and film offer for the reimagining of both age and gender, Goggin and Kriebernegg conclude that popular visual science fiction narratives do little to challenge dominant discourses of both. Analysing both film and fiction, in our chapter on recent anglophone narratives of longevity, we turn specifically to the relationship between ageing and long life but with a specific focus on generationalism. These narratives, making clear the centrality of age in speculative and dystopian world building, suggest that we lack alternatives to the generational imaginary, even in genres based upon imagining worlds that function according to logic different from our own.

'Discardable bodies' and inequalities are then the focus of Aline Ferreira's analysis of the machinations of biopower in fantasies of rejuvenation, employing the notion of 'precarious lives' from the work of Judith Butler, Roberto Esposito and Giorgio Agamben. Analysing Padmanabhan's *Harvest* (1997), Ishiguro's *Never Let Me Go* (2005) and Holmqvist's *The Unit* (2006), Ferreira concludes that these texts offer salutary warnings about the threats of the contemporary global bioeconomy. Similarly concerned with whose lives – and bodies – come to matter, the chapters by Aleksandra Pogońska-Baranowska and Stella Achilleos explore a long-standing trope of speculative and science fiction: geronticide. Pogońska-Baranowska turns to the specifically European context to consider recent 'demodystopias', novels foregrounding demographic change and the perceived threats to the social order posed by ageing populations. Pogońska-Baranowska examines contemporary representations of the long-standing dystopian trope of geronticide to situate the persistence of this idea within the context of contemporary cultural fears and anxieties about ageing. Comparing Clayton Johnson's *Logan's Run* (1967) and Christopher Buckley's *Boomsday* (2007), Achilleos then considers the changing social contexts which determine the relative value and precarity of old age in novels about geronticide.

The volume then offers a series of in-depth 'case studies' of specific texts, raising new concerns as well as developing issues explored in the earlier chapters (such as rejuvenation and demographic change). Picking up on questions about time, temporal orders and futurity already raised in the volume, Sean Seeger's discussion of Lidia Yuknavitch's *The Book of Joan* reads it as a rejection of the doctrine of progress that is often, in science fiction, expressed via the metaphor of ageing. He turns ultimately to the possibilities of queer ecology as a way out of the impasse of nature and culture.

In the first of three chapters concerned with a central issue within ageing studies – that of care – Michael Hooper focuses on dementia, ethical care and posthuman ontology in Jordan Harrison's play *Marjorie Prime*. Reading the text in performance as a 'haunted site' that offers a potentially rich location for the staging of concerns central to ageing studies, he nevertheless concludes that the play ultimately evades the ethical issues it seems to foreground. In Chapter 9, Ezster Ureczky takes the volume back to biopolitics and digital rejuvenation, but she specifically links this to the discourse of the 'crisis of care' in ageing societies through an analysis of the 'San Junipero' episode of Netflix's *Black Mirror* series, noting the potentially subversive nature of the alignment of 'passing through' and 'coming out'. Moving back to fiction, Susan Watkins focuses on a short story about elder care and generational conflict, 'Torching the Dusties'. Explicitly considering the possibilities of the dystopian mode, Watkins argues that this subgenre can offer a form of 'creative and anachronistic re-perception'.

The final chapter of the collection acts a kind of coda, returning – in a fittingly science fictional manner – to a writer whose work is so central to the challenges SF offers to our ways of imagining what it means to be human: Ursula K. Le Guin. Adopting a self-consciously speculative approach that circles around the key idea of 'narrative presence', Roberta Maierhofer explores the intersection of age and gender in two influential essays by Le Guin, 'Introducing Myself' and 'The Space Crone'.

As the different chapters within the volume show, analysing speculative and SF narratives through the prism of age and ageing studies, and bringing insights from SF scholarship to bear on our understanding of the human life course, provide new perspectives both on the concerns within the texts and on the broader social questions they raise. These range from the role of technology and AI in care to the ethical and planetary consequences of extended longevity. With this volume, we extend ageing studies to genres that may be seen as far from reality but which actually offer critical reflections on our deepest concerns about what it means to live together across time on a planet with shrinking resources.

References

Adiseshiah, S. (2019), 'The Utopian Potential of Aging and Longevity in Bernard Shaw's *Back to Methuselah* (1921)', *Age, Culture, Humanities: An Interdisciplinary Journal*, 4. Available online: https://ageculturehumanities.org/WP/the-utopian-potential-of-ageing-and-longevity-in-bernard-shaws-back-to-methuselah-1921/ (accessed 21 November 2021).

Andrews, G., and C. Duff (2019), 'Understanding the Vital Emergence and Expression of Aging: How Matter Comes to Matter in Gerontology's Posthumanist Turn', *Journal of Aging Studies*, 49: 46–55.

Bould, M., and S. Vint (2011), *The Routledge Concise History of Science Fiction*, London: Routledge.

Brand, M. R. (2016), 'Growing Old in Utopia: From Age to Otherness in American Literary Utopias', *Age, Culture and Humanities*, 3. Available online: https://ageculturehumanities.org/WP/growing-old-in-utopia-from-age-to-otherness-in-american-literary-utopias/ (accessed 20 November 2021).

Clark, S. R. L. (1995), *How to Live Forever: Science Fiction and Philosophy*, London: Routledge.

Domingo, A. (2008), '"Demodystopias": Prospects of Demographic Hell', *Population and Development Review*, 34(4): 725–45.

Falcus, S. (2020), 'Age and Anachronism in Contemporary Dystopian Fiction', in E. Barry with M. V. Skagen (eds), *Literature and Ageing*, vol. 73, 65–86, Essays and Studies, Cambridge: D. S. Brewer.

Frow, J. (2006), *Genre*, London: Routledge.

Gullette, M. M. (2004), *Aged by Culture*, Chicago: University of Chicago Press.

Gullette, M. M. (2011), *Agewise. Fighting the New Ageism in America*, Chicago: University of Chicago Press.

Hartung, H. (2017), 'Fantastic Reversals of Time: Representations of Ageing in the Fantastic Mode', *De Gruyter*, 3(2): 336–59.

Isaacson, N. (2017), *Celestial Empire: The Emergence of Chinese Science Fiction*, Middletown: Wesleyan University Press.

Katz, S., and B. Marshall (2004), 'Is the Functional "Normal"? Aging, Sexuality and the Bio-marking of Successful Living', *History of the Human Sciences*, 17(1): 53–75.

Kriebernegg, U. (2013), 'Ending Aging in the Shteyngart of Eden: Biogerontological Discourse in a *Super Sad True Love Story*', *Journal of Aging Studies*, 27: 61–70.

Kriebernegg, U. (2018), 'Time to Go. Fast Not Slow: Geronticide and the Burden Narrative of Old Age in Margaret Atwood's "Torching the Dusties"', *European Journal of English Studies*, 22(1): 46–58.

Księżopolska, I. (2020), 'Can Androids Write Science Fiction? Ian McEwan's *Machines Like Me*', *Critique: Studies in Contemporary Fiction*, doi:10.1080/00111619.2020.1851165 (accessed 4 February 2022).

Luckhurst, R. (2005), *Science Fiction*, Cambridge: Polity.

Mangum, T. (2002), 'Longing for Life Extension: Science Fiction and Late Life', *Journal of Aging and Identity*, 7(2): 69–80.

Marshall, L. (2015), *Age Becomes Us: Bodies and Gender in Time*, New York: SUNY Press.

Port, C. (2012), 'No Future? Aging, Temporality, History, and Reverse Chronologies', *Occasion: Interdisciplinary Studies in the Humanities*, 4. Available online: arcade.stanford.edu/sites/default/files/article_pdfs/OCCASION_v04_Port_053112_0.pdf (accessed 25 November 2021).

Roberts, A. (2006), *The History of Science Fiction*, London: Palgrave.

Schotland, S. D. (2013), 'Forced Execution of the Elderly: Old Law, Dystopia, and the Utilitarian Argument', *Humanities*, 2: 160–75.

Snaith, H. (2017), 'Dystopia, Gerontology, and the Writing of Margaret Atwood', *Feminist Review*, 116: 118–32.

Song, M., and T. Huters (2018), *The Reincarnated Giant: An Anthology of Twenty-First-Century Chinese Science Fiction*, New York: Columbia University Press.

Suparno, B. (2020), *Indian Science Fiction: Patterns, History and Hybridity*, Cardiff: University of Wales Press.

Suvin D. (1979), *Metamorphoses of Science Fiction: On the Poetics and History of a Literary Genre*, Ralahine Utopian Studies, Oxford: Peter Lang.

Thomas, P. L., ed. (2006), *Science Fiction and Speculative Fiction: Challenging Genres*, Rotterdam: Sense Publishers.

1

Remaking ourselves: Age, death and techno-bodies in the fiction of transhumanist immortality

Teresa Botelho

'Can it be? To live for ever?': Contemplating the death of death

In the introduction to *Death and the Serpent*, a pioneering study of representations of immortality in science fiction and fantasy, Donald M. Hassler links the engagement of the genres with the 'imperfections of the human condition' (1985: 3) represented by physical decay and death, with the haunting presence of these unavoidable futures in the experience of being human and with the hope for a reversal of their inevitability. Either by investing in exercises of extrapolation from the consensus scientific knowledge at the time of writing in the case of hard science fiction or by speculating freely on myth-based scenarios, the 'topic of change of the basic condition of mortality seems to permeate both the subject matter of the genre' and its 'tonal daring' (Hassler 1985: 4).

If one reads science fiction, in particular, as shaped by the problematization of human possibilities expressed in terms of thought-experiments that test the boundaries of probability and plausibility, it is not surprising that these limitations of the human should be attractive to the construction of imaginary projections of alternative life cycles in alternative tomorrows. The extent of this imaginative impulse to construct fictional scenarios that propose the possibility of control over the ultimate evidence of human vulnerability and precarity is attested by the significant number of works written after the first edition of Mary Shelley's *Frankenstein* (1818) listed by the editors of *Death and the Serpent* (Yoke and Hassler 1985),[1] a corpus that would probably more than double if works written in the past four decades were included in an updated version of this list.

This need and capacity to imagine a radical remaking of ourselves and our biological destiny cannot be detached from two cultural constructions of the experience of living. The first is characterized by philosopher Martha Nussbaum as 'projective disgust' towards the manifestation of age in the human body, caused by the knowledge that 'aging is the only disgust-stigma category into which every one of us will inevitably move, if we live long enough' (2017: 112) and, as Margaret Morganroth Gullette argues, by a 'master narrative of decline' that has not questioned 'the sleepy illusion that age and aging are ahistorical, prediscursive – natural' (1997: 202). Such anguish towards the ageing body has fed narratives of rejuvenation that date back to ancient myths such as Medea's rejuvenation of Aeson in Ovid's *Metamorphoses*.[2]

The second is summarized by what Stephen Cave has described as the 'mortality paradox', 'the tension between knowing of an inevitable future non-existence, while being unable to imagine it' (2012: 21), a condition which is unique to the human experience. Only humans, Cave argues, who share the 'staying alive' impulse in its basic form with other living things, have their consciousness modulated by three other capacities that set our species apart. Besides the knowledge that we must die some day, our sense of living is shaped by our awareness of ourselves as distinct individuals, carriers of memories, experiences and desires; by our idea of the future, which allows us 'to premeditate and vary our plans'; and by the capacity to 'imagine different scenarios, playing with possibilities and generalizing from what we have seen, enabling us to learn, reason and extrapolate' (Cave 2012: 22).

Zygmunt Bauman characterizes 'the offensive thought of death' (1992: 12) as 'a state without thought; one we cannot visualize and even construe conceptually' because we can never consciously experience it as anything but witnesses (1992: 14), 'signifying an interruption of the processes of making ourselves, summarized by Eugene Ionesco's King Berenger's desperate question "Why was I born if it wasn't forever?"' (Botelho 2019: 431). It is no wonder that this puzzle should have engaged the literary imagination, especially when, seemingly free from an attachment to the real and the now, fiction proposes exercises of speculative possibilities.

An analysis of the modes of addressing the possibility of life extension, rejuvenation and immortality in science fiction and speculative narratives corroborates in general terms the conclusions reached by S. Jay Olshansky and Bruce A. Carnes (2002) in their study of ageing, death and the quest for immortality, where they argue that two opposing patterns that precede the influence of modern science and philosophy can be detected. These may be summarized by two descriptors – fatalistic and prolongevitist – though most recent examples of transhumanist and post-singularity discourses may be seen to challenge this simplified dichotomy, as this chapter will discuss. A fatalistic approach, articulated in the early history of religion, science and philosophy, is characterized by 'an acceptance of aging and death as an inevitable and perhaps even desirable end to earthly life', from which idealized 'notions of what life could and perhaps should be like' can be drawn (Olshansky and Carnes 2002: 11). They trace this mode back to the philosophy of Epicurus in the fourth century BC, which proposed that 'a tranquil life could be attained by removing the fear of death' and embraced the premise that it was 'futile to live for ever because life offered only a limited number of gratifications' (2002: 14), and to Stoic philosophy, which suggested that 'the length of life was of no importance'[3] and that death itself 'should be embraced because it was natural and necessary for the proper function of the universe' (2002: 15). Early medical thought that still influences modern thinking about ageing and death followed a similar track, from the Hippocratic physicians to the AD first-century Persian philosopher and medical researcher Avicenna, who defended that maintaining health did not imply 'averting death' or 'securing the longest longevity possible', but 'guiding the body to its natural span of life' (Gruner 1930: 361).

Against this acceptance of the natural limits to life embraced by the fatalists, early prolongevitists asserted, according to Olshansky and Carnes, that age and death could be 'amenable to modification' (2002: 35) and that longevity could be extended through human intervention, a school of thought first shaped by third-century BC Taoist philosophy and alchemist practices until it found its best known expressions in the work of Francis Bacon on the possibility of age reversal and the restoration of long lifespans that were believed to have been common centuries before.[4]

These two positions also highlight the interconnection between the ageing body and the death it seems to herald since projections of a fulfilled existence without death also tend to require young, functional bodies. One example is the Struldbrugs of Luggnagg in *Gulliver's Travels*, who are condemned to immortality from birth[5] and who after forty, the normal lifespan in the country, 'have not only the follies and infirmities of other old men but many more which arose from the dreadful prospect of never dying' and are 'uncapable of friendship and dead to all natural affection' (Swift 1988: 252). At ninety, they lose all their teeth, hair and capacity to taste and are subject to all the diseases they cannot cure, and after they reach two hundred, they can no longer remember enough to hold a conversation (Swift 1988: 253). The interdependence of these two desires – youthful and competent bodies and a transcendence of what Swift called the 'calamity of human nature' – explains why most fictions of longevity, predicated either on the stopping of the ageing process or on the creation of methods of rejuvenation, also aspire to immortality and why narratives of immortality also incorporate the triumphant defeat of the destiny of the biological body.

To the question of what science fiction projections have to offer between these two modes of interpretation of the ethics of shattering the boundaries of what is imagined as the natural, Stephen Clark in *How to Live Forever: Science Fiction and Philosophy*, a study which examines 'the ways in which science fiction writers have imagined immortality', replies by complicating the premises and arguing that science fiction can be seen as a potential resource for 'general philosophical exploration of the possibility' (1995: 7) by revealing its 'inherent complexities' (1995: 8). The study also suggests that the available corpus can be organized in terms of two broad arguments – 'reasons not to want to live forever', which he sees as reflecting the majority view coming from moral philosophy (1995: 10), and its opposite, 'reasons for wishing to live forever' (1995: 18), which mirrors inputs from transhumanism and longevity advocates.[6] These argue that, as the philosopher Nick Bostrom, a co-author of the Transhumanist Declaration (2009),[7] explains, 'human nature is a work-in-progress, a half-baked beginning that we can remold in desirable ways' and that 'by responsible use of science, technology, and other rational means we shall eventually manage to become post-humans' (2005: 4).

The urtext of the first approach is easy to identify – Mary Shelley's short story 'The Mortal Immortal' (1833). This imagines an unintended defeat of death, which reveals itself to be personally devastating as Winzy, the alchemist's apprentice who drinks an immortality elixir thinking it is a love potion, comes to see eternal youth as a destroyer of his personal happiness. He wonders, as he marks his 323rd year, 'Am I, then immortal?', 'For ever! Can it be? To live for ever?' (Shelley 1891: n.p.) while living 'desirous of death, yet never dying' (1891: n.p.).

The hypothesis of the desirability of immortality would be further tested half a century later by Walter Bessant's *The Inner House* (1888), which looks at the outcomes of permanent youth and the end of death on a global scale, moving from the domain of the individual to the domain of the social and the political (see Botelho 2019). The novel begins by introducing a problem that will be central to the discussion of the transhumanist texts of the twentieth and twenty-first centuries – who will have access to the bodily rejuvenation and immortality technology once it is achieved? For Professor Schwarzbaum, the creator of 'the

Prolongation of Vital Energy' formula, whom we see at the beginning of the novel explaining the discovery of the anti-ageing elixir in a public lecture at the Royal Institution, it should not be available to all although he intends to donate it to the world. It is meant to 'prolong life only until a person has enjoyed everything they desire' and until, after two or three centuries, users agree to 'put aside the aid of science' and, contented and fulfilled, 'sink into the Tomb' (Bessant 2017: 11). Longevity, he suggests, should be offered only to the deserving, the 'salt of the earth, the flower of mankind', and not to those who are 'a burden to themselves and the world' (Bessant 2017: 10). Excluded would be those deemed physically and mentally incapable – 'the crippled and the imbecile' – those who lack social status and usefulness – 'the criminals', 'the stupid' and 'the frivolous' – but most significantly those whose economic status should automatically preclude their access to longevity – 'the poor' (Bessant 2017: 10–11). How the 'deserving' interpret the new possibility of long lives of pleasure opened by science is evidence of the capacity of speculative fiction to weave the 'complexities' of the philosophical debates mentioned by Clark.

As the narrative moves to a post–Great Discovery future, it becomes clear that the elixir has been used not to prolong life but to assure immortality since no one has stopped taking it to embrace the tomb as its creator suggested should happen. Its early adoption had been reserved for the young, frozen at a specific age (twenty-five for women, thirty for men), which set the ground for an elimination of all older citizens who might compete for resources in a genocide known as the Great Slaughter. The new immortals, living in a perpetual sameness, are described as living with no joy, no creativity and no aims, having abandoned all forms of individual expression and producing no art and losing all interest in the 'old foolish pursuit of literature' since they are 'no longer interested in their past or their future'. With 'nothing to hope for and nothing to fear', they have reached 'true happiness' since 'life has been reduced to its simplest form' (Bessant 2017: 26), in a paralyzing denial of time and age.

The novel eventually offers a form of rebellious individuality, but the fact that its agent is a young girl whose birth had exceptionally been allowed,[8] who has no memory of the past and is moved by a romanticized vision of a pre-immortality aristocratic past, only attests to the premise proposed by the novel of the suffocating consequences of any radical interference with the natural destiny of the organic body, be it life extension or the abolition of its end. This fatalistic approach is consolidated when the rebellion leads not to change but to retreat as the small band of rebels walk away from the immortality paradise to settle on a faraway island to live with joy and love and die as nature intended.

The undisguised conservative undertone of the narrative, which celebrates a nostalgic association between individuality and social hierarchy challenged by the seemingly stagnant equality of the imagined post-death world, does not obfuscate its allegiance to the dominant trope in early immortality fiction – living forever would be infinitely mind numbing and unbearable for the individual and paralyzing for societies.

The embrace of this proposition by nineteenth-century texts, framed by an insurmountable gap between the limits of contemporaneous scientific plausibility and what could be imagined, raises the question of whether and how this approach is reaffirmed, interrogated or challenged by late twentieth- and twenty-first-century science fiction influenced by the discourses of transhumanism and post-singularity utopianism. The discussion that follows will therefore analyse texts that might be understood, in terms of Clark's dichotomy, as generally sustaining the 'reasons for wishing to live forever' argument, scrutinizing the role the tropes of longevity and immortality play in the landscapes they offer.

Living with immortality

In a critical diagnosis of the sense of future and progress that contemporary Western societies increasingly embrace,[9] Joel Dinerstein warns that for the proponents of the promises of the GNR triad (genomics, nanotechnology and robotics) the source of progress has moved away from the domain of the social to that of the individual and that 'the Enlightenment utopia of the mind – as the rational host of self-control, self-mastery, and perfectibility – has shifted to the body'. 'As self-actualization now seems possible, through technological advance', he clarifies, 'the body has become the locus of consumer desire and the (literal) base for layers of technological prosthetic' (Dinerstein 2006: 573–4).

This focus on a body-centred remaking and reinvention of futures finds its most articulate and challenging statement in the hopes articulated by transhumanist thinkers and futurists who, like RayCed Kurzweil, predict that we will overcome the fragility of 'our version 1.0 biological bodies ... frail and subject to a myriad of failure modes' and that, through genetic enhancement and fusion with non-biological components, 'we will transcend the limitations of our biological bodies and brains' and 'gain power over our fates. Our mortality will be in our hands ... [and] we will be able to live as long as we want' (2006: 9).

Fiction centred on the promises of future bodies with unlimited possibilities of actualization and upgrading and on lives partially dependent on the continuity of consciousness beyond the borders of the biological self frequently ignores the societal processes, disruptions and consequences of the end of ageing and death, opting to take the reader on a speed ride through technological developments towards post-singularity worlds, as is the case in Charles Stross's *Accelerando* (2005), or plunging them directly into utopian futures where mind uploading, body cloning and nanotechnology have already created post-scarcity societies[10] where old age and death are optional, as happens in Cory Doctorow's *Down and Out in the Magic Kingdom* (2003). The discussion that follows analyses three alternative visions of those projected outcomes, focusing not only on the desirability of the future landscapes they imagine but also on the maps that lead to them.

The first novel, *Holy Fire*, by Bruce Sterling (1996; hereafter cited by page number), imagines and scrutinizes the new power relations and social landscapes that extreme longevity and immortality may foster. The novel depicts a late twenty-first-century world dominated by a political–medical–industrial complex devoted to gerontological research that is already able to offer life extension and rejuvenation treatments to its 'deserving' citizens with the ultimate objective of achieving a cure for mortality. In this global order, privilege is equated with access to longevity, which in turn is measured in terms of embodied 'worthiness', revisiting and revising Professor Schwarzbaum's exclusion recommendations in Bessant's *The Inner House*. For those identified by a medical surveillance apparatus as undeserving – like Martin, a 96-year-old film director who has enjoyed a life dedicated to the pursuit of 'irresponsible' body-destroying pleasures (including alcohol and narcotics) – there is no escape from natural ageing and death. If once 'having money almost guaranteed good health ... nowadays mere wealth guaranteed very little' (49) 'unless you live like a little tin saint', he explains. It is your medical records, 'splashed all over the net', that condemn you to your biological destiny (11). If, on the other hand, you are a productive, dependable and submissive supporter of the medical state and have 'objectively demonstrated your firm will to live', as demonstrated by your medical records (47), you are rewarded with permanent medical upgrades and rejuvenation treatments that keep you looking and feeling young.

The narrative follows one such exemplary citizen, Mia, a 94-year-old medical economist from California, living a meticulously planned existence devoid of pleasure and joy. Describing herself as a 'functionary' (13), a late twenty-first-century post-sexual and post-womanly technochrome, she summarizes her life thus: 'I don't have lovers. I don't love anyone. I don't look after anyone. I don't kiss anyone, I don't hug anyone, I don't cheer anyone up' (16). This exemplary behaviour makes her the perfect candidate for the ultimate experimental treatment which will grant her new biological youth, a restoration of all metabolic drives, and immortality, on condition she lets herself be examined and constantly medically monitored after the procedure. 'You are', her doctor explains, 'going to be a ninety-five-year-old woman who can look, act and feel like a twenty-year-old girl' (57).

Thus, the twenty-year-old girl who emerges from the treatment is not exactly the youthful-looking nonagenarian woman who volunteered for it. The difference is located not only in the body but also in the divided mind, now both old and young. While she certainly retains her sense of self, she recognizes that she is not the same. 'The Mia thing', her former 'meek ... and accommodating bundle of habits' self (63), is no longer bearable. 'Something has snapped', she recognizes when contemplating her new life; 'I can't live like this. This isn't living. I'm out of here' (66).

Following the impulsiveness and desires of her new body and double consciousness, and renaming herself Maya, the once-passive Mia escapes the medical surveillance team and heads to Europe, looking for 'holy fire', an excitement about life and its possibilities she had never missed before. There, Maya finds avenues of defiant self-expression in the company of communities of irreverent 'real young' anarchic bohemians who, unable to defeat the power of the artificially young, look for 'vivacious' alternative creative lives, sometimes seeking a different kind of immortality in virtuality and occasionally finding in suicide the most radical gesture of protest against the disruptive neo-gerontocratic order.

Experimenting with new types of pleasure and sexual delectations, Maya/Mia's embodied performance of youth will eventually exhaust its promises, falling prey to the contradiction identified by philosopher Bernard Williams. He argues that contentment in a youthful non-dying body would be necessarily elusive as an endless cycle 'of supposedly satisfying states and activities' would prove unendurably boring to anyone who remained conscious of themselves and 'who had acquired a character, interests, tastes and impatiences in the course of living' (Williams 1993: 87). If Maya's twenty-year-old self 'knows what her 94 years have taught her', 'being both the same and not the same turns her potentially immortal life into both a continuous and a discontinuous experience' (Botelho 2019: 434). Finding no long-term satisfaction in her performance of youth, she returns home and attempts to live disconnected from the system that gave her what she no longer feels she really wants, knowing full well that this break will mean ageing and eventually death. This choice, as Teresa Magnum observes, also asks readers 'to consider the emptiness of the identity "youth" by comparing the effects of rejuvenescent technology to fashion and thus suggesting that chemical simulation, like dressing young, cannot animate the fantasy or essence or abstraction of what we call youth' (Magnum 2002: 78). The text exposes its performativity in terms of accessorized reinvention – when Mia is about to become Maya and receives a number of fashion instructions on what she should wear to fully inhabit 'youth', these include, among other things, the stern indictment 'especially *no watch*' (34), suggesting the new irrelevance of time for her new twenty-year-old simulation. When the reader last sees Maya, she seems to be reclaiming time by photographing ageing Amish communities who have never embraced the reversal of the 'natural' ways, accepting the inevitability of decay and death.

If *Holy Fire* directs its critical gaze towards the scrutiny of a post-ageing and post-death world in terms of its effects on divided selfhoods and on the unfair distribution of the privilege which creates new social hierarchies based on behaviourally based worthiness, it does not attempt to trace back the social processes that made the new reality possible and acceptable to mainstream society. Imagining paths towards the transhumanist project of the end of ageing and death is the object of two twenty-first-century novels that map radically different futures – *The Transhumanist Wager* (2013, hereafter cited by page number) by American futurist Zoltan Istvan and *Walkaway* by Canadian writer Cory Doctorow (2017).

A critical approach to Istvan's text inevitably requires a consideration of the extremely controversial presence of its author in transhumanist circles. A founder of the Transhumanist Party in 2014, Istvan ran in the US presidential election of 2016 on a platform that listed as its first pledge the allocation of resources to scientific and technological efforts to 'overcome human death and aging within 15–20 years' (2014).[11] The decision to create a specific political platform dominated by a libertarian stance was greeted with dismay by many thinkers associated with other interpretations of transhumanism (see Chen 2014; Fuller 2017), which, according to James Hughes, range from anarchist to democratic and libertarian (2012). Istvan ran in subsequent elections on different party platforms (in 2016 as a Libertarian Party candidate and in 2020 as a Republican).[12] The novel, his first and only work of fiction, was self-published after having been rejected, according to its back-cover blurb, 'by more than 500 publishers around the world'. The work is difficult to classify, mixing elements of speculative fiction with a political and philosophical pamphletarian quality, and stands as a unique example of what Rick Searle of the Institute for Ethics and Emerging Technologies has denounced as a disturbingly anti-human, authoritarian investment in a form of 'technological fetishism' (2013).

What *The Transhumanist Wager* proposes, with no visible sense of critical distance or irony, is a Randian power fantasy about the virtues of a particular libertarian and individualistic interpretation of transhumanism set against the caricatured narrow-mindedness of mainstream human beliefs and actors, and the inevitable future violent clash between the two. It follows the actions of Jethro Knights, whom we first meet as a young philosophy student about to reach his own conclusions about what he sees as the Transhumanist Wager: 'We love life and therefore we want to live as long as possible – we desire to be immortal' (59). As doing nothing to achieve this aim would not help the odds of attaining immortality since it seems evident that 'we're going to die someday and possibly cease to exist', the logical solution would be 'to attempt something scientifically constructive towards ensuring immortality beforehand' (59). From this logical proposition, Knights develops an extropian philosophical system, first sketched in a course essay entitled 'Rise of the Transhuman Citizen', which he names Teleological Egocentric Functionalism and explains in these terms: 'Teleological – because it is every advanced individual's inherent design and desired destiny to evolve. Egocentric – because it is based on each of our selfish individual desires, which are of the foremost importance. Functional – because it will only be rational and consequential'. In practical terms, this means that this 'guiding and comprehensive individualist philosophy' will not be 'fair, nor humanitarian, nor altruistic nor muddled with unreachable mammalian niceties' (84). Not a fictional device but a literal transposition of the conceptual apparatus developed by the author in his public life, the approach implied by these juxtaposed concepts also mirrors Istvan's Three Laws of Transhumanism, the first of which unambiguously states that 'a transhumanist must safeguard one's own existence above all else'.[13]

Guided by these principles, which clearly identify the self-centred hierarchy of the values of Jethro's version of transhumanism, repeatedly accentuated by constant assertions of a personal desire for immortality at any price – at a certain point he admits without any hesitation that if the death of the woman he loves would grant him the assurance that we would not die, he would take the bargain – he launches an 'assertive, direct action organization' called Transhumanist Citizen, tasked with leading a 'global uprising', an 'undertaking of war' as he describes it, 'to connect today to the tomorrow we want, regardless of the cost', an endeavour that will require absolute dedication to a single cause and purpose: 'We will subordinate our nation, our families, our friends and our wealth to this victory. Nothing will stand in our way' (85).

Under the radical fundamentalism of his leadership and guided by a morality 'decided and defined by the amount of time we have left to live' and not by 'democracy, decency, altruism, kindness or notions of humanity' (85), his demands for more and more funding for research on longevity and immortality inevitably clash with the purposes and values of mainstream society. The US government (and others as the movement becomes global) is not inclined to abandon their budget priorities and follow Knight's advice to 'divert resources to the genuinely gifted and qualified' rather than using them 'on the losers of the world, or the mediocre, or the downtrodden or the fearful who will only drag us down' (127–8). The religious establishment panics, and a cartoonish Evangelical leader organizes terrorist acts of violence, attacking scientists and facilities engaged in longevity and immortality research.

As world governments join the anti-transhumanist campaign, cutting research funds and cancelling programs, rather than retreat from the fight, Knights responds to the global rejection of the old world that cannot see the future ahead by creating his own nation, supported by the unlimited funds offered by a Russian oligarch. Transhumania, a floating city-state peopled with the best scientists money can buy, becomes a utopian beacon for research on the cure for death. The dystopian anti-human and anti-social grounding for this utopia is exposed when, after Transhumania is attacked militarily by a UN coalition, the counter-attack that grants transhumanists final global supremacy destroys, in a barbaric act of cultural vandalism, most of the civic and cultural/religious landmarks of the old world, including the Vatican City, the Kaaba in Mecca, Notre Dame Cathedral, the Kremlin, Buckingham Palace, the Wailing Wall and the United Nations Building. At the end of the novel, addressing the world, Jethro Knights, finally triumphant having fulfilled his ambition to be an 'omnipotender' (80), announces to the 'people of Earth' in a fifteen-page-long speech that 'death is not destiny. Death is neither inevitable nor natural. ... Death is a malfunction of the human experience.' He asks them to choose between two possibilities – 'die or join us' (271), framing that option with considerations about the evils of altruism and religion, and the benefits of eugenics to stop the 'least valuable of you to procreate' and stand in the way of the coming new world (278). One year later, under Knights's leadership, the international borders of the six populated continents are forced to open and the whole world is declared Transhumania (287).

This dystopian imposition of the victory-over-death hypothesis, steeped as it is in what Searle calls 'fascist transhumanism' (2013), could have been used rhetorically as a denunciation of a particular interpretation of the premises of life extension, but as many critics who embrace different approaches to the philosophy stress, the undisguised tone of the text disallows that hypothesis, celebratory as it is of the deeds of Knights, the *ubermensch*, who at the end of the novel awakens from a seven-year cryonic suspension and is about to enter his new life as an immortal.[14]

If, as many Transhumanists who embrace very different perspectives fear, readers of the novel might be led to 'envisage transhumanism as the callous and potentially authoritarian enterprise' that the novel makes it out to be (Blackford 2014: 91), an alternative view of its core promises and potentials emerges in Cory Doctorow's *Walkaway* (2017; hereafter cited by page number). This text aligns itself with a future-positive, techno-optimist, radical approach frequently identified with both democratic and anarcho-transhumanism, sharing an emphasis on the creation of a 'more equal, empowered and united world' through a 'fairly regulated and distributed, freely exercised technology' (Hughes 2004: 195) and defending a praxis of open sourcing of technological advances[15] as a tool towards those envisaged futures (Gillis 2021: 419).

Walkaway, as the author has stated, is a prequel to the ambiguous post-singularity utopia created in *Down and Out in the Magic Kingdom* (2003), which takes the reader to the post-scarcity scenario of a decentralized adhocracy where nanotechnology guarantees the fulfilment of basic needs and work is an optional activity done mostly for pleasure and personal reputation. More importantly, in this future ageing, sickness and death have been made optional by a combination of mind-uploading and body-cloning processes that have turned death into a short-lived inconvenience as one's downloaded thoughts and memories can be transferred to a new body in a matter of hours. The ambiguous texture of this future is nevertheless scrutinized by testing Bernard Williams's hypothesis of the unbearable boredom of eternity[16] and by problematizing the continuity of the self inherent in the disembodied mind trope, 'introducing a degree of instability in the process of body reassignment and mind uploading' (Botelho 2014: 78).[17]

Walkaway offers a view of the process that leads to a post-death and post-scarcity future, stepping back a hundred years to its origins. In the world the novel constructs, after a general climate catastrophe, the concentration of power-enhancing technology lies in the hands of a very small elite, the zottas (for zottarich), who implement automated production systems that radically diminish the need for human labour, thus resulting in a three-tiered social structure. On top are the 'deserving' mega-rich, who justify their privilege by recycling the old 'self-serving circular' argument that claims: 'we are the best people we know, we're on top, therefore we have a meritocracy. How do we know we're the best? Because we're on top' (43). On the second level are those who still have jobs, hanging on to the conventions of respectability, 'well-behaved' and 'clinging to the ultimate self-deception' that 'they are going to be able to change anything with a paycheck' (27–8). Around and below them are the surplus, those surviving in the 'world of no-work' (9).

But outside this 'default' life, there are others. Those who leave, walk away and drop the interface devices that track their movements and who stand for a quasi-bohemian alternative tech-savvy dissent. Spread throughout the badlands, the devastated landscapes created by climate change, forming ad hoc nomadic communities, walkaways invest in the same technology that made the zotta even more privileged, but its use is guided by very different values, geared towards a post-scarcity gift economy.[18] Hacked and repurposed open-source hardware and software, 3D printing and nano-assemblers provide for basic needs such as food, clothes and building materials, and the codebase created by the UN High Commission on Refugees to help those left homeless by climate catastrophes is used now to find and convert the wreckage of the old world into the basis of the creation of 'the first day of a better nation' (48). This imperfect and messy utopia on the move, with diversified iterations around the world, is revealed to the reader through the eyes and experiences of three young 'noobs', whose walkaway decision traces the shift from 'default' to the new possible – Herbert Etc. (so named because his parents gave him 20 first names, hoping to confuse surveillance schemes); Seth, his younger friend who fears the departure from the 'beautiful children demographic' to the 'non-work' world (9); and Natalie, the disenchanted daughter of a zotta, who in her new life changes her name to Iceweasel, a clear reference to the open code internet navigator.

The zottas tolerate the walkaway dissenters as long as they can be dismissed as 'solving themselves by removing themselves' rather than staying and being a problem to be tackled (69), but this attitude changes when the walkaways' scientific and technological practices become entangled with the only underachievement that taints the self-satisfaction of the 1 per cent. Although they have dedicated part of their fortunes to life-extension treatments for themselves, including 'selective germ plasm optimization, continuous health surveillance, genomic therapies, preferential transplant access', their wish to ensure that 'when you are rich you don't have to die' is still unfulfilled (66). Limpopo, a veteran walkaway, tells the new arrivals a story that introduces the reader to what will become the central tension of the novel. The story concerns a zotta in a vat, a man worth more than most countries, who, 'just organs and grey matter', waits in 'perpetual agony' in a fortified clinic in a walled city inhabited only by the best scientists that could be recruited, for one of them to solve 'his nerve thing' (67) rather than ask to be switched off and die.

Walkaways are not troubled by the prospect of immortality as such, and in fact see it with wonder – 'When you think you might be able to live forever – your kids might live forever – everyone you know might live forever', one of them muses, 'something happens' (141). What they find unbearable is the idea of its exclusivity, the thought that immortality 'should belong to someone', that the zottas, 'who've been set on keeping immortality to themselves', might 'have the power to decide who dies, when no one has to die, ever' (141). As a walkaway scientist puts it:

> It's one thing to imagine a life of working to enrich some hereditary global powerbroker when you know that you've got eighty years on the planet, and so does he. ... But the thought of making those greedy assholes into godlike immortals, bifurcating the human race into infinite Olympian masters and mayflies. So they not only get a better life than you could ever dream of but get it forever. (141–2)

The design to avoid this plan and to arrive first at the cure for death so that they can share and viralize it (167), making it available to everyone, mobilizes discontented scientists and techs who gather in walkaway universities creating hubs of shared knowledge. This, in turn, unleashes the fury of the default world, starting a violent campaign against walkaway hubs, sending against them mercenary armies, bombs and all and any surveillance and destructive technology available.

It is from the ruins of one such attack, against the Niagata Peninsula Walkaway University (after a number of previous attacks against other campuses working on the same agenda), that the first success in this endeavour emerges. Resilient and prepared for the worst, the walkaways had saved their most important asset – the downloaded mind of one of the bombing victims, Dis, now a rebooted sim who can communicate by a synthesized voice, her words transcribed on a screen. The experience of existing that way is confusing to Dis's mind – she has to be told that she is 'meat-dead' (134) – but what puzzles this version of her is the continuity of the self or, to put it in its/her terms, the fact that she does not feel as confused and puzzled as she thinks she should be, which makes her question her status. 'I just don't understand', the rebooted mind says, 'how a meat person can contemplate what I've become without a smidge of existential angst. It's not natural' (137). She also projects the question into the future by pondering, sometime later when she is better adjusted to her new existence, on how the permanence of the body she misses shapes her perceptions. If, she admits, we are all 'meat following rules' and 'the way you feel is determined by your gut, the hairs on your toes and your environment', not having these things implies feeling differently from when she 'was meat', maintaining nevertheless a 'continuity with the meat-me' that her mind remembers (146).

This interrogation about the contingency of the recognition of selfhood is further teased out when its terms shift, proposing a reading of ageing as a tension between a sense of self and a changing body. Many years after the first successful mind rebooting, Seth, now approaching what is conventionally considered old age, looks in the mirror and is troubled by the same dysfunction that had afflicted Dis: 'This isn't me. I am a young man. ... This isn't how I see myself' (424). He reasserts the hypothesis of an inevitable complex Cartesian duality between body and mind, whereby consciousness can be seen as independent from restrictions of the 'meat machines' that enclose it, so common in the cyberpunk tradition.

Eventually, as the alternative immortality project evolves and the savvy cooperation between the various dissenting communities wins the race against the zottas, the downloading and rebooting of mind techniques are made available to all through the walkaway cloud. At the novel's end, thirty years later, the growing of new bodies into which those scanned brains could be backed, guaranteeing the defeat of death and old age, creates the new hopeful post-zotta utopia that *Down and Out in the Magic Kingdom* had already revealed with all its flaws and imperfections.

Conclusion

Sherryl Vint has argued, in *Bodies of Tomorrow*, that science fiction is commonly understood to be about the moment contemporary to its production, 'the anxieties and anticipations that form that moment' (2007: 22). If anxieties about ageing and dying are by no means exclusive to our time, as the texts discussed in the first section of this chapter demonstrate, the apparent possibility of life extension through the promises of research on regenerative medicine dedicated to extended longevity and rejuvenation, as practised by the Calico Longevity Lab or the SENS Research Foundation,[19] or the hopes of the promises to 'pause the dying process' through cryonics, as defended by Alcor or the Cryonics Institute, seems to have brought to the fore these agendas.[20] If, as Vint also points out, science fiction is 'particularly suited to exploring questions of post-human futures, since it is a discourse that allows us to concretely imagine other concepts of bodies and selves otherwise', estranging 'our commonplace perception of reality' (2007: 19), these contemporary texts can be seen as testing grounds for the new hypotheses.

What appears to surface in the three recent works analysed is how far they go beyond the basic dichotomies of natural versus artificial, fatalist versus prolongevitist stances, by projecting the over-the-horizon possibility of longevity and immortality into social and cultural landscapes and directly linking it to power distribution, layering the what-if speculative scenarios they propose with the more complex questions of who will benefit from those futurities, how they might be accepted (or enforced) and how they might change perceptions of the self and the body. The ethical challenges they pose, dependent on different interpretations of the horizons and methodologies of transhumanism, may help make sense of the options before us as we stand at the crossroads of new possibilities and have to collectively decide what, to quote Cory Doctorow, the 'first day of a better nation' would be like.

Notes

1 In the appendix to the volume, the editors list 266 works, including novels and short stories, classified as science fiction in a broad sense, that directly engage the hypothesis of physical immortality.
2 See *Metamorphoses* Book VII: 234–93.
3 As the authors point out, as the average length of life in Rome, in the second-century AD was about twenty-five, and between one-third to one-fifth of all children born reached their first year, this may seem to be a justification for the cruelty of life experienced by their contemporary Romans (Olshansky and Carnes 2002: 14).
4 See Bacon's *The Cure of Old Age and the Preservation of Youth* (1683).
5 A circular red spot on their forehead is 'an infallible mark that they would never die' (Swift [1726] 1988: 246).
6 Transhumanism is used here in the general sense proposed by Nick Bostrom, namely, 'the intellectual and cultural movement that affirms the possibility and desirability of fundamentally improving the human condition through applied reason, especially by developing and making widely available technologies to eliminate aging and to greatly enhance human intellectual, physical, and psychological capacities' (2003: 4).
7 The Declaration was adopted in 2002 by the World Transhumanist Association, which has since changed its name to Humanity+.

8 In the post–Great Discovery world, no new births are allowed except to replace individuals who have been killed by uncontrollable accidents.
9 The argument is centred on a reading of techno-optimism in the United States, but its diagnosis is seen as applicable also to Europe and other Western nations.
10 Post-scarcity economics is a speculative theoretical post-capitalism economic model in which goods and services are universally accessible due to advanced productive automated systems, namely, nanotechnology, which is seen as enabling the production of most human needs by molecular assemblers or nanofactories with little human labour and depletion of resources.
11 Zoltan Istvan's name was not on any ballot in any state, and he was voted as a write-in candidate. He gained only ninety-five votes in the national ballot (seventy-six in the state of New York and nineteen in Florida). See '2016 General Election' (2016) available at https://www.thegreenpapers.com/G16/PresidentVoteByParty.phtml.
12 In 2016, Istavan's candidacy for the California Gubernatorial Race as the Libertarian Party won 0.2 per cent of the votes (14,462). His candidacy for the Republican Presidential Primaries was also a write-in process and was lost during the Republican National Convention.
13 The second and third laws state, 'A transhumanist must strive to achieve omnipotence as expediently as possible – so long as one's actions do not conflict with the First Law' and 'A transhumanist must safeguard value in the universe – so long as one's actions do not conflict with the First and Second Laws.' See http://www.zoltanistvan.com/TranshumanistWager.html.
14 See the very critical reviews of the book by Russell Black, editor-in-chief of the *Journal of Evolution and Technology* (2014), and by Giulio Prisco (2013), who identifies himself as a radical transhumanist.
15 This very frequently implies the defence of computer and bio-hacking.
16 One of the characters, after having lived for eighty years in a 20-year-old body, wishes to die and rejects the hypothesis of immortality as a process of becoming a 'post-person'. This is not presented in the novel as an exceptional rebellion, as is demonstrated by the widely available solution of deadheading, a process that lets individuals be preserved in a state of non-life for a few centuries and then return to life to try new experiences.
17 This results, in the novel, from uncertainty over the sameness of the downloaded mind in a copied body and the loss of memory during the time frame of the process of death reversal.
18 Gift economy is understood in the novel in the sense of a model of exchange of goods and services given rather than sold or exchanged, without the expectation of a payback.
19 See https://www.calicolabs.com/, https://www.sens.org/ and Aubrey de Grey (2007).
20 See https://www.alcor.org/ and https://www.cryonics.org/.

References

'2016 General Election Presidential Popular Vote and FEC Total Receipts by Party' (2016), *The Green Papers*. Available online: https://www.thegreenpapers.com/G16/PresidentVoteByParty.phtml (accessed 2 December 2021).

Bacon, F. (1683), *The Cure of Old Age and the Preservation of Youth*, trans. R. Browne, London: Tho. Flesher and Edward Evets.

Bauman, Z. (1992), *Mortality, Immortality and Other Life Strategies*, Cambridge: Polity.

Bessant, W. ([1888] 2017), *The Inner House*, Scotts Valley: CreateSpace.

Blackford, R. (2014), 'Book Review: Zoltan Istvan's *The Transhumanist Wager*', *Journal of Evolution and Technology*, 24(2): 89–91.

Bostrom, N. (2003), *The Transhumanist FAQ: A General Introduction*, London: World Transhumanist Association.

Bostrom, N. (2005), 'Transhumanist Values', *Review of Contemporary Philosophy*, 4(May): 3–14.

Botelho, T. (2014), 'Reimagining the Body in Post-Singularity Techno-Utopias', *Spaces of Utopia: An Electronic Journal*, 2(3): 70–83.

Botelho, T. (2019), 'The Cure of Death: Fantasies of Longevity and Immortality in Speculative Fiction', in M. S. Ming Kong and M. do Rosário Monteiro (eds), *Intelligence, Creativity and Fantasy*, 431–6, Leiden: CRC Press.

Cave, S. (2012), *The Quest to Live Forever and How It Drives Civilization*, New York: Crown.

Chen, T. 'The Political Vacuity of Transhumanism', *Stanford Politics*, 15 December, 2014. Available online: https://stanfordpolitics.org/2014/12/15/political-vacuity-transhumanism/ (accessed 2 December 2021).

Clark, S. R. L. (1995), *How to Live Forever: Science Fiction and Philosophy*, London: Routledge.

de Grey, A. (2007), *Ending Aging: The Rejuvenation Breakthroughs That Could Reverse Human Aging in Our Lifetime*, New York: St Martin's.

Dinerstein, J. (2006), 'Technology and Its Discontents: On the Verge of the Posthuman', *American Quarterly*, 58(3): 569–95.

Doctorow, C. (2003), *Down and Out in the Magic Kingdom*, New York: Tor Books.

Doctorow, C. (2017), *Walkaway*, London: Head of Zeus.

Fuller, S. (2017), 'Philosopher's Corner: Does This Pro-Science Party Deserve Our Votes?' *Issues in Science and Technology*, 33(3): 31–2.

Gillis, W. (2021), 'Anarchy and Transhumanism', in G. Chartier and C. van Schoelandt (eds), *The Routledge Handbook of Anarchy and Anarchist Thought*, 416–28, London: Routledge.

Gruner, O. C. (1930), *A Treatise on the Canon of Medicine of Avicenna, Incorporating a Translation of the First Book*, London: Luzac.

Gullette, M. M. (1997), *Declining to Decline: Cultural Combat and the Politics of the Midlife*, Charlottesville: University of Virginia Press.

Hassler, D. M. (1985), 'Introduction,' in C. B. Yoke and D. M. Hassler (eds), *Death and the Serpent: Immortality in Science Fiction and Fantasy*, 3–6, Westport: Greenwood.
Hughes, J. (2004), 'Democratic Transhumanism 2.0', in *Citizen Cyborg: Why Democratic Societies Must Respond to the Redefined Human of the Future*, 187–220, Cambridge: Westview.
Hughes, J. (2012), 'The Politics of Transhumanism and the Techno-Millennial Imagination, 1626–2030', *Zygon: Journal of Religion and Science*, 4(4): 757–76.
Ionesco, E. (1963), *Exit the King*, New York: Grove.
Istvan, Z. (2013), *The Transhumanist Wager*, Brookings: Futurity Imagine Media.
Istvan, Z. (2014), 'Should a Transhumanist Run for U.S. President?', *Huffington Post*, 8 December. Available online: https://www.huffpost.com/entry/should-a-transhumanist-be_b_5949688 (accessed 27 November 2021).
Kurzweil, R. (2006), *The Singularity Is Near: When Humans Transcend Biology*, London: Gerald Duckworth.
Magnum, T. (2002), 'Longing for Life Extension: Science Fiction and Late Life', *Journal of Aging and Identity*, 7(2): 69–82.
Nussbaum, M. (2017), *Aging Thoughtfully: Conversations about Retirement, Romance, Wrinkles and Regret*, Oxford: Oxford University Press.
Olshansky, J. S., and B. A. Carnes (2002), *The Quest for Immortality: Science at the Frontiers of Aging*, New York: W.W. Norton.
Prisco, G. (2013), 'Book Review: *The Transhumanist Wager*', *Kurzweil*. Available online: https://www.kurzweilai.net/book-review-the-transhumanist-wager (accessed 2 December 2021).
Searle, R. (2013), 'Betting against the Transhumanist Wager', *Utopia or Dystopia*, 14 September. Available online: https://utopiaordystopia.com/2013/09/14/betting-against-the-transhumanist-wager/ (accessed 20 November 2021).
Shelley, M. ([1818] 2018), *Frankenstein: The 1818 Text*, London: Penguin.
Shelley, M. ([1833] 1891), 'The Mortal Immortal', in *Tales and Stories*, 148–64, London: William Paterson. Available online: https://www.gutenberg.org/files/56665/56665-h/56665-h.htm (accessed 20 November 2021).
Sterling, B. (1996), *Holy Fire*, London: Phoenix.
Stross, C. (2005), *Accelerando*, New York: Penguin.
Swift, J. ([1726] 1988), *Gulliver's Travels into Several Remote Nations of the World*, London: Marshall Cavendish.
The Transhumanist Declaration (2009), *Humanity+*. Available online: https://www.humanityplus.org/the-transhumanist-declaration (accessed 12 November 2021).
Vint, S. (2007), *Bodies of Tomorrow: Technology, Subjectivity and Science Fiction*, Toronto: University of Toronto Press.
Williams, B. (1993), 'The Makropulos Case: Reflections on the Tedium of Immortality', in J. M. Fischer (ed.), *The Metaphysics of Death*, 73–90, Stanford: Stanford University Press.
Yoke, C. B., and D. M. Hassler, eds (1985), *Death and the Serpent: Immortality in Science Fiction and Fantasy*, Westport: Greenwood.

2

Ageing and youthing: Portrayals of progression and regression in science fiction film and TV

Peter Goggin and Ulla Kriebernegg

In January 2020, the Star Trek franchise released a new streaming TV series, *Star Trek: Picard* (*STP*).[1] The iconic former captain of the starship USS *Enterprise*, Jean-Luc Picard (played by Patrick Stewart) is now retired to his idyllic vineyard home in France to live out his remaining years in peaceful melancholy. Then, a young woman on the run from assassins shows up looking for his help, and Picard rediscovers a sense of purpose that will take him back to the stars. 'I haven't been living', he says, 'I've been waiting to die' (*STP*, 'Remembrance').

Living and ageing are presented here as a kind of antagonism: even though the retired admiral has taken to wine-making in the sunny Bordeaux region and seems to be enjoying 'the good life' at Chateau Picard, an old-fashioned, yet high-tech vinery, he is lacking a sense of purpose. Before leaving Starfleet, his life had been characterized by extreme interstellar mobility, strength, courage and heroic youthfulness. Picard, suffering through his (seemingly) complacent retirement, 'safely mothballed on that vineyard of his', as Starfleet security director, Commodore Oh (played by Tamlyn Tomita), expresses it (*STP*, 'Maps and Legends'), seems to require none of these qualities. Even Picard's friends, Laris and Zahban, Romulan refugees who live with him as his housekeepers, already perceive him to be a failing old man. 'Is it dementia?' his friend asks when Picard announces that he is going to return to Starfleet. 'Do what you are good at. Go home,' he is told when enquiring about getting a spaceship for a new rescue mission (*STP*, 'Remembrance').

'Lack of movement is characteristic of decrepit age,' Kathleen Woodward argues: 'If movement bespeaks life, immobility – lack of movement – is akin to death, and inertia verges dangerously on the inert' (1983: 53). While the romanticized notion in film and literature of ageing characters yearning to break free from the tyranny of advanced age and reboot their lives is somewhat of a cliché, it constitutes a trope in cultural representations dealing with age and ageing, especially in road movies. Picard's return could be read as an interstellar 'road trip' that challenges the notion of old age as being static and immobile. It can be argued that Picard's narrative counteracts the myth of immobility in old age and celebrates the protagonist's resistance to the inertia forced upon him by his idyllic retirement. 'I tried my best to belong to this place. But I don't think I ever truly felt at home here,' he says about his chateau before deciding to rejoin Starfleet to take care of unfinished business. Picard's decision can be read as constitutive of a courageous activity narrative by promoting a new narrative of resistance. He is 'declining to decline' (Gullette 1997) and takes control of his own as well as the United Federation of Planets' destiny.

What is significant about *STP* is that the new series represents a dramatic departure from all previous series. Since 1966, when *The Original Series* (*TOS*) first aired, *Picard* is the first series in the franchise in which the primary character is not only an older man but is also played by an older actor (Patrick Stewart). And while various starship captains in the series have been portrayed (briefly) as older for episodic plot purposes, the Picard character is his actual older self without heavy make-up, hair dye and wigs to create the effects of ageing.[2] This new development, the series' success and an ageing Picard's popularity, might reflect the fact that a large number of 'Trekkies', too, are ageing.[3] It also reflects the fact that older men are becoming more and more visible on screen. Yet, it is a fairly new phenomenon in popular film and TV science fiction.

What is also notable is that *STP* generally avoids the two-dimensional stereotypes of ageing so prevalent in previous productions and other science fiction blockbusters (decrepitude, senility, decay) but does not avoid the subject of ageing itself, and while acknowledging limitations that come with advancing years (especially compared with Jean-Luc's youthful and far more agile companions), it embraces the visibility of an old man as a hero, facing his challenges and his future in a new phase in his life. Still, in the realm of popular science fiction films and series, *Picard* is quite an anomaly. This is particularly curious as representations of old age, body swapping (of older minds into youthful bodies and vice versa) and rapid ageing and reverse-ageing processes are common tropes in the genre.[4]

In this chapter, we analyse the confluences of ageing and de-ageing and discuss the potential of a rhetorical view of science fiction through the lens of ageing studies. That is, how portrayals of ageing are suasive constructs for not only sustaining and perhaps challenging contemporary notions of advanced age but also projecting and perpetuating these notions to imagined futures. Although we focus on portrayals of ageing in fictional drama contexts, and in those contexts we limit our focus to primarily human characters, as theoretical physicist and feminist theorist Karen Barad would argue (2007), our exploration is situated in a much broader intra-active cosmos. Science fiction drama engages us through complex connections and multiple knowledges that are intertwined within co-constructed material and imagined realities, not only in the drama of films and series themselves but also in real-world temporal spaces and places in the production and viewing of the films and series. What can we learn from the ebb and flow, the tidal change from young to old and from old to young, that a genre such as science fiction allows for due to its speculative character? Banerjee and Paul have observed that 'from media discussion and academic discourses to biopolitical, bioethical, and biomedical frameworks we are constantly confronted by the rhetorics of ageing' (2015: 269) and that although 'experiences of ageing are increasingly being differentiated … even these discourses are ultimately deeply rooted in an understanding of old age as a challenge or slight, and thus as a deficient period of life' (Banerjee and Paul 2015: 269). Based on the theory that age, like gender, is a cultural construct, analysing representations of ageing and youthing in science fiction allows us to explore anxieties and desires concerning concepts of longevity, immortality and youthfulness that are constructed in the visual media and distributed in the domain of popular culture.

The constitutive aspects of ageing and de-ageing at the interface of reality and fictional representation are thus not just interactive but intra-active. As Barad also states, 'Discursive practices and material phenomena do not stand in a relationship of externality to each other; rather the material and discursive are mutually implicated in the dynamics of intra-activity' (2007: 152). Time progression, for instance, both in the dramas and in their production as films and series, is not always chronologically linear. Series often start in the 'middle' of an imagined future timeline and loop backwards and forwards. The *Star Wars* series, for example, 'begins' in production release time with the first episode in the original trilogy, *A New Hope* (referred to as 'episode 4' in the *Star Wars* film series saga, as conceived by George Lucas). Then, after progressing sequentially and chronologically to episode 6 *(Return of the Jedi)* goes back in time to a prequel trilogy beginning with episode 1 (*The Phantom Menace*). After progressing sequentially and chronologically again to episode 3 (*Revenge of the Sith*), the series leaps forward to episode 7 (*The Force Awakens*). The 'final' (so far) three episodes are then interspersed in production release with films that are not part of the original series but backstory additions to the Star Wars saga, *Rogue One* and *Solo*. Thus, while the universe of the Star Wars saga itself is chronologically linear, its real-world rollout is not, as it is affected by production releases and by new episodes and alternative media productions such as animated series, fan fiction, video games and streaming television series. Other popular science fiction and fantastical franchises such as *Star Trek* and *Marvel* are similarly chronologically fluid, with multiple interconnections and intersections between characters, timelines, origin stories and alternative versions and reboots. Within these real and imagined flows of non-linear time is the ageing of the characters and actors themselves, both real and imagined, and our perceptions of them as they get older and younger before our eyes. As the audiences age, as younger audiences join and as society changes, those perceptions continuously change and are reinvented with those audiences through the intra-action of actual and conceptual ageing processes. And non-linear chronology and ageing are not limited to the human actors and imagined characters. As this chapter interrogates, imagined spacecraft, worlds, weaponry, real-world production and viewing technologies and even culturally what it means to watch and identify with various characters in these series are woven and fluid in such a network of intra-action. Ageing and de-ageing are thus articulated in both the materiality and imaginings of science fiction as ontological co-constituents. Such a fluid perspective asks us to consider how assumptions about human ageing, and thus life, might be rendered visible in trans- and posthumanist worlds.

Ageing as a speculative plot feature is a major trope in popular science fiction films and series, in terms of both progression and regression. Despite being a subgenre of speculative fiction that imagines futures based (if sometimes tangentially) on actual scientific and technological knowledge, science fiction appears to demonstrate little imagination for the future of ageing beyond already well-established stereotypes.[5] Ageing and older persons are feared, pitied and generally marginalized; older characters are frequently portrayed as senile, curmudgeonly, infirm, dangerous, corrupt or benignly simple.

What distinguishes ageing in science fiction from other genres is the notion of acceleration, that is, through external forces, the rapid or instantaneous transformation from youthfulness to old age and vice versa and, in some cases, extreme deceleration of ageing. It renders visible that ageing is often seen as a merely physical, embodied process. As Josephine Dolan points out, although not with reference to science fiction but to *The Curious Case of Benjamin Button*, in which reverse ageing is central to the plot, 'through this device of reverse ageing the film effectively uncouples old age and chronological age, destabilises life course framings and establishes fertile terrain for age appearance adjudications and chronological confusions' (Dolan 2017: 225). Unlike *The Curious Case of Benjamin Button*, though, the tropes of accelerated or decelerated ageing in science fiction usually couple ageing with decline and do not openly challenge the fact that there is little or no inherent meaning in chronology itself. In the following section, we will address the cultural constructedness of ageing and especially old age in more detail, focusing on how gender plays out in ageing science fiction characters.

Intersections of age and gender in science fiction

We use the term 'older characters' here to refer to characters who are specifically created to convey identities based on older age that are not the norm of the younger or middle-aged characters that dominate the genre. Younger characters are always presented as 'unmarked' in the hegemonic sense of 'normal' in terms of age; they are usually embodied by actors in their twenties to early forties who are perceived to be neither particularly 'young' nor 'old', where 'age' as a category is usually not a clearly visible identity marker. As such, conspicuously absent in most mainstream science fiction films and series are older human hero protagonists, bar a few of the various Whos in the long-running *Doctor Who* series. Wise old Obi-Wan Kenobi of *Star Wars*, the venerable Ambassador Spock of later *Star Treks*, powerful Yoda in the *Star Wars* films and the fierce warrior Bre'tac in the *Stargate SG-1* series are also noteworthy exceptions, though most are aliens, and while they are major characters, they are not the primary protagonists.

And old women action heroes? With relatively few exceptions, lead older women characters are practically non-existent, though they are often employed as mediators of wisdom for the protagonist or cunning evildoers in the tradition of the good witch/bad witch trope. Their invisibility on screen, however, is not due to any magical properties that allow them to deliberately vanish whenever they are in danger, but to a metaphorical 'cloak of invisibility' in the sense of public ignorance and a general overlooking of older women as viable action heroes.[6] In science fiction, older female action heroes have so far not been used strategically, though promisingly, an episode in a new Amazon Prime science fiction series *Solos* features Helen Mirren as Peg, an introspective seventy-something space explorer on a one-way journey to the far reaches of the universe. In a 1990 study of portrayals of both older women and men on primetime television, Vernon et al.

found indications 'that negative stereotypes are being replaced by more positive perceptions. However, the findings also indicate[d] that ageism continues to exist in terms of both underrepresentation and characterization' (1990: 66). They concluded: 'perhaps the most surprising finding is the preponderance of middle-aged men in focal roles in contrast to a relative lack of middle-age women. Most disturbing is the perpetuation of the idea that women must remain youthful in appearance while men are allowed to show signs of ageing' (1990: 66–67). Some three decades later, major older women characters such as Princess Leia, who appears as a battle-seasoned resistance leader in a later series of the Star Wars franchise, and Chrisjen Avasarala, as a tough-as-nails politician and secretary general of the United Nations in the Amazon Prime series *The Expanse*, are still rare. It seems apparent that science fiction is inherently ageist, and ageism plays out differently for women and men.

Science fiction fan sites meticulously devoted to archiving data about characters clearly establish the average ages of the cast members playing those characters. One online sharing site, Imgur, shows the average ages of all the primary cast members of almost all *Star Trek* TV series to be in the low to mid-thirties at the time of launch (2013). Stephen Follows (2016), a film industry data researcher, analysed the average age of lead actors across film genres over a ten-year period and found that science fiction was among the youngest of genres for the average age of actors, along with musicals and horror films.[7] He also compares the data on age by gender and notes: 'There are extremely few older women in lead roles within sci-fi movies. Only 6.1% of the women in sci-fi films were over 50 years old, compared with 17.0% of women in dramas' (2016). Now, the gender bias in science fiction is fairly well established, and the literature on this subject notes that memorable strong female leads in major science fiction franchises – such as Ellen Ripley (*Alien*), Sarah Connor (*Terminator*), Rey (*Star Wars*) and Katherine Janeway (*Star Trek: Voyager*) – are still exceptional (and mostly youthful). Female characters, though apparently increasing in number, are still far more likely to be kick-ass sidekicks or plot accomplices, rather than the heroes. Things may have progressed somewhat since the days of compliant 'sex-kitten' *Barbarella*; however, despite an apparent increase in strong female characters in popular broadcast science fiction, and even some low-key nods to sexual, gender and racial identity beyond a white, hetero, male/female binary, these are still relatively rare, and even when they do show up, they have little to do in terms of exploring gender, race or sexuality as a primary motivator of plot. By comparison, in science fiction novels, short stories, graphic novels and comics, these concepts have fared much better, having been explored by such noted authors, writing in the vein of second-wave feminism, as Ursula le Guin, Octavia Butler, Joanna Russ, Samuel Delaney, Margaret Atwood and Katherine Forrest.

Interestingly, and as an apt example of the intersection between gender and ageing in science fiction, is the character of Jadzia Dax (Terry Farrell) in the *Star Trek* TV series *Deep Space Nine*. Jadzia is a Starfleet officer and a Trill, a humanoid species, who is host to a non-humanoid Trill symbiont. The symbionts are very long lived and are implanted in succeeding generations of Trill hosts as each ages and dies. Each successive host has their own identity but also retains the full memories and, to some extent, shared personalities of preceding hosts through their symbiont. Jadzia's symbiont, Dax, thus imparts to Jadzia memories and attributes of former male hosts, the most recent being Curzon Dax, whom Captain Sisko refers to as 'old man'. Jadzia thus dwells in co-existing identities as both a man and a woman, and as a young officer and older Federation ambassador. In addition to exploring these complexities of age and gender, DS9 went where no one had gone before in the franchise, and in one episode, Jadzia is reunited with her 'wife' from a previous host and forms an intimate relationship with her (DS9, 'Rejoined'). More importantly for our purpose in this chapter, Jadzia represents a chronological confluence of both youthing and ageing in the form of the youthful but ageing Trill host and old and renewed symbiont, though the representation of this confluence is still portrayed for the viewing audience by a physically young, attractive character.

Science fiction and the imaginary of the 'fourth age'

Admiral Picard, the aged hero, returns to Starfleet to save the world. His independence and activity characterize what Peter Laslett has called the 'third age' (1989: 3). It is, as Paul Higgs and Chris Gilleard explain with reference to Laslett, a stage of life that can be seen as an era of post-retirement freedom, achievement and personal fulfilment and, even more importantly, a phase characterized, among other aspects, by 'its active exclusion of "old age" and "agedness"' (2015: 12). Interestingly, while science fiction lacks representations of characters in the 'third age', rapid age progression as a narrative device allows for depictions of characters in the 'fourth age'. This kind of 'agedness', which is only hinted at in Picard, occupies centre stage in the following examples that showcase the 'fourth age' as 'an era of final dependence, decrepitude, and death' (Laslett 1991: 4), which is not often visually represented in other genres of film and fiction.

Gilleard and Higgs analyse the 'fourth age' with metaphorical concepts taken from the realm of outer space:

> The fourth age is important as a cultural and structural component of aging but it is not constructed around the same coordinates as those of the third age. It is not simply the terminus of the third age, nor some kind of third-age anti-matter – the unsuccessful but necessary counterpart to successful aging. One way of approaching this issue is to consider the fourth age as a kind of social or cultural 'black hole' that exercises a powerful gravitational pull upon the surrounding field of aging. (2010: 121–2)

Gilleard and Higgs address the difficulty of representing the oldest age by explaining it as a 'black hole', a metaphor that signifies a place, or rather a space-time, where gravity is so strong that anything that approaches it is endangered: nothing can escape. This concept, sociologist Amanda Grenier explains, 'confronts the invisibility of the fourth age and the void of cultural space allocated to this group' (2012: 174). The use of the metaphor of a black hole, interpreted as a place of atemporality, highlights the sense of threat emanating from this phenomenon and seeks to explain the cultural 'othering' of those in this phase of life. In science fiction, characters who reach the fourth age are also othered and thus face a major threat to their selfhood but one that is not necessarily terminal because of the very speculative nature of the genre itself. In science fiction, it is through rapid age progression that we get to explore this imaginary. In all these narrative representations, old age is associated with frailty and depicted as an abject state. As Gilleard and Higgs note,

> This re-alignment of abjection and agedness arises not from a disgust attached to the visible signs of bodily aging (grey hair, wrinkled skin, and sagging muscles) nor from disdain for the demonstrable difficulties that aging bodies display. Rather, we have argued, it arises from the perceived loss of agency and bodily self-control and the failure to achieve any restoration of that loss – in short, the impotence to mount a transgression of agedness.
>
> This lack of control, and by implication lack of social agency that it implies, limits the potential of the abject aged body to challenge the position in which it is placed. The sense of threat associated with old age more generally is focused now by the social imaginary of a fourth age that appears to have lost it – to have become 'sans everything'. (2011: 141)

Despite the 'deus ex machina' of technological salvation (see Picard, among others), for the most part, rapid age progression in science fiction is portrayed negatively and painfully as degeneration and deterioration, even if it is part of the journey to transformation. One frequent plot trope is exposure to alien technology and time manipulation. In the ending of Stanley Kubrick's epic *2001: A Space Odyssey*, for example, astronaut Dave Bowman is transported to an alien caretaker 'zoo' and sees himself rapidly age to the 'fourth age' signifying decrepitude and death, whereupon he is reborn as the Star Baby, the next stage of human evolution. Rebirth provides an avoidance of the responsibility and discomfort of confronting the fourth age on both a personal and a social level. It is interesting to note that caregiving is an irrelevant concept and that solutions are in the technology.

In the *Stargate SG1* episode 'Brief Candle,' Colonel Jack O'Neill is infected by alien nanites that rapidly transform him into extreme old age in a matter of days. He also rapidly acquires all the stereotypical mannerisms of crotchetiness, stubbornness and frailty. Of course, he is eventually 'cured' and happily transformed back to his more youthful self. 'Don't worry', says the re-youthed O'Neill referring to old age, 'aside from a little prostate problem we won't go into, it's not so bad'. In the film *Looper* (2012), a crime syndicate sends victims back in time to be murdered and their bodies disposed of by a hired assassin called a 'Looper'. The Looper is under contract to 'close the loop' by murdering their older future self once their usefulness to the mob has ended. The younger Looper thus lives a life of crime and indulgence while faced with the certainty of their death by their own hand, while the old Looper, after having experienced years of murdering and indulgence, has to face (and resist) the certainty of a prescribed, violent death and fulfilment of the contract. Neither character is particularly sympathetic as youth and ageing are telescoped by the paradox of time travel. As with Dave Bowman's rebirth in *2001: A Space Odyssey*, *Looper* highlights the inconceivable possibility of living a good life in old age.

Another popular trope to fend off the unpleasant reality of the fourth age is genetic manipulation. The rare genetic disorder Hutchinson–Gilford syndrome, for instance, which causes the appearance of rapid ageing in children, appears to be the inspiration for the film *Blade Runner*'s 'Methuselah Syndrome' in the character J. F. Sebastian, a genius genetic designer whose 'glands grow old too fast'. Prohibited from travelling to the Offworld colonies because of his disability, Sebastian, who lives alone and faces accelerated ageing and an early death, is the target of manipulation by the Nexus 6 bioengineered replicants he helped create and with whom he empathizes as they attempt to avoid a similar fate of a genetically engineered early death built into their DNA. Oh, and when he fails to help them, they kill him.

Cosmic radiation is the source of the portrayal of rapid ageing in perhaps the most old-age-phobic episode in TOS of *Star Trek*, 'The Deadly Years'. While on an away mission to a planet, members of the command crew are subject to radiation from a passing comet that causes them to age by decades and rapidly deteriorate in a few days. Not only are they made to look excessively wrinkled, infirm and frail, but they are also subject to rapid senility and loss of functional and leadership abilities, especially Captain Kirk who is removed from command under protest. 'I admit, I'm getting a little gray', he argues, 'but radiation will do that to you'. Saved at the last minute by an adrenaline serum and reverted back to their youthful selves, Kirk muses to his officers that their experience is one that they will remember in their old age – 'which', he quips, 'won't be for some while' (*TOS*, 'The Deadly Years'). Gilleard and Higgs's notion of old age as an abject state 'sans everything' (2011: 141) becomes very clear in the scene where Captain Kirk's confusion is evident to everyone but himself. He, too, represents the 'old fool'. Like the old man described in Jacques's soliloquy, 'All the world's a stage' from Shakespeare's *As You Like It*, he enters a second childhood, 'Sans teeth, sans eyes, sans taste, sans everything' (Shakespeare [1623] 2012: 33) – and is forced to give up control of the starship. Kirk is of course 'cured' of ageing, which is clearly seen as pathological in this series, highlighting that in science fiction, characters usually do not die of old age, not even when ageing rapidly. The 'fourth age' is portrayed stereotypically but can be avoided by time travel, genetic manipulation or technology – which can be a blessing, but also a curse, as we discuss below.

Youthing and immortality: The Promethean curse

Aligned with rapid ageing scenarios are numerous plots in science fiction feature films and TV series (also many novels and short stories in the genre) that involve curing, or at least delaying, the 'disease' of ageing and mortality, such as digitally transferring and storing one's memory and biodata as a form of digital immortality. The TV series *Altered Carbon*, *Black Mirror* and *Caprica* all include examples of this. Suspended animation or stasis for decades and even millennia is another common method, employed in such series as *Star Trek*, the comedy *Red Dwarf* and the animated *Futurama*. Ageing and older persons are portrayed as disabled and as characters to be feared, pitied and in some cases eradicated, as in the classic science fiction film *Logan's Run*, where reaching the age of thirty is a death sentence. In the DS9 episode, 'Distant Voices', Dr Bashir faces his thirtieth birthday, of which he states, 'the thirtieth birthday is considered a sort of landmark. It marks the end of youth and the beginning of the slow march into middle age ... in two days I turn thirty. If I choose to be grumpy about it, that's my prerogative.' As this example makes clear, a purely chronological definition of ageing is foregrounded: Dr Bashir associates his decade anniversary with crisis. Decade markers have special significance, as Margaret Gullette points out: 'The decade anniversaries – fifty, forty, thirty', she writes, 'are increasingly flamboyant and critical dates, potential "crises" decorated with black balloons' (2004: 31–2). Dr Bashir interprets his thirtieth as such, as it marks, he argues, the end of youth, which he mourns. The next stage of life, middle age, seems to be threatening as he associates it with decline. After being telepathically attacked by an alien called a Lethean, Bashir enters a nightmare state where all the stereotypes of science fiction rapid ageing play out: decrepitude created with an abundance of make-up, senility, being patronized and humiliated, even breaking his hip when he falls. Being thirty doesn't seem so bad by comparison.

By contrast, age regression, or 'youthing', tends to be portrayed as both a blessing and a curse, depending on who is doing that youthing and what their motives are. For characters who intend no harm, the transformation is usually constructed positively – at least initially. For less savoury characters, youthfulness comes with a heavy price, for themselves and for others. Either way though, getting or staying young typically comes with a warning about tampering with nature and as a burden for carrying the weight of immortality. Again, there are exceptions that are contrastive, allowing for not only reflection on the physiological and psychological aspects of ageing and youthing but also the contextual in terms of the role of ageing in state and social systems and structures.

In one relatively positive reverse ageing episode of *Star Trek: The Next Generation* titled 'Rascals', a transporter malfunction converts four members of the crew, including Captain Picard, to twelve-year-olds, though they retain their adult personalities. Picard is distraught to no longer have adult authority, and Keiko is distraught to be a twelve-year-old with a husband and a baby daughter who does not recognize her. But Guinan and Ro revel in their newfound freedom to run, jump, skip and play. 'I haven't been young for a long time', exclaims Guinon, 'and I intend to enjoy every minute of it!' The four use their outward appearance and status as children to outwit aliens who board the ship and capture the rest of the crew. But youthing is replaced by instantaneous re-ageing as Starfleet duty calls, and the youngsters are 'cured' back to maturity via the now reprogrammed transporter. Social responsibility and the institutional expectations of marriage and family as well as the duty and loyalty of Starfleet officers to the Federation techno-utopia outweigh individual desire to cheat ageing and embrace a second lifetime as their younger selves. By comparison, in the Stargate SG1 series, which is set in the present rather than in the distant future, a more cynical outlook on state and social structures allows for a more nuanced relationship between childhood and adulthood. In the case of the episode 'Fragile Balance', Colonel O'Neill is cloned by Loki, a rogue Asgard scientist. The clone, a teenage O'Neill, has all the memories of the original and is essentially a much younger Jack O'Neill with an adult mind. As with the STNG episode (above), young O'Neill is frustrated by adults not taking him seriously, treating him like a child and not recognizing his adult discourse, wisdom and experience. Without the appearance of physical adulthood, he is denied its systemic authority. Still, young O'Neill is allowed to start life again on his own terms with the blessing of older O'Neill, though they will not stay in touch because, as they agree, 'that would be weird'.

Both ageing and youthing fare even better in the highly optimistic 1985 film *Cocoon*, as the senior residents of a retirement home enjoy youthful rejuvenation in the life-force-giving swimming pool of their beneficent Antarean alien neighbours. Unlike typical portrayals where those who dare partake of the fountain of youth must eventually revert back, the seniors travel back to the Antarean home world with their hosts, where they will never grow older and will never die. Gerontology scholars Karasik et al. point to *Cocoon* as an important example of a portrayal of older characters that challenges stereotypes of ageing as synonymous with 'disengaging with society' (2014).

Characters who experience rapid or sustained age regression, however, generally fare much worse in popular science fiction productions. As we noted, the act of cheating on ageing and mortality is depicted as something that goes against the laws of nature, and the price a character, often a 'bad guy', pays for the vitality, strength, beauty and virility of ill-gotten youthing is portrayed in extreme rapid ageing and death. Such is the case in the *STNG* (*Star Trek Next Generation*) episode 'Man of the People,' in which a Federations ambassador preys on women by telepathically transferring all of his unwanted thoughts and emotions to them. This keeps him young, self-focused and confident, but his victims suffer horrible age regression and dependency and eventually die while he moves on to another. Once discovered by his latest victim, Counselor Troi, who is now portrayed as extremely old and dying, all the ambassador's negative vibes flow back into him, and he rapidly shrivels and dies, vampire-like, while Troi regains her youthful self.

Again in *STNG*, in the episode 'Too Short a Season', a thoroughly unpleasant older Starfleet admiral, the actor heavily made-up to look cartoonishly old, returns to a planet that forty-five years previously he had helped plunge into a devastating civil war. He takes a rejuvenating drug that reverses his ageing and even takes his wife's dose, leaving her to remain older. But the drug destroys his body, and in an ironic twist, he dies from the very source that had restored his youthfulness and vigour. The episode concludes as Captain Picard sums up the waste of it all to his second-in-command, Commander Riker: 'The quest for youth, Number One. So futile.'

There are many more such examples of portrayals of the confluence of chronological loops and fluidity of youthing and ageing in contemporary science fiction dramas, but we would be remiss here not to mention the 'Benjamin Button effect' in the *Voyager* episode 'Innocence'. Lieutenant Tuvok is marooned on a planet where he meets up with three young Drayan children. The biological peculiarity of the Drayans is that in avoiding the psychological trauma of their awareness of impending death in old age, they revert to youthful innocence both mentally and physically as they age. Tuvok, once he gains understanding of this process, aids them in their final journey to join the 'infinite energy'. Death is thus portrayed, as the title of the episode suggests, as beautiful in its innocence as regression to youthfulness. Ageing is again represented and naturalized as traumatic.

But all of these portrayals are dependent on the real-world technologies of ageing and de-ageing for video and film. Cloning, transporters and nanoprobes are the stuff of technological possibility, but in the world-making and character-making and ageing of science fiction, they remain, for now, fictional constructs. Yet the real-world technologies, digital and material, of video and filmmaking often amplify stereotyping for plot through the overzealous use of make-up, prosthetics and props to indicate ageing of younger characters through ample applications of hair dye, wrinkles, jowls, humps and skin mottling, along with canes, walkers and wheelchairs, which theatrically equate ageing with infirmity and, for the most part, look fake. Similarly, youthing older actors provides its own production challenges, though typically with much more positive stereotypical indicators manufactured with dark hair dye, heavy pancake make-up and prosthetic musculature. Until recently, the appearance of age fakeness has seemed an acceptable aspect of the science fiction visual genres. However, innovation in the technologies of digital enhancements is perhaps changing expectations and increasing the demand for realistic portrayals of ageing and de-ageing in visual media. Of recent note is the Netflix production of *The Irishman*, which allowed actors in their late seventies and early eighties to realistically portray younger versions of themselves across a span of fifty years solely through the use of enhanced digital visual effects (VFX) and no make-up. Such technologies may allow even more realistic portrayals of rapid ageing and de-ageing to come in science fiction films and series, though the evolving production technologies alone are no guarantee that stereotypes of ageing will evolve along with them. Still, at least the potential exists for a positive step towards challenging visually pejorative portrayals of older spaceship captains. It may be that, now in his eighties, actor Patrick Stewart may continue playing Jean-Luc Picard and even younger flashback versions of himself. Or it may be that the ageing Stewart is put out to pasture and that younger actors can portray the older Picard for as long as the series is viable.

Conclusion

For the most part, popular mainstream science fiction productions continue to reflect and project our fears and cultural assumptions about ageing and old age. There is hardly any subversive reading or watching possible – many of the scripts and visual representations speculating on the future of humanity are quite ageist when analysed through the lens of ageing studies. Space, it seems, is not the final frontier for stereotypes of ageing, whether it be perpetual youth via digital memories downloaded into 'sleeves' (cloned bodies accessible only to the very wealthy in *Altered Carbon* – the poor must age and die) or outright euthanasia via disintegration (*Logan's Run*). In popular science fiction films and series, speculation is surprisingly limited and reductive in this regard and attitudes towards the future of ageing are not presented as significantly different from the past or present.

As the foreshadowing in Season One of *Picard* already indicates, Season Two, which came out just as this chapter was being finalized, also features the old admiral who resists inertia and is declining to decline, but in doing so, he must suffer the consequences of his actions and not knowing his place in society. Also, the old admiral, viewers learn, is severely ill. After asking his doctor to certify him to Starfleet as fit for interstellar service, Picard learns that it might not be a good idea, as his illness, a defect in his parietal lobe, is progressing rapidly as he ages: 'I don't know what trouble you're planning to get into', his doctor warns him, 'but maybe if you're lucky it will kill you first' (*STP*, 'Maps and Legends'). Picard actually dies from his fatal brain disease at the end of Season One, but he does so not as an ailing man, but as a hero who, just before dying, saves the galaxy. Most importantly, however, his brain, including his entire consciousness, lives on in a new synthetic body that looks just like his own body would have looked had it not died. As John Orquiola points out, 'His new synthetic frame is identical to Picard's organic 94-year-old body – meaning no super strength or other enhancements (citing that Picard wouldn't want to get used to anything new at his age). This is a sly cheat to explain why they didn't make Picard younger so that 79-year-old Patrick Stewart can continue to play him as age-appropriate' (2020: n.p.).

The genre of science fiction is devoted to imagining the possible and impossible in future science and technology, and the limitations and endless potentials for human development and exploration. Yet, popular science fiction video and film series that largely continue to sponsor heteronormative, white, male and youthful characters are indicative not only of existing hegemonic social values and ageism but also of how those values are visually represented in imagined futures. Series with female leads, people of colour and non-heteronormative, non-heterosexual characters have become more common in recent years though are still noteworthy as exceptions. Even in such series, ageing and older characters are rarely represented beyond existing ageist perceptions. At least, for now. The future of popular science fiction has yet to be written, but such series as *Picard* (and more recently, *Solos*) give us a glimpse of future possibilities and a reimagining of future representations, for better or worse, of ageing and old age.

Notes

1 The first season of the series was released on the streaming service CBS All Access (later renamed Paramount+).
2 In later films featuring the Enterprise crew from TOS, namely *Star Trek V: The Final Frontier* in 1989 and *Star Trek VI: The Undiscovered Country* in 1991, the actors are much older and paunchier. Attempts to make them appear younger are so noticeable as to make the films the subject of parodies, such as in *The Simpsons* episode 'Itchy and Scratchy: The Movie', where 'Star Trek XII: So Very Tired' is advertised on TV, featuring aged characters. Note that *The Simpsons* series itself is no stranger to offensive stereotypes of older persons.
3 Josephine Dolan discusses the 'emerging silver audience' in her book chapter 'From the Silvering of Audiences to the Silver of Spin-Offs' (2017: 31–69), arguing that even though the film industry has started to recognize the benefit of older audiences, 'the

production and release of films with older protagonists and storylines that engage with contemporary issues of ageing has lagged behind the emergence of the silver audience' (2017: 35).

4   We note this trope in speculative fiction is different from the popular concept of 'soap opera rapid ageing syndrome', the practice of rapidly ageing or de-ageing a character over episodic timelines that conflict with real-world time progression. In these cases, the rapid ageing and youthing is for the purpose of editorially hastening a dramatic story line (e.g. abbreviated pregnancy to birth and maturity from adolescence to adulthood) usually unrelated to the rapid ageing/de-ageing process itself as a plot feature.

5   Our position on defining science fiction and speculative fiction is that the latter is an umbrella term that encompasses subgenres of 'what if' fiction, including science fiction, fantasy, horror and the multiple subgenres within those genres. The *Oxford Research Encyclopedia of Literature* describes this view of speculative fiction as 'a super category for all genres that deliberately depart from imitating "consensus reality" of everyday experience' (Oziewicz 2017: n.p.).

6   As always, there are notable exceptions to the general trend. Auntie Entity in the apocalyptic Mad Max franchise (*Mad Max beyond Thunderdome*), the much older Princess Leia in *Star Wars* and President Laura Roslin in the *Battlestar Galactica* remake. Prominent ageing studies scholars Sally Chivers (2011) and Josephine Dolan (2017) have pointed to the ambivalence of increased portrayals of ageing women in popular films.

7   Follows' survey notes that Westerns and animations are the oldest in age averages for performers.

Filmography

2001: A Space Odyssey (1968), [Film]. Dir. Stanley Kubrick, USA, MGM.
Alien (1979), [Film]. Dir. Ridley Scott, USA, 20th Century Fox.
Altered Carbon (2018), [TV Series]. USA, Netflix.
Barbarella (1968), [Film]. Dir. Roger Vadim, USA, Paramount Pictures.
Black Mirror (2011–), [TV Series]. United Kingdom, Channel 4 and Netflix.
Blade Runner (1982), [Film]. Dir. Ridley Scott, USA, Warner Bros.
Caprica (2009–10), [TV Series]. USA, NBC.
Cocoon (1985), [Film]. Dir. Ron Howard, USA, 20th Century Fox.
Doctor Who (1963–), [TV Series]. United Kingdom, BBC Studios.
Logan's Run (1976), [Film]. Dir. Michael Anderson, USA, MGM.
Looper (2012), [Film]. Dir. Rian Johnson, USA, TriStar Pictures.
Red Dwarf (1988–99), [TV Series]. United Kingdom, BBC Two.

Rogue One: A Star Wars Story (2016), [Film]. Dir. Gareth Edwards, USA, Walt Disney Studios Motion Pictures.

Solo: A Star Wars Story (2018), [Film]. Dir. Ron Howard, USA, Walt Disney Studios Motion Pictures.

Stargate SG-1 (1997–2007), [TV Series]. USA, MGM.

Stargate SG-1 (1997), [TV Series]. Season 1, episode 9, 'Brief Candle'. Dir. Mario Azzopardi, USA, Showtime. Aired 19 September 1997.

Star Trek: The Original Series (TOS) (1966–9), [TV Series]. USA, Norway Productions, Desilu Productions, Paramount Television.

Star Trek: The Original Series (TOS) (1967), [TV Series]. Season 2, episode 12, 'The Deadly Years'. Dir. Joseph Pevney, USA, NBC. Aired 8 December 1967.

Star Trek: The Next Generation (STNG) (1987–94), [TV Series]. USA, Paramount Domestic Television.

Star Trek: The Next Generation (STNG) (1988), [TV Series]. Season 1, episode 16, 'Too Short a Season'. Dir. Rob Bowman, USA, Broadcast Syndication. Aired 8 February 1988.

Star Trek: The Next Generation (STNG) (1992), [TV Series]. Season 6, episode 3, 'Man of the People'. Dir. Winrich Kolbe, USA, Paramount Domestic Television. Aired 5 October 1992.

Star Trek: The Next Generation (STNG) (1992), [TV Series]. Season 6, episode 7, 'Rascals'. Dir. Adam Nimoy, USA, Paramount Domestic Television. Aired 31 October 1992.

Star Trek: Deep Space Nine (DS9) (1993–9), [TV Series]. USA, Paramount Domestic Television.

Star Trek: Deep Space Nine (DS9) (1995), [TV Series]. Season 3, episode 18, 'Distant Voices'. Dir. Alexander Singer, USA, Paramount. Aired 10 April 1995.

Star Trek: Deep Space Nine (DS9) (1995), [TV Series]. Season 4, episode 6, 'Rejoined'. Dir. Avery Brooks, USA, Paramount. Aired 30 October 1995.

Star Trek: Voyager (STV) (1995–2001), [TV Series]. USA, United Paramount Network.

Star Trek: Voyager (STV) (1996), [TV Series]. Season 2, episode 22, 'Innocence'. Dir. James L. Conway, USA, United Paramount Network. Aired 8 April 1996.

Star Trek: Picard (STP) (2020), [TV Series]. Season 1, episode 1, 'Remembrance'. Dir. Hanelle Culpepper, USA, CBS. Aired 23 January 2020.

Star Trek: Picard (STP) (2020), [TV Series]. Season 1, episode 2, 'Maps and Legends'. Dir. Hanelle Culpepper, USA, CBS. Aired 30 January 2020.

Star Trek V: The Final Frontier (1989), [Film]. Dir. William Shatner, USA, Paramount Pictures.

Star Trek VI: The Undiscovered Country (1991), [Film]. Dir. Nicholas Meyer, USA, Paramount Pictures.

Star Wars I: The Phantom Menace (1999), [Film]. Dir. George Lucas, USA, 20th Century Fox.

Star Wars III: Revenge of the Sith (2005), [Film]. Dir. George Lucas, USA, 20th Century Fox.

Star Wars IV: A New Hope (1977), [Film]. Dir. George Lucas, USA, 20th Century Fox.
Star Wars VI: Return of the Jedi (1989), [Film]. Dir. Richard Marquand, USA, 20th Century Fox.
Star Wars VII: The Force Awakens (2015), [Film]. Dir. J. J. Abrams, USA, Walt Disney Studios Motion Pictures.
Terminator (1984), [Film]. Dir. James Cameron, USA, Orion Pictures.
The Curious Case of Benjamin Button (2008), [Film]. Dir. David Fincher, USA, Paramount Pictures.
The Expanse (2015–), [Television Series]. USA, Syfy and Prime Video.
The Irishman (2019) [Film]. Dir. Martin Scorsese, USA, Netflix.
The Simpsons (1992), [Television Series]. Season 4, episode 65, 'Itchy and Scratchy: The Movie'. Dir. Rich Moore, USA, Fox. Aired 3 November 1992.

References

Banerjee, M., and N. W. Paul (2015), 'Aging Beyond the Rhetoric of Aging', in M. Oró-Piqueras and A. Wohlmann (eds), *Serializing Age: Aging and Old Age in TV Series*, 269–72, Aging Studies 7, Bielefeld: Transcript Verlag.
Barad, K. (2007), *Meeting the Universe Halfway: Quantum Physics and the Entanglement of Matter and Meaning*, Durham: Duke University Press.
Chivers, S. (2011), *The Silvering Screen*, Toronto: University of Toronto Press.
Dolan, J. (2017), *Contemporary Cinema and 'Old Age': Gender and the Silvering of Stardom*, London: Palgrave Macmillan.
Follows, S. (2016), 'How Does the Average Age of Actors Differ between Genres?' *Stephen Follows*. Available online: https://stephenfollows.com/age-of-actors/ (accessed 3 December 2021).
Gilleard, C., and P. Higgs (2010), 'Aging without Agency: Theorizing the Fourth Age', *Aging and Mental Health*, 14(2): 121–8. doi:10.1080/13607860903228762.
Gilleard, C., and P. Higgs (2011), 'Ageing Abjection and Embodiment in the Fourth Age', *Journal of Aging Studies*, 25(2): 135–42. doi:10.1016/j.jaging.2010.08.018.
Grenier, A. (2012), *Transitions and the Lifecourse: Challenging the Constructions of 'Growing Old'* Ageing and the Lifecourse, Bristol: Policy Press.
Gullette, M. M. (1997), *Declining to Decline: Cultural Combat and the Politics of the Midlife*, Age Studies, Charlottesville, VA: UP of Virginia.
Gullette, M. M. (2004), *Aged by Culture*, Chicago: University of Chicago Press.
Higgs, P., and C. Gilleard (2015), *Rethinking Old Age: Theorising the Fourth Age*, London: Palgrave Macmillan.
Imgur (2013), 'Star Trek'. Available online: https://imgur.com/a/D7mQL (accessed 23 February 2021).

Karasik, R. J., R. Hamon, J. Writz and A. M. Reddy (2014), 'Two Thumbs up: Using Popular Films in Introductory Aging Courses', *Gerontology and Geriatrics Education*, 35(1): 86–113. doi:10.1080/02701960.2012.749253.

Laslett, P. (1989), *A Fresh Map of Life: The Emergence of the Third Age*, London: Weidenfeld and Nicolson.

Laslett, P. (1991), *A Fresh Map of Life: The Emergence of the Third Age*, First Harvard paperback edition, Cambridge, MA: Harvard University Press.

Orquiola, J. (2020), 'Star Trek: Picard Season 1 Ending & All Twists Explained', *Screenrant*. Available online: https://screenrant.com/star-trek-picard-season-1-ending-explained/ (accessed 16 March 2021).

Oziewicz, M. (2017), 'Speculative Fiction', *Oxford Research Encyclopedia of Literature*. Available online: https://oxfordre.com/literature/view/10.1093/acrefore/9780190201098.001.0001/acrefore-9780190201098-e-78 (accessed 3 December 2021).

Shakespeare, W. ([1623] 2012), *As You Like It*, Dover Thrift edition, Newburyport: Dover.

Vernon, J. A., A. J. Williams, T. Phillips and J. Wilson (1990), 'Media Stereotyping: A Comparison of the Way Elderly Women and Men Are Portrayed on Prime-Time Television', *Journal of Women and Aging*, 2(4): 55–68.

Woodward, K. M. (1983), 'Instant Repulsion: Decrepitude, the Mirror Stage, and the Literary Imagination', *Kenyon Review*, 5(4): 43–66. Available online: http://search.ebscohost.com/login.aspx?direct=true&db=aph&AN=10891837&site=ehost-live (accessed 20 July 2021).

3

Ageing and generation in recent narratives of longevity

Sarah Falcus and Maricel Oró-Piqueras

Introduction

From Jonathan Swift's *Gulliver's Travels* ([1726] 2013) to Neal Shusterman's young adult *Arc of a Scythe* series, namely, *Scythe* (2017), *Thunderhead* (2019), *The Toll* (2020), authors have narrated and imagined future worlds in which some kind of 'cure' for ageing has been found. The quest for youthfulness in the form of longevity or immortality has long been central to speculative and science fiction. As Teresa Mangum points out, 'The search for immortality forms almost a subgenre of this literature' (2002: 70; see also Yoke and Hassler 1985; Clark 1995; Slusser et al. 1996). Variously read as narratives about class conflict, hubris and human desire, what is sometimes overlooked in discussions of these texts are their explicit and complex explorations of what it means to live in and across time.

This chapter focuses on four recent anglophone texts about longevity – *Super Sad True Love Story* by Gary Shteyngart (2010), *The Postmortal* by Drew Magary (2011), *Everything Belongs to the Future* by Laurie Penny (2016) and the film *In Time* by Andrew Niccol (2011) (hereafter novels cited by page number). Published or released within a few years of each other, these texts depict future or alternative worlds that have been fundamentally altered by a novum (Suvin 1979) that has resulted in extreme longevity, with the ageing of the body halted (or massively slowed) at a point in the life course, usually in young adulthood. Longevity is, in these texts, not only about longer life but also about extended physical youthfulness. The 'cure' (as named in Magary's *The Postmortal*) or 'fix' (as named in Penny's *Everything Belongs*) is then imbricated in a capitalist system that either controls time (the individual allocation of time or the treatment that will extend life) or leads to unequal distribution of the scarce resources that result from huge demographic change.

Ageing cures and the pursuit of immortality are, in these texts, then inextricably linked to economics, privilege and issues of inequality. Crucially, struggles over inequality and relative privilege are closely connected to and represented by forms of generational disruption and conflict. In his essay 'Longevity as Class Struggle', Frederic Jameson considers what he calls 'the longevity plot' as disguising 'historical change, radical mutations in society and collective life itself' (2005: 335). For Jameson, the longevity novel is about 'History' itself and reflects 'the increasing class polarization of the advanced countries of late capitalism' (2005: 342). This story of 'class struggle' is central to all four texts addressed in this chapter. The ramifications of social change – directly or indirectly linked to increased longevity – mean that the characters in these novels find themselves in a constant struggle to maintain their lifestyles, or even to survive at all, within a hostile social and economic global capitalist system. These novels, therefore, represent the relationship between longevity and inequality in a capitalist society; as Richard Lebow summarizes this relationship: 'money equals power, and immortality, if a scarce good, will be available primarily, perhaps only, to the rich' (2012: 248). Jameson also, however, recognizes the longevity novel's wider significance as part of the 'near-future sub-genre':

> On this level, it does not seem farfetched to argue that the motif of some special privilege of long life offers a dramatic and concentrated symbolic expression of class disparity itself and a way to express conveniently the passions that it cannot but arouse. But here one would want to add in something of the history of the form and suggest that the new paradigm marks a modification of the older, only-too-familiar near-future paradigms of overpopulation, ecological disaster, and the like. The longevity novel would thus stand as an enlargement of the possibilities of the near-future sub-genre, deploying the attempt to imagine future technologies in the service of the expression of deeper and more obscure fears and anxieties. (2005: 342–3)

Following this hermeneutic approach, we argue in this chapter that the deeper fears and anxieties addressed in longevity narratives are also those that are – at the representational level – most explicit: ageing, mortality and lives in time.

In Magary's *The Postmortal*, the anti-cure group 'the Greenies' forcibly carve original dates of birth on the arms of those who have taken the cure, ostensibly ageing the body accurately in a way that the cure prevents. But the coercion and crudeness of this process also draw attention to the fact that ageing is not simply biological and chronological and that living through time, ageing, is both a subjective and an intersubjective process shaped by everything from biology to economics and even climate change. What this example illustrates are the ways in which narratives of longevity are not simply warnings about mistaken human desire, but are explorations of what it means to live a life in time. As Mangum argues, 'while all narratives are profoundly preoccupied by time ... rejuvenation promises and fantasies ... often ... turn outward and become embroiled in larger concerns about time' (2002: 80). Undeniably critical of inequality and functioning as warnings about the science of life extension, the four texts here expose in various ways the temporal structures on which we depend – generation, life course markers and age stages. The 'anxieties' Jameson talks about may actually be existential and yet also social and economic concerns about age and time itself. In this chapter, we explore, in particular, the ways in which these texts both interrogate and depend upon a generational imaginary in their narratives of longevity. Conflicts that may be read as class-based are, in longevity narratives, also those of generations. The narrative propulsion provided by these generational conflicts may, though, disguise the more complex ways in which generationalism underpins the stories in these texts. They suggest that this kind of temporal ordering is central to the ways in which we understand and experience our lives in time, indicating our lack of alternatives to the generational imaginary, even within a genre based upon imagining worlds that function according to logic different from our own.

This chapter begins by exploring the concept of generation itself and the role it plays in the organization and experience of a human life in time. We then widen our scope to discuss age and ageing in these texts about longevity, recognizing that the texts critique the anti-ageing discourse that underpins rejuvenation and yet also depend upon an ageist imaginary. And, finally, we move to explore the centrality of generation within these texts and the fundamental role it plays in their treatments of longevity and time.

Generational time and identity

Generation emerged as a powerful concept in the West in the period following the First World War, beginning with the articulation of a 'war generation' (Erll 2014). It was soon after this that Karl Mannheim's influential 1927/8 essay 'The Problem of Generations' emerged, an essay still important to those interested in the study of generation. Mannheim makes clear that generation and generational identity are, though grounded in birth and death, inherently shaped by social and cultural forces. His comparison between generation and social class makes this clear. And generation itself is a complex and plastic idea. As Jane Pilcher (1994) points out, there is some terminological confusion in Mannheim's own use of generation. His use of the term is closer to the meaning of cohort: 'people within a delineated population who experience the same significant event within a given period of time' (Pilcher 1994: 483). But generation is also understood in terms of kin and reproduction, in other words, parents and children forming generations. Astrid Erll uses the terms 'generationality' ('generational identity') and 'genealogy' to express these two understandings of generation, pointing out that the latter is a much older use of generational understanding, linked as it is to kinship and family identity (2014: 385). What this conflation of ideas shows us, though, is that the notion of generation functions in our social imaginary, in our social life and in our ways of articulating the future in intersecting and overlapping ways, something we exploit in this chapter to explore a broad understanding of the ways in which generation secures – or attempts to secure – our sense of temporal identity.

Generationality and generational identity differ according to time, place and individual life course. As Pilcher's definition of cohort (above) makes clear, generational groups and collectivities may emerge from and be understood in relation to specific historical events, as June Edmunds and Bryan S. Turner (2005) argue about the 1960s generation that still functions as a powerful symbol of generational identity. 'Generationality' accommodates the different ways in which generational labels and identities come to be formed: 'The term "generationality" … has a twofold meaning. On the one hand, it refers to characteristics resulting from shared experiences that either individuals or larger "generational units" collectively claim for themselves. On the other hand, it can also mean the bundle of characteristics resulting from shared experiences that are ascribed to such units from the "outside"' (Reulecke in Erll 2014: 387). Generational identity is utilized socially, culturally and often rhetorically for many purposes, as seen in terms such as 'millennials' and 'baby boomers'. The perceived privilege of baby boomers is a good example of the ways in which generational identity linked to age cohort is used 'from the outside' to both homogenize and demonize particular groups of people. As Jennie Bristow argues, this cohort is negatively represented in cultural discourses for a number of reasons: as a retrospective interrogation of the 1960s generation that it comes to represent, in relation to twenty-first-century anxieties around the perceived economic cost of supporting and caring for this cohort and also in relation to a wider sense of demographic concern that is founded upon statistics (2016: 576). This generation is therefore constructed as a 'cultural and ... an economic problem' (Bristow 2016: 576). Similarly, Margaret Morganroth Gullette (2004) refers to the constant confrontation between 'Xers' and 'Boomers' that has been created by the media in recent decades. For Gullette, 'When Boomers are present in Xer discourse, they serve as the Other. They exist without question. They were said to hold all the good jobs, gobble the perks, and dominate the media, harping on themselves. ... They are the plutocratic sellouts with dental plans and pensions. Powerful but undeserving: "deadwood"' (2004: 43). Thus, generational identities and generational conflict are discursively constructed for particular purposes and with specific effects.

But generation functions in other ways, too. Familial generations (genealogy) are shaped in relation to each other – parents and children, for example – whilst intersecting with wider senses of generational collectivity and identity. Familial generations, like those based upon age cohort, contribute to social and individual identities in complex ways, not least because of their association with a heteronormative vision of futurity: the child as the future (Edelman 2004; Sheldon 2016). Generation in terms of both generationality and genealogy is, therefore, central to the ways in which we understand the life course and ageing itself. Bristow articulates this wider understanding of the idea of generations: '"generationalism" – "the systematic appeal to the concept of generation in narrating the social and political" ... – cannot be considered narrowly, as a description of the historical experience of particular birth cohorts: it should also be understood as a way of thinking and knowing' (2016: 575–6). In this chapter, we adopt that broad sense of 'generationalism' as a way of thinking and knowing to explore how speculative, dystopian fiction exposes our reliance on the temporal ordering of generation as both generationality and genealogy. Mannheim posits that 'the best way to appreciate which features of social life result from the existence of generations is to make the experiment of imagining what the social life of man [sic] would be like if one generation lived on for ever and none followed to replace it' (1972: 292). Whilst the texts we analyse here do not all go as far as to imagine one endless, non-replicating generation, they all offer experiments in imagining what it would be like for generational identity, generational succession and, more broadly, generational temporality to be disrupted by extreme longevity. In the process, they remind us that generational thinking and generational understanding are central to the ways in which we imagine a human life in and across time, for good or for ill.

Age and ageing in narratives of longevity

The texts analysed here might all be categorized as what Mangum calls 'rejuvenescence narratives': they 'bargain with rather than conquer time' and 'insist that readers imagine the consequences should technology succeed in reversing the aging process' (2002: 70). As such, they take – like so many rejuvenation narratives – a less-than-straightforward approach to ageing itself. In all of these texts, longevity is figured as a way to stay young, to stop physical ageing. It is based on a very narrow biological and physiological view of ageing that depends upon a Cartesian mind–body dualism. In these depictions of longevity, the texts engage with and tend to critique the scientific, cultural and capitalist interest in anti-ageing and life extension. In recent years, the proliferation of techniques to maintain a youthful appearance together with the advances in science that extend longevity seem to bring the promise of eternal youth closer to being achieved. As John A. Vincent, among others, has stated, in the past decades, the quest for anti-ageing techniques has been related to a mostly liberal economy in which 'successful ageing' is mainly understood as staying young or youthful and active for as long as possible. In this way, then, as Vincent argues, the sciences of 'anti-ageing' contribute to the negative cultural discourse of ageing (2008: 331). Anti-ageing is, as the term suggests, a movement – or ideal – that aspires to overcome ageing as decline (Gullette 2004).

Like many contemporary and classic narratives of longevity (see Mangum 2002; Lebow 2012), these four texts suggest that stopping or massively slowing physical ageing is inherently negative – both for the individual and for society. Explicitly challenging anti-ageing discourses, they might then be seen to implicitly challenge the ageism that underpins these. In all of the texts, longevity results in boredom, anxiety, repetition, insecurity and forms of undesirable social and organizational change. Vidal relates classical depictions of immortality, which link it with 'everlasting torments', as in the cases of Prometheus and Sisyphus, to modern fictions that 'associate immortality, if not necessarily with punishment and suffering, at least with situations that make everlasting life a troublesome, not altogether rewarding state of being' (2016: 667). In this scenario, the promises of eternal youth often turn into some kind of hell, a turn that Mark R. Brand has identified as inextricably attached to narratives of longevity: 'the existential nature of death, and the hard limits and motivations we attribute to it in the physical world, suggest an inescapable narrative overdetermination: a world of immortal humans – or worse, some immortal humans – must rapidly devolve into dystopia rather than eutopia' (2016: 3). The desire for youth is depicted as a hollow form of stasis – on social and individual levels – in our chosen texts. Longevity does not, though, simply condemn those experiencing it to repetition and boredom but also hampers the progress of narrative itself. There can be no longevity utopia here – inevitably, dystopia must become the driving force of these texts.

The satirical *Super Sad True Love Story* explores the protagonist, Lenny's, obsession with youth and beauty. Working at the Post-Human Services division of the Staatling-Wapachung corporation, Lenny tries to sell immortality to 'High Net Worth Individuals' whilst attempting to bolster his own fortunes and thereby fund his own life extension. High-tech vertical and lateral surveillance, which includes the sharing of financial and health data, ensures continual anxiety and conformity in this highly stratified, dystopian, crumbling United States. Brand defines the novel as 'satirically play[ing] with longevity as the ultimate advertising campaign backed by a youth-obsessed, nostalgia-fuelled culture industry' (2016: 8). However, as Simon Willmetts (2018) argues in his analysis of the novel, it is not only a matter of paying for rejuvenatory techniques and products. In the novel, individuals must also engage in close 'surveillance' of the ageing of the body and acquire youth 'culture' (2018: 272), echoing Stephen Katz and Barbara Marshall's (2004, 2013) argument about the consumerist surveillance of the ageing body and lifestyle that lies at the heart of 'successful ageing'. Laurie Penny's *Everything Belongs to the Future* adopts a conflict-driven narrative as it imagines a world where a technological development allows people to 'fix' their physical ageing at a point in the life course; in other words, people can decide to halt the ageing of their bodies. Access to the technology is controlled by capitalist elites, and a form of class conflict drives the narrative. This text explicitly addresses the commodification of and conflict over time itself:

> Consider that time is a weapon. Before the coming of the Time Bomb, this was true. It was true before men and women of means or special merit could purchase an extra century of youth. It has been true since the invention of the hour-glass, the water clock, the wristwatch, the shift-bell, the factory floor. Ever since men could measure time, they have used it to divide each other. (11)

As with the other texts, in *Everything Belongs*, stopping the ageing of the body leads to anxiety, boredom and alienation, best expressed in the position of Daisy, one of the earliest to receive the longevity treatment, who is trapped and alone in a consumerist and performative world.

Like *Everything Belongs*, *The Postmortal* imagines a world where a 'cure' halts physical ageing. The novel exposes the fear of ageing that lies at the heart of the desire for the cure. John Farrell, the main protagonist, wants the cure because he does not want to die and his fear of death is very much based on a vision of physical decline and ageing: 'I was eighty-five years old on my deathbed, fat nurses sponging off my rotten skin' (9). As Farrell's father sums it up: 'It's not that people don't want to die. It's that they don't want to grow old' (22). The long time span of the novel (June 2019 to June 2079) increasingly depicts a completely disordered society where popular access to the cure for ageing brings about scarcity of resources (including food and space), the appearance of terrorist groups (related to the pro- and anti-cure lobbies), gang violence, ecological disaster and increasingly brutal ways of controlling population numbers. Farrell works in the 'end-specialization industry', which ranges from providing a form of euthanasia to those desiring death to terminating the lives of undesirables. The novel's dystopian vision, like that in *Super Sad*, depicts the terrible social consequences of the desire to stop bodily ageing and, in its repetitious, chronological story of Farrell's life, explores the individual aimlessness and sense of stasis that result from extreme longevity.

Niccol's *In Time* provides an even more blatant representation of capitalist conflict linked to longevity as it turns time itself into a commodity to be bought, sold and purloined. The population have clocks in their wrists which start counting down once they get to their twenty-first birthday; thus, everyone looks young, but they have to keep on gaining time in order to continue being alive. The population is divided into time zones, which correspond to social classes; those who have money and live in the privileged zones have longer lives than those who have to earn their daily time. This film depicts the sense of inertia and repetition that comes with extended life. According to Johann A. R. Roduit et al., 'the wealthy have forgotten how to live' in the film; it 'raises the fact that life enhancement may be boring, not because people will not have new experiences, but because they might look and behave the same for the rest of their lives' (2018: 292). A seemingly clear representation of Jameson's argument about longevity and class conflict, the film is also, like the other texts under discussion, a critique of the desire to remain physically young looking, a desire inextricably linked to capitalist consumption.

These texts are, then, critical of the desire to extend life through technological and other more nefarious means. As noted previously, the promise of a prolonged or even eternal youth may be read as a critique of the ageism that is central to anti-ageing – and even to successful ageing. Nevertheless, their treatment of ageing is more complex than this. In all of the texts, youth, when embodied in ageing selves, is, as Mangum (2002) notes in relation to other rejuvenesence narratives, exposed as performative. Anti-ageing takes the form of the performance of youth, very much as Katz and Marshall (2013) describe successful ageing. Though this undoubtedly functions as a critique of anti-ageing and the desire to reject the ageing body, at the same time, the texts all set up an ideal of youth that is opposed to a performative version, namely, a 'natural' form of youth. Their critique then is as much of the unnatural, or anachronistic, nature of anti-ageing as it is of the ageism that underlies the desire for longevity.

One of the key ways in which the texts present this ambiguous position on age and ageing is their use of an ageist imaginary. Ageing and figures of age are central to the aesthetics of the texts. Stopping age may be represented as 'unnatural' and against the order of things, but ageing is nevertheless grotesque, terrible and to be feared. Very often, this imaginary is expressed through the disjunction between youth and age. The sense of uncanniness that comes from the juxtaposition of age and youth is quite literally seen in the characters in *In Time*. As a visual text, the film depicts characters who are youthful in appearance (played by younger actors) but chronologically old (made clear in characterisation and plot). As viewers, we hold in tension the characters' youthful or middle-aged appearances with our knowledge of their chronological ages and life experiences, making viewing the film an odd process of engagement and defamiliarization that employs the kind of cognitive estrangement theorized by Darko Suvin (1979). In other texts, the young/old disjunction is, however, more disturbing, even horrific, indulging in an imaginary that associates ageing – specifically into very old age – with the grotesque. In *The Postmortal*, for example, Oscar Wilde's *The Picture of Dorian Gray* ([1891] 2003) is used as an intertext, explicitly and implicitly. The duality and anachronistic disjunction of age and youth is experienced by Farrell in terms that echo Dorian's lived body and painted image: 'I feel like this skin of mine is just a shell – that if you knocked against it, it would crack and chip. You could peel it away and all you'd see underneath would be a sick, wrinkled old man. This body is just a hiding place' (271). This dualism of body and mind achieves its grotesque impact on the reader because of the 'unnatural' juxtaposition of youth and age: the appearance of youthfulness encases the reality of ageing as decline.

In the case of Shteyngart's *Super Sad*, it is the character of Joshie, the owner of the Staatling-Wapachung corporation, who is described in uncanny terms. For the narrator, Lenny, Joshie's face is a kind of mask that hides his real age: 'I saw his face in profile, and noticed the confluence of purpled veins that made him look momentarily old again, that produced a frightening X-ray of what burbled up beneath that handsome new skin tissue and gleaming young eyes' (222).

A similar uncanniness around age and ageing appears near the end of *Everything Belongs*. Having weaponized ageing through a time bomb that rapidly physically ages its victims, Nina becomes the reverse of the recipients of the fix: a young woman in an old woman's body. Seen through the eyes of duplicitous Alex, Nina is described as a grotesque, aged woman: 'She laughed, a terrible ancient-lady laugh that shook her small body like a bunch of twigs' (109). Specifically, and emphasizing the intersection of ageing and gender, her potential sexuality is threatening and disgusting. As a former girlfriend of Alex, and to make fun of him, she asks for some porn: 'She ran a dark, unthinkable tongue over her thin lips. Alex clenched his jaw to keep from shuddering' (109). Despite having been madly in love with Nina before the time bomb turned her into a very old woman, he is horrified by her appearance, a feeling that is probably meant to be shared with the reader. A further example of this juxtaposition of youth and age is found in Alex's hand; although he has kept a younger body, his hands are crippled from the time bomb episode: 'He was holding open the hatch when the Time Bomb hit. According to his doctors, Alex now had the hands of a ninety-eight-year-old – twisted arthritic stumps, aching constantly' (111). As with Nina, a sense of grotesque emerges in the prematurely aged hands attached to Alex's younger body. In contrast, Daisy, the scientist who created the fix as well as the time bomb and who had been taking the fix for a good number of years, is, at the end of the text, presented as a 'handsome middle-aged woman in a leather jacket, her mousy hair cut short' (112). The time bomb has repaired her previously anachronistic identity as a young body/old self and left her with a physical appearance which is closer to her chronological age.

All of these texts critique anti-ageing technology and the desire for longevity represented as endless, commodified youth. At the same time, they rely upon anxieties about age in their dystopian critiques, emphasizing that 'ageing itself [is] fundamental to dystopian writing' (Falcus 2020: 66). And the complicated expressions of lives in time that are central to these narratives are inevitably linked to generation and the generational imaginary.

Generational disorder and anachronism

Just as we get an ambiguous representation of age and ageing in the texts, so they depict generationalism in contradictory ways. Their critique of anti-ageing, longevity and its consequences is less an interrogation of ageism than it is a critique of anachronism and a celebration of the 'natural' order of youth and age, of generations, an order secured by heteronormative futurity. As Mary Russo (1999) explains when defining anachronism in ageing studies, 'Not acting one's age, for instance, is not only inappropriate but dangerous, exposing the female subject, especially, to ridicule, contempt, pity, and scorn – the scandal of anachronism' (21). When one's age is impossible to determine by physical appearance (as happens in these texts through 'the cure', 'the fix' or 'the clock-system' that stops biological ageing), anachronism becomes the scandalous norm that threatens social order itself. And this challenges not only the present but also the vision of future (as an extension, or replication, of the present).

The texts' speculative narratives of dystopian futures rely on disruptions to the futurity that is guaranteed through generational succession. This operates at the level of both form and content, something *The Postmortal* draws attention to in its self-reflexive comments on the relationship between ageing and narrative (see Gullette 2004 on ageing and narrative). In the novel, an embedded online post about redefining baseball records in the face of the cure concludes: 'How can you be a success or have a legacy if your career – nay, your entire life – has no definitive story arc?' (110). This is precisely what Farrell, the main protagonist, experiences in physical terms: 'This is how I look now. This is how I'll look when I die' (31). Years later, he takes his photo repeatedly to check for changes, and looking back at the photos, he reaches the conclusion that 'the time span is invisible. It's as if I haven't lived at all' (75). Thus, he expresses the sense that the life course no longer has meaning without physical change and that this is a failure of narrative: 'There's no story. You can't tell a damn thing' (76). As Farrell makes clear in his realization that with no physical change, there is no story, narrative fails in the face of longevity since it cannot go forward; instead, the lives of these characters, and by extension of humanity itself, seem to be stuck in endless repetition and stasis. In many ways, it is generational security, order and identity that promise the story arc for the characters in these texts and underpin the plots that drive them. Thus, ageing is both feared and necessary in these narratives – without it, life (and plot) has no meaning.

Familial ordering and reproduction are central to the ways in which we imagine time and the life course. But these things are fundamentally disrupted by extreme longevity in these four texts. Long-living characters undermine the model of generational succession and blur familial generational identities. The discomfort caused by generational anachronism is well expressed in *In Time*. This is seen and exploited in specifically generational terms in scenes between protagonist Will and his mother. The physical appearance of the actors suggests no great difference in age, despite their familial generational positions, creating a sense of dislocation for the viewer as a younger actor seemingly performs the role of an older mother to an adult son. The disjunction is odd and awkward, making clear our own reliance upon generationalism. Will then experiences the same uncertainty and discomfort when he meets Sylvia, his future girlfriend. A man we come to realize is her father asks: 'Is she my sister, my mother or my daughter? Colluding times. They say it was easy in the past.' Drawing attention to the (potential) gap between chronological and experiential age, and the appearance of the body, these moments clearly reinforce the sense of youth as a physical performance and interrogate what it means to age at all, but they also draw attention to the generational temporalities on which we rely to make sense of our own and others' lives in time.

Magary's *The Postmortal* explores generational security in ways that suggest a reliance on what Lee Edelman (2004) calls reproductive futurity, where the future is always imagined through a heteronormative generational model that precludes alternatives to this temporal ordering. Thus, even if citizens are freed from the constraints of a traditional human lifespan, the world of *The Postmortal* still organizes itself through the traditional family structure. This sense of genealogical identity is clear in the alignment of Farrell's son, David, growing and developing, with Farrell's dying father (disease and accidents can still kill). Generationally determined life and death are juxtaposed here as entirely natural processes, upon which the sense of human identity is founded. The cure disrupts this vision of genealogy. One of the unintended consequences of extended lifespans is a huge growth in divorce rates as partnership for life becomes difficult to sustain over such a long time period (36–7). Part of the reason for this trend is a specifically age-related result of the cure: since there is no prospect of growing physically old, men (in particular) do not invest in relationships for care and companionship in old age, instead preferring multiple, successional relationships (79).

The repercussions of multiple relationships are complex familial, generational structures. Farrell's sister, Polly, finds these challenging. She has a new family and partner but struggles with a sense of generational anachronism and disorder: 'And shouldn't this kid be my grandchild? Shouldn't I be handing him off to some nice, sensible daughter-in-law somewhere? How many more husband iterations am I going to go through?' (283). The novel does explore other, more optimistic visions of this new generational model. Toni (Farrell's father's carer) describes her family as a 'family rain forest': 'I'm gonna make a family so big that it's gonna need its own government. I told my husband I don't want a family tree; I want a family rain forest. I've watched my kids raise their kids and I'll watch their kids raise their kids, and their kids raise their kids, and on and on and on' (170). This optimistic vision of generational repetition and collectivity is something made possible by the cure. Nevertheless, overall the novel positions familial generational disorder as part of the dystopian consequences of the longevity revolution, disrupting lives in time in detrimental ways. This is underlined by the terminal illness of Farrell's father. His father states that he is 'at peace with the idea' of death and links this acceptance to generational security – he has seen his children grow and grandchildren arrive (150). This vision of generational order and succession (through mortality) underlines the way that the text positions generational disorder as a threat not only to social organization but also to the human experience of a life in time.

Shteyngart's *Super Sad* is more ambivalent towards genealogical security and familial roles. Lenny's parents represent generational order and security, hard won in the face of their experiences as immigrants. Lenny's ambivalent attitude to them explores both the desire to secure the identity genealogical order offers and the rejection of the conservative vision they represent. Lenny's generation's obsession with youth and bodily maintenance (represented through the company where he works) contrasts with a visit he pays to his parents in which they talk about politics openly and eat as much as they like, without trying to monitor their bodies for foods that may provoke premature ageing: 'The toast put to rest, unraveled in some happy political mumbling, we shoveled in the food without reservation, all of us from countries historically strangled by starvation, none of us strangers to salt and brine' (137–8). Lenny is, by his own admission, both comforted and constricted by his family. They have a shared history – encapsulated in their prized house filled with the Romanian furniture they have imported from Russia – but they represent a generation from which he feels removed, both because he does not directly share their Russian past and because his life has moved in a direction different from theirs. Despite this ambivalence, when Lenny discovers that his parents have survived the violence and upheaval of 'the Rupture' – as the fragile national and global order further unravels – and finds them older and frailer, he reflects: 'Who was I? A secular progressive? Perhaps. A liberal, whatever that even means anymore, maybe. But, basically – at the end of the busted rainbow, at the end of the day, at the end of the empire – little more than my parents' son' (292). That movement to acceptance of his generational role and identity is part of Lenny's eventual rejection of the violent, consumerist, anti-ageing world in which he lives. Lenny's parents represent the story arc in which he locates his own life narrative and through which he becomes critical of the extreme staying-young-forever politics that are satirized in the novel. That acceptance of genealogical meaning and order is reinforced by the emptiness of the pseudo-family offered by Joshie. Lenny recognizes Joshie as a father figure (his 'ersatz papa' [326]), and Joshie himself, when telling Lenny that his younger partner, Eunice, has left Lenny to live with Joshie, proffers that the three of them ' "could be like a family some day" ' (319). Lenny immediately recalls his own, biological family, his 'real father, the Long Island janitor with the impenetrable accent and true-to-life smells' (319). *Super Sad* recognizes the ambivalent emotional and psychological facets of genealogical relationships but ultimately emphasizes the significance of genealogical order for the ways in which we articulate our human identities and experience in time.

The vision of genealogical order is intrinsically linked to futurity in these texts, as in much speculative, dystopian fiction. At the beginning of Penny's *Everything Belongs*, Daisy revises an old video of herself announcing the changes that the 'fix' she had just designed would mean to the world: 'it remains to be seen what the effects of this miraculous technology will be on the world our grandchildren inherit – although perhaps I shouldn't use the word "inherit", since I fully intend to be around to see it myself' (21). This statement encapsulates the problem of generation in these texts: grandchildren represent futurity in a generational and reproductive model, but longevity will result in the coexistence of generations that will undo that very futurity. That sense of loss of futurity is represented as the basis of and articulated through generational conflict. At an event centred around the celebration of the 'fix', Daisy watches the other attendees, describing them as 'rich kids and their parents, who were all just so grateful for her research. At least, the parents were. The kids probably hated her – sure, they got to be young and healthy for an extra half-century, but Mummy and Daddy got that same half-century to spend the inheritance. Without that, they were having to find other ways to maintain the lifestyles to which they had become accustomed' (17). As *Everything Belongs* shows through Daisy joining a terrorist group to try to reverse 'the fix' and playing a central role in creating generational revolution, all of the texts analysed here question our reliance on generational order at the same time as they present it as the only organizational unit in which an individual seems to feel his/her life to be less futile and meaningless.

In Time utilizes these fears about a lack of future as the basis for its youth-orientated plot. Spatially and temporally, the film juxtaposes the movement of youth with the stasis of age (represented by the long-living gerontocracy). The meaningless of life for the latter is expressed in the film through the character (aged more than one hundred) who gives Will all the time he has on his 'clock' because 'the day comes when you've had enough. Your mind can be spent, even if your body's not. We want to die. We need to.' Following this gift, the plot is driven by the escapades of two chronologically young protagonists (significantly, a heterosexual couple) as they try to escape and ultimately overcome the force and power of the elite. The fast pace of the thriller narrative – encapsulated in car chases and physical escapades – is premised on and also reinforces this sense of temporal ordering founded upon young people as representative of the future. The future is, quite literally in this film about the commodification of time, what these young people are fighting for.

A more frank and terrifying articulation of the threat generational disorder poses to the future is expressed in the president's speech in *The Postmortal*:

'Our men and women fought not only for their fellow countrymen but for future generations – generations they knew they'd never live to meet face-to-face.

But there aren't going to be future generations anymore. Not after this. There will only be us. One infinite generation, forever growing and reaching an unknown and incomprehensible size.' (66–7)

The 'infinite generation' (a narrative realisation of Mannheim's injunction to imagine a world without generation) is a terrifying, dystopian image of a world without temporal ordering and succession. Sara Ahmed argues that in the absence of an alternative, humans need the sense of 'species being' in order to articulate a future that makes sense in the present and gives us hope (2010: 183). The ever-expanding generation here is both a misnomer and a horrific nightmare – disbanding the whole notion of generation (which is intimately founded on succession and reproduction), it transforms species being from future-orientated and hopeful to stasis and hopelessness.

The novels and film, then, showcase the disruption among generations that extended longevity would bring about, and this is inherently related to the future itself, something under threat in all of these dystopian and even apocalyptic worlds. Generational order depends upon heteronormative succession, with the future symbolized by the young. This model ensures, perhaps paradoxically, that the future will resemble the past. As Edelman's critique of reproductive futurity makes clear, this 'organizing principle of communal relation' prevents the exploration of alternatives and 'queer resistance' (2004: 2). Ironically, Lenny's initial extreme, anti-ageing stance offers a direct challenge to what Edelman identifies as the conservatism of reproductive futurity. As Lenny proclaims at the beginning of the text: 'The children are our future only in the most narrow, transitive sense. They are our future until they too perish' (2). Over the course of the novel, Lenny comes to reject this view and value generational identity and the future as conceived through a model of mortality and succession, something symbolized by his return to the 'old' world of Italy, a culture represented as connected to the past and grounded in materiality – both of the body and of the physical, non-human world. In all of these texts, then, time and ageing are grounded in generationalism underpinned by reproductive futurity that guarantees a return to the stability of past social orders.

Generationality and collectivity

Mannheim makes a distinction between generational location (shared by those in the same space and time) and the formation of a sense of generation: 'Whereas mere common "location" in a generation is of only potential significance, a generation as an actuality is constituted when similarly "located" contemporaries participate in a common destiny and in the ideas and concepts which are in some way bound up with its unfolding' (1972: 306). The actualizing of generations is key to some of the conflicts in these texts. In *Everything Belongs*, for example, a young generation of rebels pursues what is effectively a class-based battle with the gerontocratic elite that it sees as stealing time. The union of the young rebels in the face of inequity produces a sense of generational identity and collectivity. Similarly, the construction of the older elites as a kind of gerontocracy – in the minds of the young rebels – articulates them as an imagined generation. A similar class-based generational conflict unfolds in *In Time*, in the hierarchically organized society made up of those with less time and those with more. The protagonist of the film represents the chronologically young battling with the stasis of the gerontocratic wealthy. The film celebrates the dynamism of youth – in character and plot – and opposes this to the performativity of youth seen in the gerontocracy who have benefitted from life-extension treatment. The way that the film presents stasis versus movement (on screen and in the plot) underlines that – 'real' young people move, transgress, drive fast, whilst older people are seen in perfectly sculpted locations, largely static.

At the same time, one consequence of extreme longevity is a loss of cohort generational identity. In *Everything Belongs*, Daisy, who is portrayed as being around 110 years old and one of the very early people to be 'fixed', is left without a sense of generational collectivity and identity. Her lover, colleagues and friends are dead, and her only generational contemporary is Parker Tremaine, an ambitious and duplicitous man she cannot bear. Yet, he is the only person with whom she can share memories of the past and with whom she has 'shared experiences' (Reulecke in Erll 2014: 387). This sense of access to a shared past and to a common narrative of historical change is expressed as they look out over an Oxford changed across the decades during which both have lived. She recognizes that no one else around her can share her sense of the past and history, especially the chronologically young: 'None of these kids necking free cocktails would remember' (19). Daisy's reliance on an old recording of a speech she gave in the early days of longevity technology – full of optimism and possibility – indicates that it is only through technology (ironically, since this is what has caused her anachronistic situation) that she can access and bear witness to the past. Otherwise, she is stuck within her own accumulating memories of a past that no one shares.

That sense of alienation from generationality and a shared history is also depicted in *The Postmortal*. The novel has a sixty-year timescale that takes the reader through four stages of the longevity revolution, making clear the link between longevity and dystopian plot: prohibition, spread, saturation and correction. In a typical SF manner (akin to Offred's tapes, discovered after the cessation of the society of Gilead in Atwood's *The Handmaid's Tale* [1985]), the narrative is presented as a found text, discovered in 2090, after the 'cure' is made illegal. Like Offred's account in *The Handmaid's Tale*, this one has been 'edited and abridged', presumably for the benefit of a new anti-cure society. Nevertheless, the edited tale of Farrell's journey from a 29-year-old who illegally receives the cure to an older man living through the apocalyptic events that ensue makes clear the repetitive and alienating nature of infinitely extended life. Farrell's narrative becomes increasingly cyclical, if also increasingly terrible and violent, as he moves from one job to another and from one location to another, divorced from any sense of generational identity and, with the increasing complexity of his own family – including the deaths of both his father and his first son – a lack of genealogical identity. The narrative's relentless drive towards apocalypse does not disguise – in fact, exacerbates – its sense of temporal aimlessness, as Farrell becomes increasingly unmoored in time and space. In the final words of his diary, Farrell remembers a traveller he once met who told him he would outlive not only time but also any conflict and disease created by humankind. Farrell's reflection when he is about to be killed is that it was a lie, something that he has known since he took 'the cure' when he was in his twenties: 'I've always known it was lie. You cannot hide from the world. It will find you. It always does. And now it has found me. My split second of immortality is over' (365).

In Shteyngart's *Super Sad*, generationality is, like genealogy, central but ambiguous. From the beginning of the novel, Lenny struggles with generational identity, and the novel satirizes generationalism based upon consumerist practices, largely technologically enabled. The hapless Lenny sees his own cohort as already too old (all of them in their very late thirties, as he himself is), and he falls in love with Eunice for her youth and freshness. He expresses this in his reflections on the first night they spend together: '"Oh, Lenny," she said, a little sadly, for she must have sensed just how much her youth and freshness meant to me, a man who lived in death's anteroom' (23). Thus, he tries to be part of Eunice's age cohort but experiences only alienation and unhappiness. He feels that Eunice's generation speak a different language on social media (something reinforced by the contrast between Eunice's online posts and Lenny's diaries in the novel). Lenny also finds himself at odds with his younger partners working in Post-Human Services. In an episode in which they refuse even to share the lunchroom with him, Joshie, his boss, tells him: '"You have to stop thinking and start selling. That's why all those young whizzes in the Eternity Lounge want to shove a carb-filled macaroon up your ass. … And who can blame them, Lenny? You remind them of death. You remind them of a different, earlier version of our species"' (64–5). Joshie, for his part, performs his identification with Eunice's generation. When he meets Eunice, he is equally mesmerized by her youth, and he performs his age in order to feel closer to Eunice's generation. Joshie seduces Eunice solely with the intention of having 'youth' around. As Eunice tells her friend, 'He kept looking at me with this kind of sweet, lustful face, like he wants to whore me out, but gently, like I'm his daughter and his sex toy at the same time' (225). Generationality is exposed in this novel as a performative construct that is intrinsically linked to the consumer and youth-driven dystopian world of the novel.

By the end of the novel, Lenny recognizes the value of cohort identity grounded in shared experiences and history when he realizes that not only has the longevity treatment sold by Post-Human Services failed but also ageism is inherent in the liberal capitalist system founded on the desire for the new, something he tries to escape by moving first to Canada and finally to Italy. He moves to Italy because he wants to be in a place 'with less data, less youth, and where old people like myself were not despised simply for being old, where an older man, for example, could be considered beautiful' (326). Lenny's epilogue is characterized by nostalgia, emphasized by the appeal of the 'old' world expressed by Lenny when he visits some of his friends in an old rural farmhouse. In the epilogue, he feels distanced from the younger generation in Italy; he sees them as not understanding the past, something that he comes to value, as he articulates on his return from Italy to his apartment in New York:

I live in the last middle-class stronghold of the city, high atop a red-brick ziggurat that a Jewish garment workers' union had erected on the banks of the East River back in the days when Jews sewed clothes for a living. Say what you will, these ugly co-ops are full of authentic old people who have real stories to tell.' (49)

Leaving behind his earlier fear of older bodies and selves, Lenny's recognition of cohort identity is based upon shared experience linked to ageing across time, something that the extreme liberal America ends up destroying and which ultimately causes the destruction of the country itself. Nevertheless, the novel's satirical nature should warn us of taking this at face value. Lenny's *volte-face* and embrace of ageing and the old may simply be another performative gesture in his bid to find generational collectivity and community in an alienating world.

Conclusion

These contemporary narratives of longevity follow earlier examples in their ambivalence about ageing itself: critiquing the desire to remain young, they nevertheless depend upon an ageist imaginary that presents physical ageing, in particular, as grotesque or uncanny. Whereas in Shteyngart's *Super Sad*, Joshie is presented as both anachronistic and uncanny while trying the new youthing technologies that his enterprise is developing, the protagonist, Lenny, constantly finds himself out of place in his efforts to fit into age cohorts younger than his own. Similarly, uncanniness defines the main characters in Penny's *Everything Belongs* when they become victims of the time bomb, and the long-living characters in *The Postmortal* and *In Time*, whose appearance and chronological age are often radically at odds.

This ambivalence about ageing extends into the exploration of generational disorder in the novels. Generationalism is presented in the texts as the only plausible way of ordering our lives in time. The texts suggest that futurity is guaranteed only through generational security, which relies on heteronormative reproduction and familial roles, with *Super Sad* perhaps offering the most ambiguous approach to this in its nostalgic epilogue that explicitly positions the future as a return to the past. Within the four longevity narratives, lack of generational order results in chaotic consequences that threaten and make unsafe both the protagonists of the texts and the whole societies in which they live. Whilst it is easy – and justifiable – to critique this as a dystopian conservatism that cannot imagine the future except as the selfsame, we need to acknowledge the different facets of generationalism in these texts. They may lament the loss of a sometimes nostalgic, heteronormative vision of genealogical ordering and rely upon generational conflict to drive their plots, but they also suggest that genealogy and generationality are important to our sense of history – social and individual – and to our ability to perceive ourselves as part of a collectivity. Generationalism is also crucial to the dystopian form, as it constructs visions of social collapse and human responses to the past, present and future. Generationalism and our generational imaginaries may need to be expanded and critiqued, but we are not yet ready, it seems, to do without them as we make sense of our lives in time.

References

Ahmed, S. (2010), *The Promise of Happiness*, Durham: Duke University Press.

Atwood, M. ([1985] 1987), *The Handmaid's Tale*, London: Virago.

Brand, M. R. (2016), 'Growing Old in Utopia: From Age to Otherness in American Literary Utopias', *Age, Culture and Humanities*, 3. Available online: https://agecultur ehumanities.org/WP/growing-old-in-utopia-from-age-to-otherness-in-american-literary-utopias/ (accessed 20 November 2021).

Bristow, J. (2016), 'The Making of "Boomergeddon": The Construction of the Baby Boomer Generation as a Social Problem in Britain', *British Journal of Sociology*, 67(4): 575–91.

Clark, S. R. L. (1995), *How to Live Forever: Science Fiction and Philosophy*, London: Routledge.

Edelman, E. (2004), *No Future: Queer Theory and the Death Drive*, Durham: Duke University Press.

Edmund, J., and B. S. Turner (2005), 'Global Generations: Social Change in the Twentieth Century', *British Journal of Sociology*, 56(4): 559–77.

Erll, A. (2014), 'Generation in Literary History: Three Constellations of Generationality, Genealogy, and Memory', *New Literary History*, 45(3): 385–409.

Falcus, S. (2020), 'Age and Anachronism in Contemporary Dystopian Fiction', in E. Barry with M. V. Skagen (eds), *Literature and Ageing*, vol. 73, Essays and Studies, 65–86, Cambridge: D. S. Brewer.

Gullette, M. (2004), *Aged by Culture*, Chicago: University of Chicago Press.

In Time (2011), [Film] Dir. A. Niccol. USA: 20th Century Fox.

Jameson, F. (2005), 'Longevity as Class Struggle', in *Archaeologies of the Future: The Desire Called Utopia and Other Science Fictions*, 328–44, London: Verso.

Katz, S., and B. Marshall (2004), 'Is the Functional "Normal"? Aging, Sexuality and the Bio-marking of Successful Living', *History of the Human Sciences*, 17(1): 53–75.

Katz, S., and B. Marshall (2013), 'New Sex for Old: Lifestyle, Consumerism, and the Ethics of Aging Well', *Journal of Aging Studies*, 17(1): 3–16.

Lebow, R. N. (2012), *The Politics and Ethics of Immortality*, Cambridge: Cambridge University Press.
Magary, D. (2011), *The Postmortal*, London: Penguin Books.
Mangum, T. (2002), 'Longing for Life Extension: Science Fiction and Late Life', *Journal of Aging and Identity*, 7(2): 69–80.
Mannheim, K. ([1927/8] 1972), 'The Problem of Generations', in P. Kecskemeti (ed.), *Karl Mannheim: Essays*, 276–322, London: Routledge.
Penny, L. (2016), *Everything Belongs to the Future*, New York: Macmillan.
Pilcher, J. (1994), 'Manheim's Sociology of Generations: An Undervalued Legacy', *British Journal of Sociology*, 45(3): 481–95.
Roduit, J. A. R., T. Eichinger and W. Glannon (2018), 'Science Fiction and Human Enhancement: Radical Life-Extension in the Movie "In Time"', *Time, Medicine, Health Care and Philosophy*, 21(3): 287–93.
Russo, M. (1999), 'Aging and the Scandal of Anachronism', in K. Woodward (ed.), *Figuring Age: Women, Bodies, Generations*, 20–33, Bloomington: Indiana University Press.
Sheldon, R. (2016), *The Child to Come: Life after the Human Catastrophe*, Minneapolis: University of Minnesota Press.
Shteyngart, G. (2010), *Super Sad True Love Story*, London: Granta.
Shusterman, N. (2017), *Scythe*, New York: Simon and Schuster.
Shusterman, N. (2019), *Thunderhead*, New York: Simon and Schuster.
Shusterman, N. (2020), *The Toll*, New York: Simon and Schuster.
Slusser, G., G. Westfahl and E. S. Rabkin, eds (1996), *Immortal Engines: Life Extension and Immortality in Science Fiction and Fantasy*, Georgia: University of Georgia Press.
Suvin D. (1979), *Metamorphoses of Science Fiction: On the Poetics and History of a Literary Genre*, Ralahine Utopian Studies, Oxford: Peter Lang.
Swift, J. ([1726] 2013), *Gulliver's Travels*, London: Penguin.
Vidal, F. (2016), 'Desire, Indefinite Lifespan, and Transgenerational Brains in Literature and Film', *Theory and Psychology*, 26(5), 665–80.
Vincent, J. A. (2008), 'The Cultural Construction of Old Age as a Biological Phenomenon: Science and Anti-ageing Technologies', *Journal of Aging Studies*, 22(4): 331–9.
Wilde, O. ([1891] 2003), *The Picture of Dorian Gray*, London: Penguin.
Willmetts, S. (2018), 'Digital Dystopia: Surveillance, Autonomy, and Social Justice in Gary Shteyngart's *Super Sad True Love Story*', *American Quarterly*, 70(2): 267–89.
Yoke, C. B., and D. M. Hassler, eds (1985), *Death and the Serpent: Immortality in Science Fiction and Fantasy*, Westport, CT: Greenwood.

4

Biological slaves: Discardable bodies in dystopia

Maria Aline Ferreira

Science fiction and utopian narratives have always been deeply interested in the avoidance of ageing, speculating on how to achieve longer lifespans and even immortality, while also considering the dangers and pitfalls attendant upon this dream. Fantasies of rejuvenation, including acquiring new organs and, more radically, new bodies, have become increasingly common in fiction and film, articulating a deep-rooted wish to extend life and eventually defeat death. This aspiration, however, can often be achieved only by using the organs or the entire bodies of underprivileged people, thus effectively making them biological slaves. The fictional texts to be examined in this chapter crucially revolve around who has a right to longer lifespans, on the one hand, and the precariousness of certain lives, considered of less importance and ready to be exploited, on the other.

Texts in which rampant biocapitalism and biocontrol conspire to render destitute people invisible and discardable include Manjula Padmanabhan's play *Harvest* (1997), Kazuo Ishiguro's *Never Let Me Go* (2005a) and Ninni Holmqvist's *The Unit* (2010), which share a number of topics such as organ trafficking and donation, ubiquitous bio and digital surveillance, and the exploitation of weaker, poorer citizens. These narratives give centre stage to the marginalized bodies of those rendered disposable, commodified and dehumanized as usable body parts by a biocapitalist society that serves the interests of the wealthy elites, who are aware of the existence of those disadvantaged people but often choose to ignore their suffering in the interests of their own health and comfort. Those citizens who are rendered invisible by their disposability as biological slaves alert us to the precariousness of human rights, which can be revoked without notice even in supposedly democratic regimes, as well as to the exploitation of human lives for the benefit and extension of the lifespans of other wealthier and more powerful citizens. In addition, and relatedly, the desire for a longer life interrogated in these texts can be seen as predicated on a fear of age itself, a fear strongly associated with biocapitalism, closely linked to what almost amounts to an obsession with youth, invested in consumerist practices and a denial of the ageing body. The texts accordingly delve into our malaise as ageing societies, where the pressure to stay young is intense and medical breakthroughs promise longer, healthier lives. They also crucially point out how age, namely, old age, must be seen intersectionally, in relation to wealth, privilege, gender and even nation. These bionarratives thus dramatize the intricate negotiations of biopower in near-future societies, offering a trenchant critique of some disciplinary 'power dispositives', to draw on Foucault's terminology (2003: 249), that crucially determine who lives and is allowed to grow old.

Biopolitical negotiations of power

Michel Foucault's biopolitics is centrally concerned with the technological strategies and operations of power that 'make live' (2003: 241), that is, promote and manage life in a given society, aiming to 'improve life, to prolong its duration, to improve chances, to avoid accidents, and to compensate for failings' (2003: 254).

The power of making live or letting die, which was exercised in earlier times by a sovereign, according to Foucault's analysis (2003), is now, in these near-future societies, in the hands of the state, as well as of the very wealthy and of megacorporations that, while allowing the well off to continue living and grow old with recourse to biotechnologies, force others to die. The disciplinary techniques employed by the state or private institutions to tame the bodies of those who will literally be allowed to die in order to benefit others can be seen as an extension of Foucault's biopower, now transformed into a kind of eugenicist programme,[1] grounded on a desire for longer life and the avoidance of bodily ageing and frailty. It may also crucially become a conflict of generations, between older, wealthier people obsessed with avoiding ageing and younger, vulnerable, disposable bodies.

With the incremental development of both capitalism and the life sciences, the former has inexorably shaped the latter, in particular in terms of choosing which projects to focus on and fund. The value placed on the biosciences, then, is in part dependent on the money assigned to them. McQueen (2016: 1–2) maps the transition from late capitalism to biocapitalism, arguing that biocapitalism is the 'frontline of capitalism today, promising to enrich and prolong our lives, whilst threatening to extend capitalism's capacity to command our hearts and minds', posing an increasing risk to the body's autonomy and individual freedom. As Foucault asserted, 'Life becomes the explicit center of political calculation' (2007: 79). In his view, biopower and biopolitics have become 'centred on the body as a machine: its disciplining, the optimisation of its capabilities, the extortion of its forces, the parallel increase of its usefulness and its docility, its integration into systems of efficient and economic controls' (Foucault 1998: 139), words that resonate with and fittingly apply to the main thematic concerns in these bionarratives.

In a related vein, Sunder Rajan muses (2007: 78): 'What forms of alienation, exploitation, and divestiture are necessary for a "culture of biotechnology innovation" to take root? On the other hand, how are individual and collective subjectivities and citizenships both shaped and conscripted by these technologies that concern "life itself"?' Giroux (2008: 587), discussing the biopolitics of neoliberalism, examines how it 'uses market values as a template for realigning corporate power and the state, but also how it produces modes of consent vital to the construction of a neoliberal subject and a more ruthless politics of disposability'. As he further remarks, in words relevant to the fictional narratives discussed here: 'Within this new form of neoliberal rationality and biopolitics – a political system actively involved in the management of the politics of life and death – new modes of individual and collective suffering emerge around the modalities and intersection of race and class' (2008: 587)[2] as well as age. Lopez and Gillespie (2015: 1) are similarly concerned with 'economic logics governing life and death and how certain lives and bodies are made killable and disposable'. They are troubled by the ways in which 'economic processes of commodification and capital accumulation make lives killable, and exploit bodies, lives and labor in ways that bring on premature death' (2015: 3), as is the case with the redundant Indians in Padmanabhan's play *Harvest*, selling their organs and sometimes their whole bodies to be purchased by much older, wealthy citizens. I will be using these economic logics of grievability and killability, in Lopez and Gillespie's words, to explore certain neoliberal capitalist strategies operative in these literary narratives to subjugate bodies deemed more discardable.

Whose, then, are the lives that count? These biodystopias, in taking exacerbated neoliberal biocapitalist scenarios to their radical, logical conclusions, examine how the mechanisms of biocapitalism collude to convert the bodies of those deemed less valuable into biocommodities. They give consideration to the exploitation of what Rose (2007: 6) calls 'biovalue', inserted in new configurations of 'bioeconomy' and 'biocapital' that can lead to the abuse and manipulation of those judged to be weaker and redundant. As Butler (2004a: xiv–xv) remarks: 'Some lives are grievable, and others are not; the differential allocation of grievability that decides what kind of subject is and must be grieved, and which kind of subject must not, operates to produce and maintain certain exclusionary conceptions of who is normatively human: what counts as a livable life and a grievable death?'

A related issue addressed in these narratives is the following: who is allowed to grow old and who is not? What forms of biocapitalist tyranny are at work in these biotechnological dystopias to ensure that those citizens who are wealthy or considered more valuable for society have access to the organs they need to continue to live and prosper and indeed grow old? Intergenerational conflict is inevitably at work, but whereas in *The Unit* it is the older people who are forced to sacrifice themselves for the sake of the younger generations, as might be expected, following an ageist logic, in *Harvest* and *Never Let Me Go*, the younger are the scapegoats, dying to save others, usually older people, whose aged bodies are failing.

According to Neilson (2012: 59), 'population ageing is one of the most important processes of transition bearing on the current global moment, entangling biology with processes and events such as migration and the financialization of daily life'. As he further observes, the 'processes of capitalization that have invested biogerontological research raise issues of access and of the wisdom of financing such activities on the basis of a desire to indefinitely extend life when general health care resources are already stretched' (2012: 51). Indeed, a central area where this desire is conspicuous is in the 'intersection of financially driven rejuvenation medicine and policy discourses of "healthy" or "positive" ageing' (Neilson 2012: 51), an aspect that *Harvest* investigates and problematizes.

These are some of the key questions examined in the narratives analysed here, which suggest that the market forces at work in biocapitalist societies will in all likelihood prevail, rendering exploited citizens to a large extent invisible and dispensable. Indeed, transhumanist aspirations of bypassing the aged body by transferring one's consciousness to a new, younger one are closely entwined with advanced biocapitalism. According to Ranisch and Lorenz Sorgner (2015: 7–8), transhumanism 'affirms the radical transformation of human's biological capacities and social conditions by means of technologies', a notion aptly exemplified in *Harvest*, which will be discussed now.

Padmanabhan's *Harvest*

The politics of ageing in richer countries occupies centre stage in Padmanabhan's dystopian play *Harvest* (1997), which examines how far some people are willing to go to extend their lives or even acquire a new body. One of the central ideas in *Harvest* is the philosophical and ethical question of the lengths to which we can go or would be prepared to go to achieve a long life, often with total disregard for others' welfare, in the context of unbridled capitalism and consumerism, where the retention of youth is seen as a profitable business, in contrast with other versions of capitalism where older people are blamed for using health resources.

This is a key concern in *Harvest* (1997), which uses dark humour to address global organ trading and its many and serious ramifications. The inspiration for *Harvest* was the 'flourishing illegal trade in human organs in India' (Padmanabhan 1997: 5).[3] *Harvest* is described on the cover blurb as a 'vision of the cannibalistic future that awaits the human race … a parable of what will happen when the rich denizens of the First World … begin to devour bits and pieces of the Third World poor'. The words 'cannibalistic' and 'devour' meaningfully point to the main themes of the play, the commodification and exploitation of human beings. For medical anthropologist Scheper-Hughes (2001a: 1), the global organ transplant economy is arguably a form of 'late modern cannibalism', with the body treated as an 'object, albeit a highly fetishized one, and as a "commodity" that can be bartered, sold or stolen in divisible and alienable parts', in effect a form of 'neo-cannibalism' (2001b: 1; see also Moni 2014). Padmanabhan's *Harvest* takes this cannibalistic metaphor even further, describing the ways in which a young Indian's body is bought and occupied by an older American buyer, whose consciousness takes up residence in the former.

The author herself states in the introduction to *Harvest* that the play is centrally about the body, about 'what it means to have agency over one's own personal container. It's about need versus greed', about the 'human condition'. She explains she is using the topic of the traffic of human organs to 'make a more universal point about use and abuse between people, cultures and economies' (Padmanabhan 1997: 18). The concept of the body as being constituted of pieces to be traded for profit that drives the organ-trafficking business contrasts, in a paradoxical way, with – in Frow's words (1998: 49) – the myth of the 'integrity of the body: a myth of resurrection', a fantasy of a long life after death, which ties together the notions of human sacrifice and the biblical resurrection of the body, a new lease of life for the purchaser of the body parts and sacrifice and suffering for the donors. The characters in *Harvest* are literally their body parts; they have become parts of a whole that will be dismantled, little by little, as with the clones in Ishiguro's *Never Let Me Go* or the older, discardable people in Holmqvist's *The Unit*, both works to be treated below.

Set in Mumbai in 2010, *Harvest* contrasts a wealthy Western world which, thanks to a considerable extension of life expectancy, is desperately looking for young bodies and fresh organs to supply the needs of its older citizens, with the poorest areas of Mumbai, where healthy young people are lured into selling their organs. Since those in the Western countries live much longer and the women do not bear children anymore, they either have several fresh organs from the citizens of poorer parts of the world transplanted into their ageing bodies or acquire young men's entire bodies, usually moving into them with recourse to what appears to be a kind of consciousness transfer.

In this world, society continues to be sharply divided along capitalist lines, with some bodies in the Global South transformed into biocommodities, as objects of capitalist exploitation by wealthier nations, in this case the United States. Most people in India have to endure a profoundly polluted, diseased atmosphere, while those in wealthier areas of the world that have escaped this devastation can avail themselves of the technologies that enable them to buy younger, healthier bodies that they then proceed to 'inhabit'. Poor Indians are given what to them looks like an absurdly large amount of money in exchange for what they are told will be the sale of some of their organs, while in some cases, without their knowledge, it is their whole body that will be sold.

The organ buying and harvesting process is mediated through a powerful, Big Brother–like corporation, InterPlanta, which hires desperate, jobless Indian men and women, promises them a luxurious life with Western amenities, tracks their every movement and communicates through a virtual reality gadget installed in their house, which enables the Indians to see a virtual projection of their wealthy owner. The victims are surveilled 24 hours a day by this Big Brother–like device and imprisoned in their own homes, but it still appears to them a worthwhile business arrangement, bearing witness to the insidious and widespread operation of biopower.

Eventually, they discover that they have been duped into selling their whole body, but by that stage, they have fallen totally under the sway of the carefully crafted virtual avatars of the Americans they are helping with their body parts, dazzled by the promises of luxury that materialize when their poor homes are transformed, by means of the Americans' money, into houses with bathrooms, furnished kitchens, running water and televisions, amenities their neighbours could never dream of. Enticed by the lure of capitalist gifts, comforts and gadgets, the destitute Indians are keen to accept any job or money thrown their way, no matter at what cost, even if some discordant voices in the family are raised. They are thus unashamedly exploited by the well off, privileged inhabitants of western countries like the United States, who search for a longer lease of life, jumping from body to body, strongly suggestive of vampiric, almost decadent old-age figures that prey on the young. *Harvest* thus dramatizes older citizens' dissatisfaction with their ageing bodies and their overpowering wish to regain youthful ones at the expense of underprivileged young people in India, while also critiquing the Western world's consumerist practices and corresponding determination to remain young at all costs, denying the ageing process.

Om Prakash, a young, jobless Indian man, is hired by InterPlanta to donate his organs, much to the dismay of his wife, Jaya. The video projection that becomes the centre around which the protagonists' lives revolve is of a beautiful young woman, Ginni, an avatar of Virgil, an older American who buys the right to own Om's body. To the Indian victim of exploitation, Ginni looks like a goddess he wishes to please at all costs, and in her extreme beauty and allure, he deems her worthy of even the final and most extreme donation: his whole body. However, Jeetu, Om's younger brother, arrives unexpectedly and is, apparently by mistake, taken by the company instead of Om, a turn of events that underlines the disposability of bodies that appear to be interchangeable, their only importance the profit the system will make from their biovalue.

As Virgil himself puts it, emphasizing his total disregard for the individual members of the Indian family, who matter for him only in terms of their bioavailability: 'We look for young men's bodies to live in and young women's bodies in which to sow their children' (Padmanabhan 1997: 86). Virgil now has the body of a young Indian man, Jeetu, and in that guise explains to Jaya, Jeetu's sister-in-law and lover, that his body now contains a 'red-blooded all-American man' (1997: 87) who desires her and wishes to have children with her, an idea she vehemently rejects. Since in this future United States, women can no longer become pregnant, men who wish to have children, like Virgil, have to look elsewhere, paying women in countries in the Global South, who can still reproduce, to carry their babies. They would then be the surrogate mothers for their children, preserving a Western model of hegemonic masculinity and reproduction as well as of exploitation of the impoverished victims.[4]

In Virgil's case, this is his fourth body in fifty years, since two were not successful, but he keeps trying, since he is able to 'travel from body to body' (Padmanabhan 1997: 134). New bodies for old constitutes a long-standing fantasy dramatized in, for instance, H. G. Wells's 'The Story of the Late Mr Elvesham' ([1896] 2014), where a wealthy, older man transfers his mind to the body of a young medical student, who in turn finds himself in Mr Elvesham's body. In Kureishi's novella 'The Body' (2002), in turn, the protagonist, feeling himself ageing fast, has his mind transplanted to a new, young body and starts a brand new existence, though he eventually comes to regret his decision and wishes to go back to his old life. Kelly's *The Possessions of Doctor Forrest* (2011) re-envisions Stevenson's (1886) gothic body-swapping fantasy as a present-day instance of that age-old aspiration using the tools of modern-day medicine, updating the ambition for radically extended youth and longer lifespans, which recent developments in the biosciences suggest may indeed gradually come about.[5]

This search for immortality, although present throughout human history, takes on different, more biotechnological contours in Padmanabhan's, Ishiguro's and Holmqvist's texts, which can be described as 'rejuvenescence' narratives, to adopt Teresa Mangum's terminology (2002: 70). These narratives are informed by, while also shining a critical light on, the extreme capitalist and consumerist values of contemporary, profoundly ageist societies that emphasize a prevalent, narcissistic stance, conducive to a pursuit of youth with recourse to all available means, often disregarding others' bodily integrity.

Virgil explains InterPlanta's business model as follows: 'We support poorer sections of the world, while gaining fresh bodies for ourselves' (Padmanabhan 1997: 86). InterPlanta has total disregard for the victims' loss of life.[6] While the organ donors are described by Scheper-Hughes (2002: 4) as an 'invisible and discredited collection of anonymous suppliers of spare parts', the organ receivers, in turn, are 'cherished patients, treated as moral subjects and as suffering individuals'.[7] Indeed, in *Harvest* it seems that moral concerns do not play a part in the recipients' drive to remain alive by literally acquiring new bodies. As Scheper-Hughes (2001a: 31) observes, 'Social justice and notions of the good society hardly figure' in discussions around the procuring or buying of organs for transplant, since 'bioethical standards have been thoroughly disciplined and brought into alignment with the needs and desires of consumer-oriented globalization'.[8] *Harvest* critiques some potential effects of exacerbated biocapitalism that might allow powerful biotech companies to provide radical medical procedures to wealthy, usually older clients at the expense of the lives of destitute people in poor countries. Indeed, this consumer-oriented drive for anti-ageing procedures prioritizes a youthful, healthy-looking body, prized as the highest possession in this ageist, consumer culture.

Social justice and ethical concerns around the donation and transplant of human organs and body parts are also central topics in the novel to which we now turn, Ishiguro's *Never Let Me Go*, a biodystopia in which the drive to acquire body parts in an effort to live longer, healthier lives is taken much further, to a drastic, logical conclusion where people are specially created to be organ donors.

Ishiguro's *Never Let Me Go*

The narrative of *Never Let Me Go* follows a group of friends, later revealed to be clones, who are raised together in a private school, Hailsham, where they are secluded from the outside world, living in a kind of vacuum where they are sheltered from society. In this alternative England of the 1990s, cures for most diseases have been achieved and there does not appear to be a shortage of organs for transplant. There are similar generational dynamics at work in *Never Let Me Go* and *Harvest*, where young people are forced to sacrifice themselves for other, usually older, people who prey on them and use their organs to survive and grow old, resulting in a truncated life course for the donors. The plight of the clones in *Never Let Me Go*, whose trajectory we follow from childhood to adulthood, appears particularly egregious since we first see them as children, as innocent victims of a system they unquestioningly accept.

It is clear from the beginning that these are not 'normal' children and adolescents. They have been bioengineered not to have children and are ignorant of their origins. Their biological families are never mentioned, and they do not have family surnames. Instead, they are known by their first name followed by a letter, as in the case of Kathy H, the protagonist and narrator, who is thirty-one at the start of the novel and is a carer, looking after those former Hailsham students who are going through the process of donating their organs and then completing, a euphemism for dying.[9] As the students gradually find out, they are clones deliberately created and raised to be organ donors, conditioned to accept their fate and to have their lives curtailed, deprived of the possibility of growing old. The clones are described as 'shadowy objects in test tubes' (Ishiguro 2005a: 239) and seen as biotechnological artefacts, as slaves, instrumentalized and manufactured to serve society in general.

This is then the dark, occult side of a society in which the clones, as sacrificial victims, suffer for the benefit of others, as if they were less than human and could be sacrificed without generalized remorse. How could such a horrendous practice be sanctioned?[10] It is indeed more 'convenient' if people know about it but choose to ignore the extent of their criminal exploitation of other citizens, who, despite being members of this society, appear to have no rights. Like the clones, who have been 'told and not told' (Ishiguro 2005a: 73, 80) of their situation, with their teachers and guardians careful not to reveal their secret (apart from Miss Lucy, who eventually tells them who they are and their purpose in life), citizens at large choose to forget about the existence of these clones. Indeed, in this society, 'for a long time, people preferred to believe these organs appeared from nowhere, or at most that they grew in a kind of vacuum' (2005a: 240). As one of the teachers from Hailsham, Miss Emily, explains to the clones: 'However uncomfortable people were about your existence, their overwhelming concern was that their own children, their spouses, their parents, their friends' did not die, so 'you were kept in the shadows, and people did their best not to think about you' (2005a: 240). Even though two of the teachers, Miss Emily and Marie-Claude, tried to raise public concern for the clones' plight by collecting their artistic output, which would supposedly prove they were 'fully human' (2005a: 239), while remaining complicit with a system that conspires to suppress any knowledge about the clones' predicament, with the closure of Hailsham, the public 'wanted you back in the shadows' (2005a: 242).

This is a form of what Levy (2011: 13) describes as 'bystander passivity', which can derive 'from a number of interweaving psychological attitudes. Diffusion of personal responsibility, an inability to identify with the victim, a feeling of powerlessness, and a failure to conceive of an effective intervention all contribute to the apparent indifference of bystanders standing adjacent to atrocity.' According to Cohen (2001: 4–5), in the context of psychological theories of denial: 'Denial may be neither a matter of telling the truth nor intentionally telling a lie. … There seem to be states of mind, or even whole cultures, in which we know and don't know at the same time', a state of affairs reminiscent of the situation in *Never Let Me Go* where the citizens know, but choose not to know, about the clones, an ambiguity that conceals the vexed moral and ethical conundrum associated with the clones' predicament. Cohen, referring to tragic events that are known to be happening or to have happened but which many people choose to ignore, observes (2001: 5, emphasis added):

> The psychology of 'turning a blind eye' or 'looking the other way' is a tricky matter. These phrases imply that we have access to reality, but choose to ignore it because it is convenient to do so. This might be a simple fraud: the information is available and registered, but leads to a conclusion which is knowingly evaded. 'Knowing', though, can be far more ambiguous. We are vaguely aware of choosing not to look at the facts, but not quite conscious of just what it is we are evading. *We know, but at the same time we don't know.*

These words fittingly apply to the citizens in *Never Let Me Go* who choose to overlook the existence of the clones and the fact that they have been denied the possibility of a long, fulfilled life. Cohen's words also speak to the mindset of a society which has been conditioned to unreservedly accept the suffering of some for the greater benefit of the many, following a utilitarian logic that can feel convenient but when directly confronted is experienced as morally and ethically wrong.

According to Charlwood (2018: 86), Ishiguro is 'obsessed with ageing', while Yeung (2017: 1) reads *Never Let Me Go* as a 'meditation on human mortality', noting that the clones' 'situation reflects human beings' confrontation with mortality'. As Ishiguro himself states (Matthews 2009: 124):

> Ultimately, I wanted to write a book about how people accept that we are mortal and we can't get away from this, and that after a certain point we are all going to die, we won't live forever. There are various ways to rage against that, but in the end we have to accept it and there are different reactions to it. So I wanted the characters in *Never Let Me Go* to react to this horrible programme they seem to be subjected to in much the same way in which we accept the human condition, accept ageing, and falling to bits, and dying.

This compliance with their fate, then, read through the lens of Ishiguro's words, amounts to an acceptance of mortality, even though the clones have their lives severely curtailed and are denied the possibility of old age. As Ishiguro (2005b) states: 'I was interested in the human capacity to accept what must seem like a limited and cruel fate', in effect the clones' ultimate sacrifice of their lives. In the same way as the citizens were conditioned to uncritically assent to the clones' sacrifice, the latter were trained from the beginning to unhesitatingly accept the social contract of organ donation imposed on them, which deprives them of enjoying a fulfilling old age.

Indeed, human sacrifice is at the heart of all the tales examined here. Meaningfully, Scheper-Hughes (2001a: 31) regards the 'global traffic in human organs, tissues, and body parts from the living as well as from the dead' as a 'misrecognized form of human sacrifice'.[11] In *Never Let Me Go*, the biblical echo of the age of thirty-three, when Jesus died and Kathy H will also 'complete', reinforces this concept of human sacrifice, of the clones as scapegoats, sacrificial victims, invisible and disposable bodies. While the clones' acquiescence to their fate without rebellion or attempts to run away seems almost unnatural, going against the will to live and survive, their psychological conditioning at least partially accounts for their attitude, which again can be linked to the biblical story of Jesus and His unquestioning acceptance of His death as a sacrifice to save humankind from their sins.

Jeetu and Kathy H can be seen as illustrative embodiments of what Agamben (1998) described as 'bare life', epitomized by the *homo sacer* who represents those who could be maltreated with impunity since they lacked any legal status and whose life, divested of any rights, could be taken by the state. This process of a person's inclusion or exclusion in society is also addressed by Roberto Esposito, who reflects on the 'category of person' (2012: 1), considering that 'only a life that can provide the credentials of personhood can be considered sacred or qualitatively significant' (2012: 2). What these credentials are is a matter of discussion in *Never Let Me Go*, where some teachers attempt to prove the clones' humanness through the art they produce in a vain attempt to save them from their fate.

As Butler (2009: 20) in an analogous vein remarks, in words that could also apply to Ishiguro's clones: 'The question is not whether a given being is living or not, nor whether the being in question has the status of a "person"; it is, rather, whether the social conditions of persistence and flourishing are or are not possible.' As she further notes (Butler 2004b: 39), 'When we ask what makes a life livable, we are asking about certain normative conditions that must be fulfilled for life to become life.' In the case of the clones, these conditions are certainly not fully present, so that the question posed by Butler (2004b: 17) of 'what constitutes the human, the distinctively human life, and what does not' hardly applies to the clones' lives, cut short by organ donations. This pressing question of what constitutes (and who determines) what a person and, by extension, a valuable life is, centrally addressed in *Never Let Me Go*, is also posed, although in very different ways, in *Harvest*. Whose lives are worthy of making live or letting die, to engage yet again with Foucault's expression?

Giving in almost willingly to their own captivity, these characters become paradigmatic examples of the 'precarious lives'[12] discussed by Butler (2004a). Their existence as always already exploitable and dehumanized also corresponds to what Bauman (2003) describes as 'wasted lives' and Butler (2009) as 'ungrievable lives'. Although Butler is referring to a war context, the 'ungrievable' lives she mentions can also appropriately relate to Ishiguro's clones: 'An ungrievable life is one that cannot be mourned because it has never lived, that is, it has never counted as a life at all' (Butler 2009: 38). These lives are deemed so unworthy of attention and respect that they often do not elicit remorse for the way they are treated, as in the tales discussed here.

The precarious lives of Ishiguro's clones, predicated on the willing acceptance of human sacrifice, are inscribed in biopolitical mechanisms appositely described in terms of cannibalism, as also in Padmanabhan's *Harvest*, as noted above. Noble (2011: 162) observes that the 'consumption of the human body in the twenty-first-century medical trade also gives rise to the imagery of cannibalism'; indeed, for her, it is the 'cannibalistic nature of this trade, in its frequent transgression of moral and ethical limits, which inspires the desire to sensationalize in much of the media coverage with which we have become familiar'. Karmakar and Parui (2017: 107) take this perspective further and argue that 'descriptions of human clones created in order to donate organs to the capitalist clientele pose problematic questions regarding issues such as agency, ethics and neoliberal consumption that may be classified as biocapitalist cannibalism', a view that can be applied to the clones in Ishiguro's *Never Let Me Go* who are regarded as biocommodities to be recklessly used for their biovalue, to allow others to live longer, healthier lives.

However, it is not only the young, 'third-world', colonized body that is exploited for its 'biovalue', as in *Harvest*, or the cloned bodies deliberately created to serve as organ donors as in Ishiguro's *Never Let Me Go*. In Ninni Holmqvist's *The Unit*, to which I now turn, a Scandinavian society makes unfair use of older population sectors that do not conform to certain conventional behaviours, leading to forms of abuse and manipulation of those deemed weaker and 'dispensable', significantly in order to help others lead longer, healthier lives. While the clones in Ishiguro's novel are denied a full life, including enjoyment of old age, in *The Unit*, old age is the feared time when citizens with no family attachments are regarded as more expendable than others and will be forced by the state to donate their organs, a situation that thoroughly tests democratic values.

Holmqvist's *The Unit*

Ninni Holmqvist's *The Unit* introduces a new set of related questions, portraying a society that punishes older people for having led a life, often against their own wishes, that did not conform to what society considered a worthy existence, with the state going on to deprive them of their life and liberty as a direct result of how they lived when they were younger, effectively sentencing them to an early death. *The Unit* is centrally a dystopia about ageing, where older, childless citizens, whose lives are deemed less valuable and a drain on society's resources, are forced by the state in a near-future Sweden to become organ donors, according to a utilitarian logic.

Indeed, in Holmqvist's biodystopia, proponents of utilitarian economics take these views to radical extremes, eliminating those considered a burden on society and thus saving resources needed to provide a better life for the rest of society, without widespread rebellion from citizens. This view, predicated on the ageist assumption that older lives are somehow worthless, an idea central to geronticide and dramatized in *The Unit*, stands in stark contrast with the bioethical philosophy that defends the promotion of the well-being of older citizens, an Ethics of Care. As Sara Schotland observes:

> As the population ages and as medical technology improves, there is a tension between an Ethics of Care that supports enhancing the lifespan of the elderly versus utilitarian arguments that would devote scarce dollars and therapies to younger and more productive members of society. While geronticide might seem a far-fetched, dystopian nightmare, the question of whether and how to distribute health care resources as our population ages is, of course, a topic of extensive commentary. (2013: 171)

The older, single citizens in *The Unit* are taken to special centres where they lead a comfortable life but will start to donate their organs as soon as they are needed, while also participating in medical experiments. These facilities feature very pleasant surroundings and excellent amenities, as well as ubiquitous surveillance, where the 'tiniest nook or cranny was monitored by cameras' and 'hidden microphones' (Holmqvist 2010: 3), reminiscent of the panopticon, the prison system first described by Jeremy Bentham and then updated by Foucault, where the inmate 'is seen, but he does not see' (Foucault 1977: 200), a situation also reminiscent of *Harvest*, where the Indian family is constantly monitored, and of *Never Let Me Go*, where the clones are both watched and watch each other. As Dorrit, the protagonist and narrator, remarks: 'I have no way of checking whether the surveillance is switched off or not, so it makes no difference' (Holmqvist 2010: 213). Indeed, the narratives in these texts revolve around prison-like spaces, where the protagonists are thoroughly controlled and virtually unable to escape.

Under the guise of an allegedly and ostensibly democratic society, Holmqvist's *The Unit* portrays a country that exerts the kind of inescapable control over the lives of certain of their older citizens that is more commonly associated with totalitarian states, calling into question definitions and practices of democracy and implicitly interrogating its very nature. After all, the bioexploitation was democratically voted for by the citizens, whose lives are now thoroughly manipulated by a decree approved in a democratic fashion, after debates and a referendum, following the socially sanctioned rationale of helping those worthier of organs, because they are considered more useful to society. Who, however, makes those rules? How can an allegedly democratic society like this near-future Sweden sanction this kind of practice? As Sara Schotland, in a related vein, pertinently asks: 'Should a society devote substantial resources to caring for the unproductive elderly?' (2013: 160), a question addressed in *The Unit*, which implicitly asks who matters in society, whether its older citizens are important and who should be kept alive.[13]

When, then, are people deemed 'dispensable' in this future Sweden? Women over fifty and men over sixty, single, with no children, often jobless, artistic types, are taken to the Second Reserve Bank Unit for Biological Material, a 'luxury slaughterhouse' (Holmqvist 2010: 212), as one of the 'dispensable' (2010: 48) describes it, and are forced to donate selected organs, until eventually they will donate a vital organ and, to use the euphemism from Ishiguro (2005a), which is effectively a fundamental forerunner text, 'complete'. In this 'democratic' state, then, bearing children is seen as almost compulsory if one is to be worthy of being allowed to live after the age of fifty for women and sixty for men, without their bodies being used for organ donations. Indeed, people are so frightened of remaining childless that many adolescents bear children, just to be on the safe side. Reproduction is thus a central feature in *The Unit*, as in *Harvest*, since without children there is literally no future of the species. The primacy of reproduction in these texts reveals the symbolic power of children and child-bearing and the forceful investment in the reproductive role, but this line of reasoning alone should not be responsible for the redundancy of older, childless citizens.

The protagonist, Dorrit, a single, childless woman, is taken to one of these units, where she unexpectedly falls in love and against all odds gets pregnant. Although she considers escaping and keeping her child, the pressure placed on her eventually makes her abandon those thoughts of freedom. This disturbing sense of dystopian compliance and conformity, of submissiveness and obedience in Holmqvist's *The Unit*, echoes Ishiguro's *Never Let Me Go*, with neither the dispensable nor the clones rebelling against their fate. This willing acceptance of sacrifice for the benefit of other, more 'useful' members of society in *The Unit* is perhaps even harder to understand, since they could have tried to hide somewhere or escape to another country before being collected and taken to the unit. While in *Never Let Me Go*, people know the clones exist but choose to forget about them, in *The Unit*, society is fully aware of the fate of these older, unattached citizens and has accepted this reality, making everyone complicit in their fate.[14]

Another similarity between *The Unit* and *Never Let Me Go* is the idea that people who have fallen in love may get a 'deferral' (Ishiguro 2005a) and be allowed to live for longer. In *Never Let Me Go*, there is a rumour that if two people are in love, their donations could be postponed, so that they would be able to enjoy some more time together. In *The Unit*, when Dorrit falls in love and gets pregnant, she is convinced that she will be allowed to live and be a mother to her child and even settle as a family outside the unit with the child's father, another dispensable in the unit, Johannes, but her expectations are dashed when she is told in no uncertain terms that she remains a dispensable and her child will be given up for adoption immediately after being born.

Indeed, the future society in *The Unit* is predicated on the notion of the individual 'biovalue', to borrow Rose's term (2007: 6), of its citizens, whose lives are appraised in terms of 'economic considerations' (Holmqvist 2010: 210), where 'everyone has to be profitable all the time' and older women are advised to have an abortion due to the potential risk of having a baby with health problems, which would mean a big financial burden for the state. Dorrit's foetus, in turn, is described as 'fresh human capital' (2010: 193) or 'biocapital' in Rose's (2007: 6) terms.

The possibility of growing old and enjoying the last stages of life is denied to the older, childless citizens in Holmqvist's *The Unit*, to the impoverished Indian citizens of Padmanabhan's play *Harvest* and the clones in Ishiguro's *Never Let Me Go*, with all of them, albeit in different ways, being allowed to die to satisfy the craving on the part of wealthy citizens for longer, healthier lives. These narratives alert us to the potential for inequalities in the treatment of those who become effectively first-class citizens, on the one hand, and second-class ones, on the other, the latter becoming invisible and discriminated against, sacrificed for the sake of the greater good of society at large and of those wealthy enough to exploit, often remorselessly, the bodies of underprivileged others.

The three texts briefly examined here provide a critique not only of contemporary social structures but also of future ones, as the scientific advances gradually become available for implementing biotechnological innovations that will likely benefit only the wealthier members of society, putatively preventing ageing. They can thus pertinently be read as cautionary tales that warn against extreme biocapitalist and consumerist values that radically discriminate between the richer and the poorer, deepening already existing disparities and inequalities.

Conclusion

The long-standing ambition to preserve youth and extend the human lifespan has always been a potent force driving bioscientific advances, dramatized in numerous fictional and filmic examples. The fictional narratives considered in this chapter extrapolate from our contemporary world to create societies where the presence of an ageing population exerts pressure on biocapitalism to provide means of deflecting disease and old age, often going to unacceptable lengths to ensure extended youth and well-being, while simultaneously addressing social anxieties and fears about population ageing and the potentially 'burdensome' older person.

These narratives share a number of very topical thematic concerns: exacerbated biocapitalism and enforced organ donation by some members of the society, the often hidden operations of biopower, and ubiquitous surveillance and control. The texts ask whether it could be acceptable to sacrifice people or to deceive them into donating their organs in order to benefit individuals from societies bent on achieving longer lives, in particular for wealthier citizens, at the expense of others, practices often predicated on intergenerational conflict, although not in *The Unit*, which constitutes a meaningful exception, with some older people becoming the sacrificial victims. These biodystopias are cautionary narratives, alerting their readers to a gradual increase in the exploitation of disadvantaged and predominantly young people who will increasingly become biocommodities that will be taken advantage of, providing organs and biomaterial to wealthier, usually older, citizens. Indeed, with the well-to-do population in prosperous countries living longer, the tendency will be towards greater efforts to procure organs for transplantation to meet the increased demand. This need, at least until organs can be grown from an individual's own stem cells or be 3D-bioprinted,[15] is likely to be aggressively tackled in some countries and by some biotech companies, keen on profit, to satisfy affluent patients at all costs, thereby creating wider inequalities between those who can afford life-saving biomaterial and those who cannot or are forced to donate it. Indeed, many older people will not have access to expensive medical treatments, with the biopolitics of ageing catering mostly to the desires of wealthy people to stay young as long as possible, an impulse driven by the fear of ageing itself, which permeates these texts.

The crucial biopolitical question these bionarratives ask is: who is entitled to grow old in the age of biocapitalism? In these texts, ageing is mostly about avoiding frailty and maintaining a healthy, vigorous body; this emphasis on appearing young involves deep-rooted ageist conceptions that have long been an integral part of our societies. These biodystopias warn about such extreme future medical technologies as body transfer but also about the exploitation and misuse of vulnerable people as biocommodities, practices that need to be thoroughly restricted by law and regulated to be ethically acceptable and not lead to manipulated, dehumanized lives, deprived of a potentially fulfilling existence, including the prospect of a healthy and rewarding old age.

Notes

1 Indeed, as Ehlers and Krupar (2019) insist, life-making is inextricably entwined with power relations.
2 See Cooper's (2011) analysis of 'neoliberal biopolitics' and the 'financialization' of life.
3 Vora (2008: n.p.) discusses the 'commodification of "life"' in the context of the kidney trade in India, arguing that the 'creation of excess body parts and lives through medical and transportation technologies, creates a system where Indian lives function to support other lives in the West, rather than their own', an aspect instantiated in *Harvest*.
4 The colonial/postcolonial context is central to this play, but it falls outside the scope of this article.
5 This plot is also explored to great effect in Silverberg's *To Live Again* (1969), where the consciousness of usually very wealthy citizens is stored and then transferred to someone else's body, where it remains active alongside that person's original consciousness, in some cases taking over completely. Similarly, in Rogers's *Body Tourists* (2019), a neural interface, coupled with digital memory transfer, allows the cloned brain of a dead person to take over the host brain for a limited period of time. This is also the case in Flynn's *The Companions* (2020) and in the American series *Altered Carbon* (2018–).
6 After all, as Foucault (2003: 248) remarks, 'Power literally ignores death'.
7 As Wasson (2011: 76) observes, '"Donor" and recipient often inhabit a colonising binary, human tissue flowing from East to West, from poor to the wealthy … from marginalized to powerful'. In addition, the donor is 'often nameless and effaced in medical discourse, while the transplant recipient is extensively documented and cherished' (2011: 77). Meaningfully, although the dystopian texts under consideration here address and explore this effacement of the donor, they also give donors a voice, often using their point of view, thus effectively working against their invisibility.
8 As Neilson (2012: 51) asserts, in words that could apply to Virgil, it is also possible to look at some 'radical developments as individuals being responsible for their own health and having recourse to extreme measures facilitated by powerful biotech companies'. In his words, 'users of anti-ageing medicine frequently understand themselves as exercising agency and responsibility in challenging traditional biomedical conceptions of ageing as decline and loss'.

9   In Shusterman's *Unwind* (2007), there is a very similar premise to Ishiguro (2005a). Those children and adolescents who are seen by their parents or guardians as troublesome are forcibly taken to facilities where they are 'unwound', a euphemism to refer to the organ donations they go through until they die.
10 Russell (2019: 175) asks a similar question in the context of Ishiguro's book but also in the real world, namely 'what ideological and cultural production is necessary to produce a world where practices that should seem repellant [*sic*] are, in fact, normalized and even celebrated?'
11 As Wasson (2015: 99) in an analogous vein remarks, 'In anonymous living donation the donor is often represented as a mere manufacturer of tissue, a move which elides their sacrifice. This elision has facilitated a brutal predation on poor and vulnerable harvestees worldwide.'
12 See Nayar (2020) for further fictional examples of these precarious lives.
13 This question came to the fore during the worst moments of the Covid-19 pandemic when doctors were at times forced to choose which patients were more deserving of treatment when there was a shortage of ventilators.
14 Gullette (2017) discusses a vast array of ageist practices that fittingly apply to the scapegoating of older people in *The Unit*.
15 For an overview of the main socio-ethical and regulatory issues, see Vermeulen et al. (2017).

References

Agamben, G. (1998), *Homo Sacer: Sovereign Power and Bare Life*, trans. D. Heller-Roazen, Stanford, CA: Stanford University Press.
Altered Carbon (2018–), [TV Series] Dir. L. Kalogridis, USA: Netflix.
Bauman, Z. (2003), *Wasted Lives: Modernity and Its Outcasts*, Cambridge: Polity.
Butler, J. (2004a), *Precarious Life: The Power of Mourning and Violence*, London: Verso.
Butler, J. (2004b), *Undoing Gender*, New York: Routledge.
Butler, J. (2009), *Frames of War: When Is Life Grievable?* London: Verso.
Charlwood, C. (2018), ' "Stop … and Remember": Memory and Ageing in Kazuo Ishiguro's Novels', *American, British and Canadian Studies*, 31(December): 86–113.
Cohen, S. (2001), *States of Denial: Knowing about Atrocities and Suffering*, Cambridge: Polity.
Cooper, M. (2011), *Life as Surplus: Biotechnology and Capitalism in the Neoliberal Era*, Seattle: University of Washington Press.
Ehlers, N., and S. Krupar (2019), *Deadly Biocultures: The Ethics of Life-Making*, Minneapolis: University of Minnesota Press.
Esposito, R. (2012), *The Third Person: Politics of Life and Philosophy of the Impersonal*, Cambridge: Polity.

Flynn, K. M. (2020), *The Companions*, New York: Scout.
Foucault, M. (1977), *Discipline and Punish: The Birth of the Prison*, trans. A. M. Sheridan, London: Penguin.
Foucault, M. (1998), *The History of Sexuality: The Will to Knowledge*, vol. 1, trans. R. Hurley, London: Penguin.
Foucault, M. (2003), *Society Must Be Defended: Lectures at the Collège de France, 1975-1976*, ed. Arnold Davidson, New York: Picador.
Foucault, M. (2007), *Security, Territory, Population: Lectures at the Collège de France, 1977-1978*, trans. G. Burchell, New York: Palgrave Macmillan.
Frow, J. (1998), 'Bodies in Pieces', in L. Dale and S. Ryan (eds), *The Body in the Library*, 35–51, Amsterdam: Rodopi.
Giroux, H. A. (2008), 'Beyond the Biopolitics of Disposability: Rethinking Neoliberalism in the New Gilded Age', *Social Identities*, 14(5): 587–620. doi:10.1080/13504630802343432.
Gullette, M. M. (2017), *Ending Ageism, or How Not to Shoot Old People* (Global Perspectives on Aging), New Brunswick: Rutgers University Press.
Holmqvist, N. ([2009] 2010), *The Unit*, trans. M. Delargy, Oxford: Oneworld.
Ishiguro, K. (2005a), *Never Let Me Go*, London: Faber & Faber.
Ishiguro, K. (2005b), 'SPIEGEL Interview with Kazuo Ishiguro: "I Remain Fascinated by Memory"', *SPIEGEL Online*, 10 May 2005. Available online: https://www.spiegel.de/international/spiegel-interview-with-kazuo-ishiguro-i-remain-fascinated-by-memory-a-378173.html.
Karmakar, M., and A. Parui (2017), 'Bioengineering and Cultural Identity: A Study of Kazuo Ishiguro's *Never Let Me Go*', *Asian Journal of English Studies*, 6(2): 107.
Kelly, R. T. (2011), *The Possessions of Doctor Forrest*, London: Faber & Faber.
Kureishi, H. (2002), *The Body and Other Stories*, London: Faber & Faber.
Levy, T. (2011), 'Human Rights Storytelling and Trauma Narrative in Kazuo Ishiguro's *Never Let Me Go*', *Journal of Human Rights*, 10: 1–16.
Lopez, P. J., and K. A. Gillespie, eds (2015), *Economies of Death: Economic Logics of Killable Life and Grievable Death*, New York: Routledge.
Mangum, T. (2002), 'Longing for Life Extension: Science Fiction and Late Life', *Journal of Aging and Identity*, 7(2): 70–81.
Matthews, S. (2009), 'I'm Sorry I Can't Say More: An Interview with Kazuo Ishiguro,' in S. Matthews and S. Groes (eds), *Kazuo Ishiguro: Contemporary Critical Perspectives*, 114–25, London: Continuum International.
McQueen, S. (2016), *Deleuze and Baudrillard: From Cyberpunk to Biopunk*, Edinburgh: Edinburgh University Press.
Moni, S. (2014), '"In Bits and Pieces": Bodies in Movement, Liminality and Subaltern Resistance in Manjula Padmanabhan's *Harvest*', *Journal of Postcolonial Writing*, 50(3): 316–28.

Nayar, P. K. (2020), 'Precarious Lives in the Age of Biocapitalism', in M. Thomsen, M. Rosendahl and J. Wamberg (eds), *The Bloomsbury Handbook of Posthumanism*, 425–35, London: Bloomsbury Academic.

Neilson, B. (2012), 'Ageing, Experience, Biopolitics: Life's Unfolding', *Body & Society*, 18: 44–71.

Noble, L. (2011), *Medicinal Cannibalism in Early Modern English Literature and Culture*, New York: Springer.

Padmanabhan, M. (1997), *Harvest*, London: Aurora Metro.

Ranisch, R., and S. Lorenz Sorgner, eds (2015), *Post- and Transhumanism: An Introduction*, Frankfurt: Peter Lang.

Rogers, J. (2019), *Body Tourists*, London: Sceptre.

Rose, N. (2007), *The Politics of Life Itself: Biomedicine, Power, and Subjectivity in the Twenty-First Century*, Princeton, NJ: Princeton University Press.

Russell, E. (2019), *Transplant Fictions: A Cultural Study of Organ Exchange*, Cham, Switzerland: Springer Nature.

Scheper-Hughes, N. (2001a), 'Commodity Fetishism in Organs Trafficking', *Body and Society*, 7(2–3): 31–62.

Scheper-Hughes, N. (2001b), 'Neo-cannibalism: The Global Trade in Human Organs', *Hedgehog Review*, Summer 2001. Available online: https://hedgehogreview.com/issues/the-body-and-being-human/articles/neo-cannibalism-the-global-trade-in-human-organs.

Scheper-Hughes, N. (2002), 'Bodies for Sale – Whole or in Parts', in N. Scheper-Hughes and L. Wacquant (eds), *Commodifying Bodies*, 1–8, London: Sage.

Schotland, S. D. (2013), 'Forced Execution of the Elderly: *Old Law*, Dystopia, and the Utilitarian Argument', *Humanities*, 2: 160–75.

Shusterman, N. (2007), *Unwind*, New York: Simon & Schuster.

Silverberg, R. (1969), *To Live Again*, New York: Doubleday.

Stevenson, R. L. (1886), *Strange Case of Dr Jekyll and Mr Hyde*, London: Longman's, Green.

Sunder Rajan, K. (2007), *Biocapital: The Constitution of Postgenomic Life*, Durham: Duke University Press.

Vermeulen, N., G. Haddow, T. Seymour, A. Faulkner-Jones and W. Shu (2017), '3D Bioprint Me: A Socioethical View of Bioprinting Human Organs and Tissues', *Journal of Medical Ethics*, 43(9). Available online: https://doi.org/10.1136/medethics-2015-103347.

Vora, K. (2008), 'Others' Organs: South Asian Domestic Labor and the Kidney Trade', *Postmodern Culture*, 19(1). Available online: https://muse.jhu.edu/article/270615.

Wasson, S. (2011), '"A Butcher's Shop Where the Meat Still Moved": Gothic Doubles, Organ Harvesting and Human Cloning', in S. Wasson and E. Alder (eds), *Gothic Science Fiction 1980–2010*, 73–86, Liverpool: Liverpool University Press.

Wasson, S. (2015), 'Recalcitrant Tissue: Organ Transfer and the Struggle for Narrative Control', in J. D. Edwards (ed.), *Technologies of the Gothic in Literature and Culture*, 99–112, London: Routledge.

Wells, H. G. ([1896] 2014), 'The Story of the Late Mr Elvesham', Scotts Valley, CA: CreateSpace.

Yeung, V. (2017), 'Mortality and Memory in Kazuo Ishiguro's *Never Let Me Go*', *Transnational Literature*, 9(2). Available online: http://fhrc.flinders.edu.au/transnational/home.html.

5

Contemporary perspectives on ageing in European dystopian literature

Aleksandra Pogońska-Baranowska

Introduction

At the dawn of the twenty-first century, the age of the Anthropocene and advanced global capitalism, contemporary writers seem to perceive an overwhelming necessity to warn the human race of the risks arising from its own power and audacity. As MacKay Demerijan claims, 'Our obsession with the post-apocalyptic and dystopian in contemporary fiction is an indication of a larger need to acknowledge' the risks of our own progress and 'to take into account the tremendous environmental, psychological, and sociological destruction that it has caused over the last few centuries' (2016: 5). Dystopian novels, although predominantly set in the future, represent an attempt to examine contemporary social and political issues that could, if left unattended, bring about undesirable consequences. As well as apocalyptic projections, they often represent large cultural and technological shifts and allow us to picture the future consequences of our behaviour: 'They highlight our collective fears and allow us to process them in a nightmarish fantasy' (Demerijan 2016: 5). They give a fictional voice to all the issues that appear to be too terrifying or disorienting for the collective to express outwardly. According to Edward Edinger, the author of *Archetype of the Apocalypse*, dystopian and apocalyptic visions act to move us away from damaging, yet normalized, human behaviours, in order to promote new and more viable ways of acting collectively (2002: 23). No wonder that potential hazards presented by dramatic demographic shifts stimulate the imagination of contemporary writers, some of whom base their works on catastrophic visions of the future and raise questions about the place of older individuals in the society of the future. How will our society cope with the rapidly growing population of its oldest members? Are we adequately equipped to meet the economic and political challenges of 'the demographic time bomb'? Will we be able to offer very old people the care, treatment and respect they deserve? And, finally, how far will older people be placed under pressure to 'move over' and make room for younger generations?

This chapter is focused on an analysis and comparison of contemporary European dystopian novels that represent geronticide and related practices in their exploration of demographic change and generational relationships at the dawn of the twenty-first century. The interpretation of *Gli Scaduti* (2015) by Italian novelist Lidia Ravera and *The Unit* (2006 in Swedish) by Swedish author Ninni Holmqvist is followed by an analysis of *Eternity Express* (2003) by French writer Jean-Michel Truong. The exploration of the texts in the light of key debates about ageing and ageism, preceded by a short presentation of previous articulations of the problem in the European canon of literature (including the work of Thomas Middleton, Anthony Trollope, Paolo Mantegazza and Luce D'Eramo), proves that, while geronticide might seem a far-fetched, dystopian nightmare, the question of how to face the perceived economic and social threat caused by rapid population ageing remains the subject of attention and cultural anxiety. As the population ages and as medical technology improves, there is a tension between an ethics of care that supports enhancing the lifespan of older people versus utilitarian arguments that would devote scarce dollars and therapies to younger and supposedly more productive members of society. In the end, as Andreu Domingo claims, dystopias reflect the tensions of the societies from which they emerge (2008: 731).

Demographic change and ageism

At the dawn of the new millennium, science does not perceive death as a metaphysical mystery that cannot be explained. Rather, for many in modern societies, death is regarded as a technical problem that can be solved. As Yuval Noah Harari maintains, 'In the twenty-first century humans are likely to make a serious bid for immortality' (2016: 16). With the advancement in medicine and hygiene over the past two centuries, the life expectancy of humans worldwide has almost doubled from forty to seventy. The United Nations (2019) estimate that at present, the life expectancy of the people born in the richest parts of the globe is around seventy-nine years and is still going up. Nevertheless, within the coming decades, scientific and technological developments may extend the average lifespan to numbers that seem impossible to imagine.

Paradoxically, though, this achievement has generally been received not with joy but with concern and pessimism about the 'burden' that growing numbers of older, supposedly dependent, people would impose upon a shrinking younger population, as the rise in life expectancy coincides with a fall in the birth rate. Consequently, older people have not only increased in numbers but also as a proportion of the population, which has brought about a process of rapid population ageing, a phenomenon more widespread in European countries than in other parts of the world. Europe is currently perceived as 'the oldest' continent of the globe and, according to the Organisation for Economic Cooperation and Development (OECD 2021), it is supposed to retain this position until 2060.

European governments are starting to confront the challenges posed by the dramatic demographic shift. Widespread concern is provoked by the escalating needs and maintenance costs of an ageing population, while, simultaneously, the tax base shrinks as the percentage of employed people declines. As a consequence, the oldest members of contemporary societies represent an increasing dilemma for policymakers and resource providers, which affects attitudes towards their survival and the pressure on them to 'move over'. Older people are stigmatized as useless and inefficient in a society that is based on production and consumption. The discourses that position older people as those who steal the future from the young, burdening them with the costs of their pensions and absorbing considerable economic resources, are strongly emphasized. In consequence, many problems of older people do not result directly from the effects of biological ageing, but from discriminating social attitudes towards old age.

Although age is one of the earliest characteristics we notice about other people (Fiske 1998: 358), it is far from being the only social marker that shapes our attitudes towards other individuals. As Amy J. C. Cuddy and Susan T. Fiske claim, conscious or not, we form our opinions based on sex, race and religion, among other social categories (2002: 3). However, unlike these other categories, older age is one that most of us eventually join, as every living person grows older (Ayalon 2015). Despite increased public and research attention on diversity and inclusion efforts, a closer look suggests that not all forms of diversity and inclusion have been considered equal. In particular, focus on age discrimination goes largely unchallenged and even unnoticed, as we tend to disparage older people without fear of being censored (Nelson 2016: 191–8).

As Paul Higgs and Chris Gilleard argue, ageism[1] may appear as a result of attitudes or prejudice, but it can also be understood as an aspect of an inherently discriminatory society or culture (2020: 1618–19). Such structural discrimination may be noticed in prejudicial hiring practices and social policies, the oppressions of institutional abuse, the marginalization of older people or the dominance of the decline narrative (Gullette 2004: 7) according to which old age is perceived in terms of physical and mental health deterioration. As claimed by Higgs and Gilleard, the later stages of life have been characterized as two very diverse, but yet closely related concepts of the third and the fourth age. The 'social imaginary' of the fourth age works in opposition to the cultural field of the third age, which, in turn, can be perceived as originating within the social changes of the late twentieth century and its focus on choice, autonomy, self-expression and pleasure (Higgs and Gilleard 2020: 1619). Thus, much of the active 'othering' of old age in contemporary culture seems closely related to the growth of consumer markets, lifestyle differentiation and the valorization of individual choice and agency. The 'dark side' of old age, represented antithetically as a feared and undesired fourth age, characterized by frailty and lack of choice, serves as an amplifier of those cultures. In poet and novelist May Sarton's terms, 'real' old age is something that one falls into, rather than simply another stage of life one is travelling through (1996: 15). The interconnectedness of ageing, vulnerability and frailty is fundamental to the process of othering old age. Within Western culture, old age has often been represented as a 'foreign' country that remains 'other' to most members of society. This idea was well expressed by Sarton when she wrote: 'The trouble is, old age is not interesting until one gets there, a foreign country with an unknown language to the young and even to the middle-aged' (1982: 23). What such approaches make clear is that old age is represented more often as an attribute of others than as a conscious identity of the self.

Geronticide: Killing 'the elderly'

Many prominent age studies scholars, including Margaret Morganroth Gullette, argue that the othering of social groups, including older people, can lead to extreme forms of violence. The author dedicates her latest book, *Ending Ageism, or How Not to Shoot Old People* (2017), to the problematic issue of the normalization of older people as 'burdensome hazard' (Biggs and Powell 2001: 10). The text fights against 'increasingly grave instances from the array of ageisms … [for example] glaring neglect in private or public life, grossly hostile speech, abusive images, cruel practices, threats, incitements to self-harm, or violence' (Gullette 2017: 22). As the scholar explains,

> People tend to distance themselves from individuals or groups that frighten them. Fear can be taught, heightened, or redirected: after World War II, against

communists; after 9/11, Muslims; today, immigrants. Social-identity and terror management theories, informed by age theory, explain how fear can be manipulated against old people. A handy new group to target. (2017: 21)

In public discourse, older people are being constructed as a new target group against whom injustice is gradually becoming discursively legitimated. The rhetoric of 'the silver tsunami', 'the grey flood', the 'agequake' or the 'age wave', 'amplified by the authoritative tones of medical and health policy expertise, conceives of population ageing as an imminent catastrophe' (Charise 2012: 3). Older people are 'naturalized as a liquid cataclysm whose volume exceeds the nation's ability to contain, or even guard against, an abstracted human burden' (2012: 3).

The increasing older population poses not only economic and utilitarian but also ethical questions for modern society. In *Treatise on Parents and Children*, George Bernard Shaw noted that if society wishes to continue what he called 'breeding', it must accept the inevitability of killing older individuals in order to make way for the young. According to Shaw, such deaths would be the only effective way of discouraging older people from seeking eternal life on earth ([1914] 2006: n.p.). Despite the fact that geronticide, understood as the deliberate and systematic killing of older individuals solely because of their age, either by others or through social pressure to commit suicide, is a modern term (see Posner 1995; Post 1991), Mike Brogden argues that there is nothing new in such homicides, since all societies have regularly condoned the killing of older people. Although legal statutes may have proscribed direct actions against older individuals, storytelling metaphors, allegories and historical moralizing suggest that older people, especially those regarded as 'senescent', have always been represented as disposable because of their lack of utility. A tradition-sanctified resolution endemic to those accounts is that terminating the lives of older members of society 'should solve the perceived problems of demography and of economics' (Brodgen 2001: 139). As Hartung notes, even in the early twentieth-century medical study of old age, *Senescence* (1922), the author, G. Stanley Hall, treats euthanasia as a possible future solution to the problem of old age (2013: 51).

Over the past few decades, fiction has come to be perceived as a useful way to understand the experience of ageing from various points of view, approaching that experience without the limits imposed by disciplines such as gerontology and sociology. Through literary texts, writers continue to confront the 'age wave' and its effects on social life using a variety of approaches, from the overwhelmingly realistic to the irreverent to the ecstatic. Some of them, inherently concerned with the exploration of lateness in the form of what Frank Kermode calls 'the sense of an ending' (1967: 368), turn to the dystopian imagination, speculate where others would fear to tread and portray life-threatening consequences of ageism. In particular, some authors of contemporary dystopian novels explore not the 'voluntary act' of euthanasia, but those occasions when other parties determine that older people should lose their fundamental right to life. In these novels, societies which otherwise preach tolerance, civility and human rights prompt elders, marked out by the social prejudices attached to ageism and by other negative stereotyping, to accept premature death.

Although twenty-first-century demodystopias[2] seem groundbreaking, it should be noted that the theme of disposing of older people as a means of population control was a recurrent motif in earlier speculative literature. Sara D. Schotland's (2013) analysis of Thomas Middleton's *Old Law, or A New Way to Please You* (1656), a tragicomedy about a law that introduces a popular programme of forced execution, provides evidence of this. Nancee Reeves notes the great increase in scenarios in which older generations are forced to commit suicide in the speculative fiction of the nineteenth and early twentieth centuries, a period that saw the development and popularization of Darwinian evolution and eugenics (2017: 103). The theme of geronticide, as related to the spectre of decline and the 'burden' of an ageing population (Falcus 2020: 124), appears in *The Fixed Period* (1882), a satirical dystopian novel by Anthony Trollope,[3] and in more contemporary texts such as William F. Nolan and George Clayton Johnson's *Logan's Run* (1967). The dumping of 'the elderly' in *Gli scaduti* (2015), the fatal donation law introduced in *The Unit* (2006) or the mass executions of older people in *Eternity Express* (2003) are, therefore, part of a long tradition of European speculative writing about ageing and enforced death.

Gli scaduti and the dumping of 'the elderly'

The image of a world in which 'fathers' are cast out from society appears in *Gli scaduti* (2015), an Italian dystopian novel written by Lidia Ravera. In a state which controls and manages the private lives of its citizens, there is no place for the supposedly burdensome aspects of old age. The discourse of crisis and burden accentuates the growing number, neediness and poverty of older people, whose volume apparently exceeds the nation's ability to contain it: 'Italy is not a country for old men. It is too inefficient, with poor welfare conditions and full of urban solitude. Nevertheless, the elderly constitute a majority of society' (Ravera

2015: 3).[4] With this bitter reflection, the author begins to outline a shocking story based on a terrifying scenario, futuristic, but full of extremely realistic images – typical of today's speculative fiction.

The story is set in Italy in the near future, where a new government introduces a law that regulates exchange between the young and older people, eliminating spontaneity of feelings, and affection, all to deal with the economic and social 'burden' of an ageing society. By using the argument of 'return to nature' (Ravera 2015: 16) and life in compliance with the rules of evolution, the anti-elderly Unique Party obligates citizens over sixty years old to retire, 'get out of the way' (2015: 17) and spend the rest of their existence in a parallel reality, extraneous to active life. People in their thirties are seen as protagonists of their own lives, whereas those who have reached the age of sixty are treated as expired and are removed from social, family and professional life, in order to make way for younger generations.

The narrator of the story invokes the slogans spread by the politicians during the political campaigns, appealing to the incompatibility of older people with the dynamic, modern world:

> Is there anything more natural than a growing weakness, a progressive disaffection with material and intellectual issues of those who have lived for over seven or even eight decades? The elderly are not able to live well in our world, they resemble disabled people living among normal individuals. Sharing the spaces of youth and maturity becomes a source of frustration and fear for those who are not capable of walking fast and finding pleasure in sex, food, performance, competition. (Ravera 2015: 72)

Ageist attitudes often frame older adults as incapable, dependent and lacking in self-determination. In a lot of ways, the ageist stereotypes are similar to ableist ones about people with disabilities, who are commonly portrayed as dependent and less capable. Not only have these issues become central to the 'decline narrative' focused on the physical and mental health deterioration of older people, but as noted by Degnen (2007: 72), the illnesses experienced in older age emphasize the 'us' versus 'them' binary opposition, more than does the representation of chronological age. When cognitive impairments are added, the individual identity that can be expressed through choice, autonomy and self-expression becomes limited, which is often described as the 'social death' of the subject (Sweeting and Gilhooly 1997: 95). At a certain age, society decides that people are not able to keep up with the changing world, which transforms them into dispensable members of society, waste destined to be scrapped. As claimed by one of the representatives of the Unique Party, in the natural cycle, human existence starts, continues and finishes, and nobody complains about it. Or, at least, not in public.

The creation of a parallel reality, where older people can live together and construct a closed society, seems to remain the only solution. Information about the logistics of this 'retirement' is scarce and remains shrouded in mystery. According to official accounts, after a solemn ceremony, pensioners are transported by train to a luxurious complex in an unknown place in the north of the continent, where they can enjoy a new, relaxed life, after many years of effort, responsibilities and competition. In reality, instead of public pension benefits, they are 'scrapped', excluded from any social participation in their secluded space, designed to contain the purportedly 'burdensome' aspects of old age. The images of the train carriages exporting the older people recall the tragic events of the deportation of Jews during the Second World War. With the echo of the tragic events of the Holocaust, the concept of the scrapping of a human being is emphasized to signal the terrible paths that can be followed by people stripped of moral values. The containment and exclusion of older people highlight the Foucaldian relationship between space, body and identity, as the ageing person is increasingly marginalized and isolated from social interaction due to the discursively constructed otherness of the ageing body. In this regard, the space of the closed retirement community is a heterotopia of deviation, an example of 'those [spaces] in which individuals whose behaviour is deviant in relation to the required mean or norm are placed' (Foucault 1986: 25). The retired residents are denied access to information from the outside world; they are forbidden to be in possession of private mobile phones or computers. As described by Umberto, one of the main protagonists of the novel, who falls victim to the new law, the residents' reality is characterized by the lack of control over time and everyday activities. The new pensioners are not treated as independent individuals but are totally deprived of their autonomy, literally waiting for death.

In the introduction to the book, the author refers to a real political event, Italian prime minister Matteo Renzi's speech, in which 'the youthful' postulated 'scrapping' all of the politics that represent the preceding generations. Lidia Ravera claims that the use of the word 'scrapping' stimulated 'a literary nerve' and inspired her to imagine a new model of reality, where the practice initiated by Renzi and his adepts is extended to the whole society (2015: 5). Despite the author's declaration, the political scene does not seem to be the only source of her inspiration. The alternative vision of the future, in which the integration of older people in the natural cycle of life in society is perceived as an act against the laws of nature, appears in 'Una proposta risolutiva' (1988), a short story by

Luce D'Eramo. Although the text was written as a response to a very different demographic context, as an exploration of Malthusian fears experienced as a result of the process of rapid population growth, it also raises the issue of the place of older people in the modern world.[5] Marianna Rizzini (2015), by contrast, notices many analogies between *Gli scaduti* and Buzzati's short story entitled 'Cacciatori di vecchi' (1966a). Indeed, while reading *Gli scaduti*, it is difficult to resist the impression that Ravera is familiar with Buzzati's works. In his short stories, Buzzati is quite cynical in representing the generation gap as a conflict in which the young give chase to and beat their parents (as in the short story mentioned above) and older people are abandoned (as in 'Orchidee ai vecchi' published in 1950) or literally thrown away like rubbish to be taken to a dump (as in 'Viaggio agli inferi del secolo' published in 1966). Nonetheless, even the war between generations becomes a victim of time, as the final lines of 'Cacciatori di vecchi' demonstrate. Having spent a night chasing their parents, the young criminals notice their silhouettes' reflections in a shop window and shiver with fear, as they realize that they have grown old, and a new gang of youngsters is approaching to beat them in turn. They suddenly come to the realization that nobody can escape time and the stages of the life cycle, and so they foresee a similar end for themselves.

At this point, it is worth noting that the Raverian story represents a sequel to *Porci con le ali* (Ravera 1976), which revisits the topic of the 1968 youth revolt in Italy, a revolt inspired by distaste for traditional Italian society. Bearing in mind the link between the two novels, the ageist attitudes portrayed in *Gli scaduti* not only represent a desire for revolution and to change the world to make it less unjust but are also motivated by rage against the old, positioned as scapegoats for the disastrous state of the world. The renunciation of the previous generation is held according to the law of *contrapasso*,[6] executed to the disadvantage of the rebels from the past. For the ex-protesters from 1968, the representatives of the successive generations have prepared a scenario of deportation. The rejected, the eponymous *scrapped* members of society are the ones who will develop their own techniques of resistance and encourage the new generations to revolt against the new social system and act in the name of the 'silent majority', who will one day also become victims of time and share their parents' fate.

In *Gli scaduti*, Elisabetta, Umberto's wife and an ex-protester from 1968, who has preserved the rebel spirit from the past, stands up to the new 'retirement' laws. She cannot passively accept the isolation from her husband, her life partner, slightly older and, hence, already sent to the retirement facility. She supposes that, contrary to the governmental claims, the retired do not benefit from the idyllic life described in the glossy brochures and decides to find out the truth by any means. As we discover in the course of events, according to the rules of the 'methodical organization of decline' (Ravera 2015: 123), the residents of the new retirement facility are routinely being prescribed drugs to keep them sedated and deprived of any expressions of individuality, any desire to react or revolt.

As is typical of dystopian genre, Ravera reverses the premises of utopian literature. From prestige and respect, present in the renowned societies created in More's *Utopia* ([1516] 2012) and Campanella's *The City of Sun* ([1623] 2007), we move to the rejection of older people from important political roles and even the total disappearance of older people and their pedagogical values, as found in Orwell's *1984* ([1949] 2000) and Zamyatin's *We* ([1924] 1993). An exceptional approach may be noticed in Wilson, the main Orwellian protagonist, who tries to communicate with an older man who constitutes the only trace of the former reality, trying to prove that the lack of contact with the representatives of previous generations deprives people of the knowledge gained from their ancestors' experience. The resonance of this view can be perceived in the female Raverian protagonist, Elisabetta, who creates a mobile phone application *My memory*, which puts all the knowledge acquired by older people at the disposal of the next generations: 'everyone possesses a personal heritage from the past. … It is a richness that cannot be earned in any other way than living. However, long life is a capital of the elderly, and we want to work for young people' (Ravera 2015: 137). Nonetheless, with the process of societal modernization, which includes advancements in technology and science, the society in the novel does not seem to perceive personal heritage as of real value.

However, we cannot ignore the glimpse of hope in the novel's dystopian reality, which lies in the final rebellion organized by Matteo, son of Elisabetta and Umberto, and the representative of the young generation, who notices that the new reality, the utopian vision created by the thirty- and forty-year-old individuals, is not based on equality. There are people who, through the use of bribes or because they belong to the powerful elite, manage to avoid deportation. Although Matteo can be seen as one of the potential beneficiaries of the new system, he feels a strong bond of affection for his parents and wishes to save them from deportation. He takes advantage of his privileged position in the organizational structures of the new state, and using his access to the communication media, he calls for revolution. With the use of slogans 'Nobody is eternally young' and 'Inform yourselves: it is your right' (Ravera 2015: 198), Matteo convinces his contemporaries to confront the real conditions endured by their retired parents. The novel concludes with descriptions of the squares full of protesters, blocked train stations and older people escaping the carriages of deportation. Although the last scene of the novel is not clear about the success, or not, of the rebellion, as Elisabetta and Umberto decide to leave Italy and set off on a long journey towards a place where older people are rarer and are therefore treated with due respect, the author of the book decides to leave her readers with at least a spark of hope, in order to carry this critical utopian stance into our new millennium (Moylan 2000: 276).

The Unit – a dystopia about the value of human life

The issue of older individuals' value in a future society reappears in the latest novel by Ninni Holmqvist, *The Unit* (2006). The author of the book creates a very radical vision of tomorrow, in which experience is no longer valued and perceived as a factor that defines individuals' roles in society. In this world, all childless individuals are classified as 'dispensable' and removed to facilities where they are forced to make a different, ultimate contribution to their society. The drastic policy was introduced by the state as a part of a multifaceted master plan to encourage fertility in a rapidly ageing society where too few babies are being born.

'It was more comfortable than I could have imagined' (Holmqvist 2009: 3) – with these words, Dorrit, a single, fifty-year-old woman picked up from her home in a metallic red SUV and transported to a luxury facility created by the government, opens *The Unit*. Her new, two-room apartment is spacious, luminous, 'tastefully decorated' (2009: 4) and is located inside an elegant complex that includes a theatre, art studios, a cinema, a library and gourmet restaurants. For the first time, Dorrit is surrounded by like-minded people and feels included rather than ostracized. At the Second Reserve Bank Unit for biological material, she is one among a community of people who couldn't, or chose not to, have children. The cost is that, for the remaining years of their lives, their bodies will be disabled through a series of medical experiments, and their organs will be removed one by one, until the final, fatal donation. Some of the residents will lose their vision to cornea transplants; others will be deprived of the sense of hearing. As a consequence of myriad experiments with psychotropic drugs, some patients will not be able to stay awake or will exhibit medication-induced Alzheimer's symptoms. However, everything seems justified because of the benefit that it offers to the community as a whole. As claimed by the slogans repeated by the main protagonist, her body is not her own: 'Life is capital. A capital that is to be fairly divided among the people in a way that promotes reproduction and growth, welfare and democracy. I am only a steward, taking care of my vital organs' (Holmqvist 2009: 123). The Swedish writer has imagined a utilitarian society, obsessed with capital, but in a human form. The body has become a good, to be allocated by the state to serve the needs of others. Those who have children or who work in the fields of healthcare or education are seen as important members of society, enabling its growth. Childless and creative individuals, like Dorrit, are considered 'dispensable' and forced to make their own biological contributions. This theme uncannily echoes its organ-donation-dystopia predecessor, Kazuo Ishiguro's *Never Let Me Go* (2005), as both novels represent extreme forms of eugenic control and imagine societies of extreme utilitarianism. However, while Ishiguro's characters belong to a humanoid species that does not exist yet, *The Unit* involves no technological novum; it is set in the here and now.

Holmqvist wrote *The Unit*, she explains in an author's note, after she turned forty-five, when she realized that she was 'completely dispensable' and that her death would leave 'no tangible empty space behind me that needed to be filled'. As a childless woman practising a creative profession, she felt obliged to write about 'how it felt to be regarded as a selfish, spoiled oddball who does not contribute to any kind of growth' (2009: 270). The novel was first published in English in 2009 and has been recently newly reissued, supposedly to take advantage of the feverish interest in reproductive dystopias aroused by Hulu's adaptation of Margaret Atwood's *The Handmaid's Tale* (2017). Nevertheless, *The Unit* seems to be an inversion of Margaret Atwood's Gilead, where fertile women are fecundated by force under biblical sanction. Here, the explanation of horror – the extraction of human organs from the childless – is secular, a capitalist democracy demanding its toll.

The novel explores the intersection of two kinds of discrimination, that is sexism and ageism, which creates the 'double jeopardy' effect (Palmore 1999: 11). Although both childless men and women are required to give their bodies up to extend the lives of younger members of society, the age at which they enter the facility is determined by gender. Women are sent to the 'Reserve Unit' at the age of fifty. Men, in contrast, are deemed 'dispensable' as they turn sixty. Several researchers have stressed that when it comes to ageing and ageist attitudes, 'culture is indeed more punishing of women' (Twigg 2004: 62). The term 'double standard of ageing', introduced in the early 1970s by Susan Sontag ([1972] 1997: 19), refers to the fact that in Western cultures, women are 'aged' far earlier than men. The double standard stems from prescribed roles and normative expectations that are different for men and women. Men's prescribed roles over the lifespan are related to employment status, whereas women's 'age status is defined in terms of events in the reproductive cycle' (Arber and Ginn 1991: 41). In gendered ageism, the perspective of double jeopardy emphasizes the dominance of patriarchal norms.

It is worth noting that the unit itself is a utopian fantasy of government welfare for ageing citizens (it offers delicious meals, culture and companionship) but with a particularly sharp, dystopian twist. And yet one of the most shocking elements of the book is the extent to which all the residents not only accept but also affirm their own status. 'All this luxury! How much is all this costing the taxpayer?' (Holmqvist 2009: 52), Dorrit's new friend Elsa remarks, aghast, when she observes the well-equipped exercise facilities. Apart from the ability to live without cost in a stylish suite, all the individuals feast in excellent restaurants, relax in a beautiful winter garden and benefit from a wide range of entertainment facilities. Although the Reserve Unit is perfectly organized and amply staffed by qualified medical professionals, it may be seen as an institution that parodies the Hippocratic Oath and the assumed goals of medical care, as its main purpose is to maintain the 'patients' for organ donation.

The horror becomes increased because *The Unit* is set in what is supposedly a Western democracy. Though the idea for 'biological reserve units' was first proposed by a fringe political party, as Dorrit recalls, it soon 'slipped into the manifestos of some of the bigger and more established parties' (Holmqvist 2009: 24) and was ultimately passed by referendum. By emphasizing the ease with which seemingly extreme points of view and policies can become widely accepted, the writer appears to stress the fact that the dystopian future does not necessarily emerge from autocracy, but it can originate in widely held beliefs taken to an extreme.

Nevertheless, there is a strong inconsistency in the state's rationale. When Dorrit finds herself unexpectedly, and almost miraculously, pregnant, she assumes that she will be freed, as by virtue of her maternal status, she is no longer 'dispensable'. In fact, however, it turns out that she is doomed by her 'dispensable stamp' never to leave the unit. Having given birth, Dorrit will be obliged to give up her child and complete her final donation. The author of the book does not offer her readers any explanation for this inconsistency. Perhaps, the regimen is not flexible enough to address any exceptional circumstance. Or the state is so determined to rid itself of older citizens that it allows no exception to the rule that entry in the unit is a death sentence, from which there is no appeal.

Nonetheless, one of the nurses assumes great risk and decides to help Dorrit and gives her the opportunity to escape. The protagonist is amazed that there are several exits from the facility that she has never seen before. It turns out that the inmates are conditioned by 'psychological methods and power games' used to control them and deprive them of any motivation to escape (Holmqvist 2009: 203). As explained by the nurse, 'If you do manage to get motivated, if you really do want to survive, then you will find those exit doors. I know it sounds crazy, but that's just how the human psyche works: we generally see what we are prepared for, what we expect to see' (2009: 203). Dorrit finally does see an exit door and manages to escape into a dark, starlit night. Yet the novel closes with Dorrit back in the Reserve Unit, where she has just given birth to an infant whom she will shortly surrender, just before her life is terminated during the final donation act. The writer leaves the reader with great uncertainty as to how and why Dorrit failed in her escape. Was it just the protagonist's dream? If she had managed to escape, was she captured and returned to the unit? Or did she return voluntarily, defeated by the system as she realized that despite apparent freedom, there was no exit?

As in a typical classical dystopia, the reader is not offered any hope, and Dorrit's inability to escape the unit stands in for her failure and that of her compatriots to protest and act against the idea of sacrificing 'dispensable' older people. At the end of the novel, the implications of the exploitation of dispensable 'others' are brought to the entire population. There is a need for a greater number of donors, and the net is widened. Individuals are so desperate to parent that babies are stolen from prams. The dispensable other has become the universal 'we'.

Eternity Express and the mass killing of older individuals

Jean-Michel Truong's *Eternity Express*, published in 2003, is just a part of a long tradition of speculative writing about ageing and enforced death. However, Truong's vision provides one of the most frightening and explicit examples of geronticide in contemporary speculative fiction. Truong's story describes a dystopian world where population has outstripped resources. As a consequence of the collapse of pension funds and Western countries' inability to pay out pensions, over 20 million 'papy-boomers' are sent to live in a Chinese Eldorado, Clifford Estates, a residential estate with a considerably lower living cost. The policy is justified by the Retired Citizens Relocation Law, described during the political campaign as a 'judicious compromise', the only way of providing retired people with decent living conditions at an affordable cost for society.

According to the new law, as 'the one hundred and sixty million people who had to pay for the retired were quite determined not to let themselves be bled dry by a generation to whom they owed nothing' (Truong 2003: 61), full management of all retirement pension funds throughout the European Union is transferred to private companies. The sum of money, corresponding to the number of retired people they take care of, is fixed after an invitation to tender. In return, the firms take on the obligation to receive in their establishments, for the rest of their lives, all the citizens who have reached the legal retirement age. Also, the companies must respect certain specifications regarding the required standards of living, food, leisure activities, medical care and even funeral services. Consequently, in exchange for a certain sum of money financed by a state loan, the European governments hand over all obligations towards ageing members of society to the private sector, thus advantageously passing on the economic risk linked to their growing longevity. The companies argue that they are able to make the business profitable with their 'financial expertise and savoir-faire in management' (2003: 63). However, nothing is said about where the contract is to be executed. Thus, given the economic situation prevailing in European countries, the retired citizens have to accept exile to more affordable countries.

All the pensioners are transported via luxury train to a supposedly luxury retirement community, and during their journey, they repeat the official arguments they have heard in the social campaigns prior to the vote for the Retired Citizens Relocation Law, which they perceive as a highly advanced social solution that emphasizes European primacy:

- 'You'll see, this law will remain in history as a fantastic social advance – just as important as paid holidays – in keeping with Europe's good old Christian and humanist tradition.'
- 'To my mind', continued an ex-teacher, 'this is the ultimate proof of the superiority of the European model of development, which has always sought to reconcile economic dynamism and social solidarity. Look at America, where the old people work till seventy, eighty, then silently die in their basements' (Truong 2003: 66).

The passengers, used to life in a society which valorizes caring for those in need, no matter their age, take for granted the adult child's duty to care for their aged parent, based on the care ethicist's approach.[7] However, among the 'nouveaux-riches' on the train, there is Jonathan, an unscrupulous doctor who is trying to escape from his dark past: having made use of 'creative euthanasia' (Truong 2003: 225), he sustained his patients' ailments in order to despoil them of their life savings. He has served a long prison sentence. While he is listening to the conversation of his travel companions and looking at a glossy brochure depicting hundreds of identical villas with gardens in front of the door and perfectly trimmed privet hedges, doubt arises in his mind – who will pay for this earthly paradise when the bank accounts are in the red? Especially if, in contrast to the utopian vision of *gerocomio*, accessible only for wealthy and well-heeled older individuals (Mantegazza [1893] 2017: 63), the 'retirement villages' receive all guests, regardless of their material status. As other passengers on the train start to carefully calculate the costs of the Clifford Estates, they realize that under no circumstances is it a profitable enterprise. One of the most insightful passengers concludes that the only factor that allows the luxury estate to lower its costs is the reduced life expectancy of its residents. A few moments later, the character is found dead and the atmosphere of the journey starts to resemble Agatha Christie's novel *Murder on the Orient Express* ([1934] 2011).

Nevertheless, when the train stops in the middle of the desert and the passengers leave it, the long-awaited arrival at the Clifford Estates seems like the reaching of the promised land, and nothing for them foreshadows the forthcoming tragedy. Champagne flows and the newly arrived inhabitants are offered a refreshing shower. As in *Gli scaduti*, the author draws on Holocaust imagery in order to emphasize the tragic condition of the 'dispensable' members of contemporary society. When the train reaches its final destination, all the protagonists are gassed and burnt. We discover that the death train has preceded the extermination of a generation of which 'society could no longer bear the burden' (Truong 2003: 292).

Eternity Express postulates a world in which older people are put to death against their will because they represent a waste of resources. The new generation adopts a utilitarian logic to justify this tragedy – it is simply unsustainable to continue the status quo, where the life chances of the potentially productive young are subordinated to maintain and extend the longevity of older generations. The reasoning is simple: there are just not enough resources to support an ageing population. Through this unanswerable logic, Truong is trying to warn us about generational conflict and narratives that characterize older baby boomers as a drain upon younger people. If we come to believe that for the majority to survive, some must die (Truong 2003: 209), we will not be able to stop the *Eternity Express* of tomorrow. The heroes of this nightmare may be the pensioners of today, as a terrifying reality revealed by the author takes place in a world not very distant from our own.

Conclusion

The rising popularity of dystopian fiction in recent decades should not undermine the long tradition of dystopian writing within which the latest trends need to be located (Falcus 2020: 138). However, it must be noted that the problems that we deal with in the twenty-first century are deeply integrated into the life of the community as a whole. The novels analysed in the chapter demonstrate that the process of rapid population ageing, which has become a phenomenon widespread in all European countries, constitutes one of the biggest challenges that humanity is facing at the dawn of the new millennium. Potential hazards caused by the consequences and menaces of ageism stimulate the imagination of contemporary writers, who imagine in their works catastrophic visions of the future. As dystopian fiction allows us to explore truths that would be otherwise outside of what is culturally acceptable, contemporary authors create inherently ageist fictional future realities that act as mirrors that reflect our collective fears. All the texts analysed in this chapter depict realities in which older people, perceived of as dispensable members of society, become a new target group of life-threatening forms of ageism. They are deported, sacrificed for the benefit of more 'productive' members of society and massively assassinated. Although all the represented visions of diverse forms of geronticide remain in the realm of the writers' fantasy, they should be perceived as a useful tool in the exploration of demographic change and generational relationships in the twenty-first century. With the common presence of comparisons to the tragic events of the Holocaust, the utilitarian approach to the issue of population control becomes aggravated and pushed to the limits in order to signal the hypothetical routes that humanity might follow.

As Margaret Atwood wrote in her collection of critical essays, 'we find dystopias a lot easier to believe than utopias', since 'utopias we can only imagine' and 'dystopias we've already had' (2005: 106). However, as they take form of what Baccolini and Moylan call critical dystopias, the texts 'maintain a utopian impulse' in their critical approach to our reality (2003: 7). They can bring about awareness and help us to play out our collective shadows in a place and time safely separate from our own, engaging in the dangers and fears of the future while addressing the challenges of the present. The recent popularity of dystopian literature does seem to signal something about our society or, as Atwood puts it, 'is a sad commentary on our age' (2005: 106). But if dystopia provides a warning, there must be some potential for change and therefore hope for the future.

Notes

1. Definitions and concepts of ageism have changed over the years. The term was introduced by the first director of the National Institute of Aging, Robert Butler, in 1969, and was described as a 'prejudice by one age group against another age group' (1969: 243). In subsequent work, Butler defined it as 'a process of systematic stereotyping and discrimination against people because they are old' ([1995] 2001: 35).
2. In 1968, the biologist Paul R. Ehrlich published *The Population Bomb* (1968), depicting population growth in the years after the Second World as a global human catastrophe. He predicted massive famines caused by an excess population and urged immediate action to stop its growth. As Andreu Domingo claims, Ehrlich can be seen as one of the principal instigators of so-called demodystopias, understood as a subgenre of dystopias where the imagined visions of the futures derive from demographic shifts, taken to an extreme (Domingo 2008: 729).
3. The novel depicts a futuristic English ex-colony called Britannula, which takes advantage of its own legislative autonomy to regulate the death of its citizens, apparently to spare them undignified suffering and to help cut down on the state's expenditure on unproductive people.
4. Due to the lack of an English edition of the novel, the chapter includes my own translations.
5. The narrator of the story is the main speaker during a conference that takes place in 2134 to discuss a dangerous increase in the number of suicides among those in the third age. According to the speaker, nature requires 'useless' older people to have the courage to disappear. Hence, old people who are relatively independent should be employed in social works or public gardens; the remaining 70 per cent can choose between voluntary euthanasia or exile to the countries of the Third World.
6. The term is derived from Latin, and it refers to the punishment of souls in Dante's *Inferno*, 'by a process either resembling or contrasting with the sin itself' (Musa 1984: 37–8).
7. Scholars have identified three major philosophical views related to the basis for filial duties. First of all, ethical tradition commands lifelong parental reverence. Secondly, parents are owed a debt of gratitude for care that they provided for their children. Finally, care for parents is the expression of friendship and love (Selig, Tomlinson and Hickey 1991: 625).

References

Arber, S., and J. Ginn (1991), *Gender and Later Life: A Sociological Analysis of Resources and Constraints*, London: Sage.

Atwood, M. (2005), *Writing with Intent: Essays, Reviews, Personal Prose: 1983–2005*, New York: Carroll and Graf.

Ayalon, L. (2015), 'Perceptions of Old Age and Ageing in the Continuing Care Retirement Community', *International Psychogeriatrics*, 27(4): 611–20.

Baccolini, R., and T. Moylan (2003), *Dark Horizons: Science Fiction and the Dystopian Imagination*, London: Routledge.

Biggs, S., and J. L. Powell (2001), 'A Foucauldian Analysis of Old Age and the Power of Social Welfare', *Journal of Aging and Social Policy*, 12(2): 93–112.

Brogden, M. (2001), *Geronticide: Killing the Elderly*, London: Jessica Kingsley.

Butler, R. N. (1969), 'Age-Ism: Another Form of Bigotry', *The Gerontologist*, 9(4): 243–6.

Butler, R. N. ([1995] 2001), 'Ageism', in G. Maddox (ed.), *The Encyclopedia of Aging*, 38–9, New York: Springer.

Buzzati, D. (1950), 'Orchidee ai vecchi', in *In quel preciso momento*, 136–44, Vicenza: Neri Pozza.

Buzzati, D. (1966a), 'Cacciatori di vecchi', in *Il Colombre [e altri cinquanta racconti]*, 145–54, Segrate: Arnoldo Mondadori Editore.

Buzzati, D. (1966b), 'Viaggio agli inferni del secolo', in *Il Colombre [e altri cinquanta racconti]*, 381–452, Segrate: Arnoldo Mondadori Editore.

Campanella, T. ([1623] 2007), *The City of the Sun*, Gloucester: Dodo Press.

Charise, A. (2012), '"Let the Reader Think of the Burden": Old Age and the Crisis of Capacity', *Occasion: Interdisciplinary Studies in the Humanities*, 4: 1–16. Available online: http://occasion.stanford.edu/node/96 (accessed 20 August 2021).

Christie, A. ([1934] 2011), *Murder on the Orient Express: A Hercule Poirot Mystery*, New York: Harper.

Cuddy, A. J. C., and S. T. Fiske (2002), 'Doddering, but Dear: Process, Content, and Function in Stereotyping of Older Persons', in T. Nelson (ed.), *Ageism: Stereotyping and Prejudice Against Older Persons*, 3–26, Cambridge: MIT Press.

Degnen, C. (2007), 'Minding the Gap: The Construction of Old Age and Oldness amongst Peers', *Journal of Aging Studies*, 21: 69–80.

D'Eramo, L. (1988), 'Proposta risolutiva', in L. Aldani and U. Malaguti (eds), *Pianeta Italia: Gli autori della World SF italiana*, 285–93, Bologna: Perseo.

Domingo, A. (2008), 'Demodystopias: Prospects of Demographic Hell', *Population and Development Review*, 34(4): 725–45.

Edinger, E. F. (2002), *Archetype of the Apocalypse*, Chicago: Open Court.

Ehrlich, P. R. (1968), *The Population Bomb*, San Francisco: A Sierra Club–Ballantine Books.

Falcus, S. (2020), 'Age and Anachronism in Contemporary Dystopian Fiction', in E. Barry and M. V. Skagen (eds), *Literature and Ageing*, vol. 73, *Essays and Studies*, 65–86, Cambridge: D. S. Brewer.
Fiske, S. T. (1998), 'Stereotyping, Prejudice, and Discrimination', in D. T. Gilbert, S. T. Fiske and G. Lindzey (eds), *The Handbook of Social Psychology*, 4th edn, 357–411, New York: McGraw Hill.
Foucault, M. (1986), 'Of Other Spaces', *Diacritics*, 16(1): 22–7.
Gullette, M. M. (2004), *Aged by Culture*, Chicago: University of Chicago Press.
Gullette, M. M. (2017), *Ending Ageism, or How Not to Shoot Old People (Global Perspectives on Aging)*, New Brunswick: Rutgers University Press.
Hall, G. S. (1922), *Senescence*, New York: D. Appleton.
Harari, Y. N. (2016), *Homo Deus: A Brief History of Tomorrow*, New York: Harper Collins.
Hartung, H. (2013), *Narrating Age*, Habilitationsschrift: Universität Potsdam.
Higgs, P., and C. Gilleard (2020), 'The Ideology of Ageism versus the Social Imaginary of the Fourth Age: Two Differing Approaches to the Negative Contexts of Old Age', *Ageing and Society*, 40: 1617–30. Available online: https://doi.org/10.1017/S01446 86X19000096 (accessed 12 August 2021).
Holmqvist, N. (2009), *The Unit*, New York: Other Press.
Kermode, F. ([1967] 2000), *The Sense of an Ending: Studies in the Theory of Fiction*, New York: Oxford University Press.
MacKay Demerijan, L. (2016), *The Age of Dystopia: One Genre, Our Fears and Our Future*, Newcastle: Cambridge Scholars.
Mantegazza, P. ([1893] 2017), *Elogio della Vecchiaia*, Firenze: Pontecorboli Editore.
Middleton, T. ([1656] 2007), 'The Old Law, or A New Way to Please You', in G. Taylor, J. Lavagnino, M. P. Jackson, J. Jowett, V. Wayne and A. Weiss (eds), *Thomas Middleton: The Collected Works*, 1335–96, Oxford: Oxford University Press.
More, T. ([1516] 2012), *Utopia*, London: Penguin Classics.
Moylan, T. (2000), *Scraps of the Untainted Sky: Science Fiction, Utopia, Dystopia*, Boulder: Perseus.
Musa, M. (1984), 'Commentary Notes', in D. Alighieri (ed.), *Dante: The Divine Comedy: Volume 1: Inferno*, 37–8, London: Penguin Classics.
Nelson, T. D. (2005), 'Ageism: Prejudice against Our Feared Future Self', *Journal of Social Issues*, 61(2): 207–21.
Nelson, T. D. (2016), 'The Age of Ageism', *Journal of Social Issues*, 72(1): 191–8. Available online: https://doi.org/10.1111/josi.12162 (accessed 19 December 2020).
Nolan, W. F., and G. C. Johnson (1967), *Logan's Run*, New York: Dial Press.
Orwell, G. ([1949] 2000), *Nineteen Eighty-Four*, London: Penguin Modern Classics.
Palmore, E. B. (1999), *Ageism: Negative and Positive*, New York: Springer.
Posner, R. A. (1995), *Aging and Old Age*, Chicago: University of Chicago Press.
Post, S. G. (1991) 'Euthanasia, Senecide, and the Aging Society', *Journal of Religious Gerontology*, 8(1): 57–65.

Ravera, L. (2015), *Gli scaduti*, Milano: Bompiani.
Ravera, L., and M. L. Radice (1976), *Porci con le ali*, Roma: Savelli.
Reeves, N. (2017), 'Euthanasia and (D)evolution in Speculative Fiction', *Victorian Literature and Culture*, 45: 95–117.
Rizzini, M. (2015), 'Rottamandi di tutto il mondo, ribellatevi. Il manifesto di Lidia Ravera', *Il Foglio*, 8 March 2015. Available online: www.ilfoglio.it/articoli/2015/03/08/news/rottamandidi-tutto-il-mondo-ribellatevi-il-manifesto-di-lidia-ravera-81611/ (accessed 19 December 2020).
Sarton, M. (1982), *As We Are Now*, New York: W.W. Norton.
Sarton, M. (1996), *At Eighty-Two: A Journal*, New York: W.W. Norton.
Schotland, S. D. (2013), 'Forced Execution of the Elderly, *Old Law*, Dystopia, and the Utilitarian Argument', *Humanities*, 2: 160–75.
Selig, S, T. Tomlinson and T. Hickey (1991), 'Ethical Dimensions of Intergenerational Reciprocity: Implications for Practice', *Gerontologist*, 5: 624–30. Available online: https://pubmed.ncbi.nlm.nih.gov/1778488/ (accessed 10 September 2021).
Shaw, G. B. ([1914] 2006), *Treatise on Parents and Children*, Project Gutenberg. Available online: https://www.gutenberg.org/files/908/908-h/908-h.htm (accessed 10 September 2021).
Sontag, S. (1997), 'The Double Standard of Aging', in M. Pearsall (ed.), *The Other Within Us*, 195–204, London: Routledge.
Sweeting, H., and M. Gilhooly (1997), 'Dementia and the Phenomenon of Social Death', *Sociology of Health and Illness*, 19: 93–117.
The Handmaid's Tale (2017), [TV series] Bruce Miller, USA: MGM Television, Hulu.
The Organisation for Economic Co-operation and Development (2021), 'Ageing and Demographic Change'. Available online: https://www.oecd.org/economy/ageing-inclusive-growth/ (accessed 10 September 2021).
The United Nations, Department of Economic and Social Affairs (2019), 'Life Expectancy at Birth by Region, Subregion and Country, 1950–2100'. Available online: https://population.un.org/wpp/Download/Standard/Population/ (accessed 10 September 2021).
Trollope, A. ([1882] 1993), *The Fixed Period*, Oxford: Oxford University Press.
Truong, J. M. (2003), *Eternity Express*, Paris: Albin Michel.
Twigg, J. (2004), 'The Body, Gender, and Age: Feminist Insights in Social Gerontology', *Journal of Aging Studies*, 18: 59–73.
Zamyatin, Y. ([1924] 1993), *We*, London: Penguin Classics.

6

Ageing and age-based extinction in twentieth- and early twenty-first-century speculative and science fiction: William F. Nolan and George Clayton Johnson's *Logan's Run* (1967) and Christopher Buckley's *Boomsday* (2007)

Stella Achilleos

Introduction

The issues of geronticide and age-based extinction as a means of population control are perhaps nowhere more powerfully or more persistently addressed than in twentieth- and early twenty-first-century speculative and science fiction. The genre includes numerous texts that have dealt with these ideas, such as Isaac Asimov's *Pebble in the Sky* (1950), William F. Nolan and George Clayton Johnson's *Logan's Run* (1967), Ira Levin's *This Perfect Day* (1970), Lois Lowry's *The Giver* (1993), Jean-Michel Truong's *Eternity Express* (2003) and Christopher Buckley's *Boomsday* (2007). Perhaps this is hardly surprising, given that the genre appears to be particularly apt for the treatment of such challenging and controversial ideas. As I will be suggesting, in enabling the authors to boldly explore the possibility of geronticide and age-based extinction, the fictional worlds imagined in their narratives also enable them – and, thereby, also invite us, as readers – to interrogate some of the most central philosophical and ethical questions in the realm of biopolitics. One way or another, the above-mentioned texts rework a familiar theme in the tradition of speculative and science fiction, with an important literary precedent found in Antony Trollope's *The Fixed Period* (1881–2) – a novel inspired in its turn by William Rowley, Thomas

Middleton, and Thomas Heywood's early seventeenth-century tragicomedy 'An/The Old Law' ([1656] 2007). Further, these works may be said to nod to a much larger tradition of texts that engaged with the idea of age-based extinction, from Plato's *The Republic* in the classical period to Jonathan Swift's 'A Modest Proposal' in the eighteenth century. Concentrating on two of the novels here, William F. Nolan and George Clayton Johnson's *Logan's Run* and Christopher Buckley's *Boomsday*, I intend to demonstrate the ways in which twentieth- and early twenty-first-century speculative and science fiction developed the theme of age-based extinction as it was treated in literary precedents, as well as how the authors in each case cast the issue into their own contemporary context.

My choice of Nolan and Johnson's *Logan's Run* is governed by the fact that the novel arguably provides the most striking twist on the idea presented in Trollope's *The Fixed Period* and in other twentieth- and twenty-first-century speculative and science fiction texts: while these engage with the idea of killing people at an age of sixty plus (the limit being set in Trollope's novel at sixty-seven), in Nolan and Johnson's text, the lifespan is set at twenty-one years. Thus, stretching the idea of age-based extinction to its limit, *Logan's Run* highlights, as I will show, the instability of such terms as 'old' and 'old age' when these are considered from the perspective of biopolitics, governmentality and population control. Buckley's *Boomsday*, on the other hand, does not involve the same kind of twist as Nolan and Johnson's novel. Neither is the plot of Buckley's text situated in the distant future as in Nolan and Johnson's novel – and, indeed, as in so many other examples of speculative and science fiction.[1] However, in holding a magnifying glass over the absurdities of modern-day politics and society (in a world in which both are largely driven by the media) and in exposing the cynicism of a society, a large part of which embraces the idea of euthanizing older members of the population, Buckley's biting satire eerily suggests that a fine line is all that separates the present from a dystopian future in which age-based extermination is normalized or legalized.

The literary tradition of geronticide

First, let me take a detour into the literary tradition of geronticide that influenced twentieth- and early twenty-first-century works of speculative and science fiction that deal with age-based extinction, starting with the important literary precedent set by Trollope's *The Fixed Period* (1881–2), a satirical dystopian novel that, as Andrea Charise notes in a recent discussion, 'overtly depicts aging as a critical issue of demographic containment' (2002: 144). The title of Trollope's text refers to the fixed period of sixty-seven years that the citizens in the Republic of Britannula, an imaginary former British colony where the plot is set, are allowed to live. The process of life termination is here euphemistically referred to as 'deposition': as part of this process, those who have just turned sixty-seven will be removed to 'The College', a place tellingly located in a town called 'Necropolis', from where they will 'depart', and after exactly one year, those 'deposed' are set to be cremated (2008). This plan for the compulsory 'deposition' of all citizens at the age of sixty-seven is said to have been voted into legislation by the first legislative assembly of the Republic that met thirty years prior to the events narrated at the beginning of the novel. At the time, the idea was supported by the overwhelming majority of the assembly, who were then young and saw 'deposition' as a way to spare the state the economic burden of unproductive people. However, the law about 'deposition' is put to the test when Britannula's oldest citizen, Gabriel Crasweller, starts to approach the end of his 'fixed period'. Ironically, Crasweller, who had once voted in favour of the idea of 'deposition', now starts to have second thoughts about it and starts lying about how old he is. John Neverbend, Britannula's president and Crasweller's friend, discovers that these feelings are in fact shared by many other citizens, who had once supported the idea but now try to come up with excuses in order to avoid 'deposition'. Despite the fact that Neverbend remains fixed to the idea (this being after all an idea that he himself introduced) and is resolved to ensure the faithful execution of the law, Crasweller's 'deposition' is conveniently halted in the text, as the carriage that is about to transport him is stopped by newly arrived British military troops who force Neverbend to free Crasweller and resign from his position as president.

This convenient repudiation of the violence of geronticide is an element also found in 'An/The Old Law', the seventeenth-century play by William Rowley, Thomas Middleton and Thomas Heywood from which Trollope appears to have drawn inspiration.[2] The plot takes place in the imaginative dukedom of Epire, a city in Greece – whose classical political philosophy, as Mika Ojakangas (2016) has pointed out, provides the origins for what has come to be known as *biopolitics*, following Michel Foucault's influential treatment of the concept in the series of lectures he gave at the Collège de France in the 1970s.[3] Indeed, as Ojakangas argues, while Foucault identifies biopower as a new technology of state power that emerged in the second half of the eighteenth century, 'the idea of politics as control and regulation of the living in the name of the security, well-being and happiness of the state and its inhabitants is as old as Western political thought itself, originating in classical Greece' (2016: 1). Providing one of the earliest straightforward treatments – if not the earliest one – of biopolitics and the issue of geronticide in English literary history, 'An/The Old Law' presents the response of the Epirean society to a law introduced by Duke Evander that 'all men living in our dominions of Epire in their decayed nature to the age of fourscore, or women to the age of threescore, shall on the same day be instantly put to death' ([1656] 2007: 1.1.132–5). In decreeing this law, the Duke is notably said to have surpassed in wisdom all the lawgivers who preceded him in ancient Greece (such as Draco, Solo and Lycurgus) and the philosophers Aristotle and Plato (whose texts are central in the tradition of classical Greek biopolitical thought traced by Ojakangas).

Referring to the rationale upon which the decision to decree the execution of all men at the age of eighty and all women at the age of sixty has been based, the Duke's proclamation with which the introduction of this law is announced explicitly states that this is 'for the care and good of the commonwealth' ([1656] 2007: 1.1.128–30). The method devised for the execution of the characters who have reached the set age is that of having them hurled into the sea from a high cliff,[4] and the law is supposedly put into action with the Duke ordering the 'Agent of death' ([1656] 2007: 2.1.132), that is the executioner, to take one of the older citizens in the play, Creon, to his death. However, it is disclosed at the end of the play that the proposed geronticide has been a kind of public test or a social experiment to try out the citizens' moral standing (an idea that, as I will go on to point out, matches the devices of speculative and science fiction and has a special pertinence in Buckley's *Boomsday*). As part of this experiment, the older citizens who were supposedly led to their execution are taken to a place of safe seclusion instead; they appear on stage still alive in Act 5, and they are given the position of judges in the Duke's restored moral order. As I have argued elsewhere though, the play's 'happy resurrection of the dead' in the final act and the Duke's disavowal of the violence of geronticide cannot easily dispel the dark and very disturbing overtones found in the rest of the play, especially as the Duke's social experiment reveals a society whose majority of citizens are cynically overjoyed at the idea of seeing close relatives executed when this will enable them to benefit financially (Achilleos 2017: 133).[5] The example of Cleanthes, a young man who is appalled by the law and tries to save his old father Leonides from execution, stands as a striking exception in a society in which cynicism, predatory instincts and the deterioration of intergenerational and familial bonds seem to prevail.

As I go on to argue, while nodding to the tradition established by Rowley, Middleton and Heywood's 'An/The Old Law' and Trollope's *The Fixed Period* (and, by extension, to the classical tradition of biopolitics that preceded them), the two texts on which I have chosen to concentrate here may also be firmly situated within the historical context in which they were produced, giving voice to their own period's preoccupations with age-based extinction and the interrelated issues of population control and biopolitics. Significantly, both texts were written not only within periods in which the question of old age had special currency in the framework of important social and economic debates, but also in a post–Second World War context in which the idea of mass extermination had acquired a terrifying set of overtones and collective memory had been marked by the horror of genocide.

Population and age-based extinction in *Logan's Run*

First published in 1967 (and turned into a film in 1976), Nolan and Johnson's *Logan's Run* offers a powerful rewriting of the idea of age-based extinction found in its literary predecessors, speaking to the social and cultural context of a period in which youth was in many ways valorized and old age was seen with suspicion and mistrust. Indeed, the authors' treatment of age and ageing in the novel cannot but be situated within the social and cultural framework of what is frequently referred to as the 1960s 'cult of youth', which was fostered during the period by the generation of the 'Baby Boomers' (i.e. those born during the post–Second World War baby boom). This generation – that, as Doug Owram remarks, 'thought of itself as a group distinct from previous generations' (1996: ix) – eagerly expressed the aspiration for social, cultural and political change by questioning established values, thereby also celebrating its own youth and youthful impulse. The distrust that, as Owram further comments, was largely shown towards 'adult judgement' (1996: 138) by the generation of the baby boomers in the 1960s is indicative of the group's broader valorization of youth at the expense of maturity or older age.

While resonating with this context, *Logan's Run* does not simply engage with the expression of mistrust towards or the denigration of older people but with the idea of exterminating all individuals above a certain age. Indeed, as I have already noted, the text stretches the idea of age-based extinction to its extremes by presenting the reader with a world in which all citizens should die at twenty-one. The method chosen for the killing of those who reach that age in the novel is chillingly reminiscent of the method that had been used for mass executions by the Nazis nearly three decades earlier: all who reach the age of twenty-one are required to report to one of the many available 'Sleepshops' where they are put to death with the use of a toxic gas. Ironically, this is said to be a joy-inducing process, as suggested early in the text by the protagonist Logan, who reflects on 'the Sleepshops with their gaily painted interiors, the attendants in soft pastel robes, the electronically augmented angel choirs, the skin spray of Hallucinogen, which wiped away a confused look of suffering and replaced it with a fixed and joyful smile' (2015: 14).

In yet another eerie allusion to the methods used by the Nazi regime, which marked Jews with a star, a person's proximity to death is here marked by the colour of the radioactive, crystal flower that is found on everybody's right-hand palm. Of course, in this case the extermination plan covers the entire population, and in order to ensure that no exceptions are made, the crystal – that is set to indicate one's age range by changing colour every seven years, from yellow to blue and then to red – is firmly embedded in the hand upon birth. On the last day of the twenty-first year, the crystal is programmed to start blinking red and black and finally to turn all black, thereby indicating that the person has reached the maximum time he or she is allowed to live. Those who attempt to escape being put to death and refuse to report to a sleepshop, the so-called 'runners', are hunted down by 'sandmen', who undertake to exterminate their targets. Being visible to all, the palm flower crystal enables those around the 'runner' to identify him or her and to raise the alarm, an element that turns the entire society into a huge surveillance mechanism. In this manner, the system presented in the book aims to minimize the possibility of the kind of deviance that is so forcefully presented in 'An/The Old Law' and *The Fixed Period*.

As in its literary predecessors, *Logan's Run* presents the decision for the extermination of those above twenty-one as one that was collectively made for the well-being of society. More specifically, the text situates the decision in relation to the problem posed by the insufficiency of existing resources to cover the needs of an ever-growing population – an issue that no doubt acquired special currency in the twentieth century, as the period witnessed an unprecedented explosion in global population, from about 1.65 billion at the beginning of the century to over 6 billion by the year 2000 (United Nations 1999: 1). The issue appears to have been particularly prominent during the 1960s, when *Logan's Run* was written, especially as the World Population Emergency Campaign (founded by Hugh Moore in 1960) sparked intense fears about the calamitous consequences of overpopulation, fears that significantly influenced policymaking in the United States.[6] Chapter 8 of the novel refers to the period 'at the end of the Twentieth Century, before the Little War, when men spawned like microbes on a culture dish'. At that time, 'the great problem was food. The fourth horseman rode the land and his name was Famine' (2015: 58). Prior reference to the 'Little War' is made near the beginning of the book, before the first chapter (numbered 10, as the chapters in the book are numbered in reverse order),[7] where it is noted:

> The seeds of the Little War were planted in a restless summer during the mid-1960s, with sit-ins and student demonstrations as youth tested its strength.
>
> By the early 1970s over 75 per cent of the people living on earth were under twenty-one years of age.
>
> The population continued to climb – and with it the youth percentage.
>
> In the 1980s the figure was 79.7 per cent.
>
> In the 1990s, 82.4 per cent.
>
> In the year 2000 – critical mass. (2015: n.p.)

However, the factors that led to the eruption of the 'Little War' and subsequently to the decision to terminate citizens' lives at the age of twenty-one are explained much later, in chapter 2. As noted here, the first major event in this war took place in Washington amid governmental attempts to regulate population growth, a measure that led to massive protests by young people in the mid-1960s:

> For over a month young people had been pouring into the city, massing for a huge demonstration to protest the Thirty-ninth Amendment to the Constitution. Like other prohibitions before it, this Compulsory Birth Control Act was impossible to enforce, and youth had taken the stand that it was a direct infringement of their rights. Bitter resentment was directed against the two arms of Governmental enforcement, the National Council of Eugenics and the Federal Birth Study Commission. Washington had no business regulating the number of children a citizen could have. Bitterness turned to talk of rebellion. (2015: 135)

According to the story, President Curtain tried to justify the governmental plans to regulate births by 'stress[ing] the severity of the food shortage, as world population spiraled toward six billion' (2015: 135). However, the young did not fail to see the hypocrisy of his calls upon them to 'exercise self-control in this crisis' (2015: 135) as, besides being overfed, the president himself was also the father of nine children. This escalated into a massive intergenerational conflict and a rebellion that the young had no trouble winning in a short period of time, as the majority of the country's armed forces were young themselves and sided with the rebels. The 'Little War' – a name that ambiguously points both to its short duration and to the young age of the rebels – saw the young take over the government of the country. This marked the beginning of 'the great debates on how best to solve the population crisis' (2015: 137). The figure who proposed the extermination of all those at the age of twenty-one was a sixteen-year-old called Chaney Moon, 'a crowd pleaser, with the talent to make the commonplace sound novel and the preposterous seem reasonable' (2015: 137). Moon's proposal soon took 'young America' and all the rest of the world by storm: as the idea came to be supported by millions, Moon himself was hailed as 'the world's savior, the new Messiah' (2015: 137). Five years later, when the 'Moon Plan' was instituted across the globe, Moon (at the time aged twenty-one) was the first one to prove his devotion to the plan and to the agreed-on solution to the population crisis by being led to his death in public. This is said to have been the beginning of 'the age of government by computer' as a machine called 'the Thinker' was programmed to enforce the 'Moon Plan'. So, by the year 2072 the population of the whole world was young (2015: 137).

No doubt, besides stretching the limits of the idea found in the text's literary predecessors, the worldwide implementation of the 'Moon Plan' and the compulsory euthanasia of all at the age of twenty-one also cast an ironical glance at the youth-worshipping culture of the 1960s. In this respect, shifting the point of extermination to the age of thirty, the story in the 1976 film adaptation of the novel offers what has been called 'a macabre fulfilment of the 1960s slogan "Don't trust anyone over 30!"' (Moody 2006: 327). At the same time, the 'Moon Plan' calls attention to the instability of the words 'old' and 'old age' when these are seen from the perspective of biopolitics: the threshold of who is considered 'old' and expendable may easily shift when the criteria involve a purely economic set of considerations. By the same token, the category of 'old age' may easily be extended to include any people who are considered to be a burden to the economy.

Also, one cannot miss the irony in the way in which the rebellion described in the novel develops: what starts as a rebellion about the infringement of young people's human rights to biological reproduction leads to a solution that is a direct infringement on the right to live and that involves compulsory death for all at what would commonly be considered a prime age of youth and vitality. Being regulated by machines, the resulting society is a dystopic world in which human contact and affection are minimized. Further, as Mary E. Theis comments, 'this futuristic society ironically deprives youth of more of their parental rights than earlier forms of government' (2009: 68). Tellingly, children are separated from their parents at birth and brought up in nurseries that are governed by machines, the 'Autogoverness[es]' (2015: 109). No doubt, the weakening of human bonding also contributes to the plan to maximize obedience to the system and ensure that people more easily accept the idea of being put to death at the age of twenty-one.

In narrating Logan's 'run' – and his shift from Sandman to Runner on his own Lastday – the novel registers the protagonist's ardent, even if belated, realization that the drive to live on and enjoy human contact is stronger than the duty to obey the system. But Logan is not the only character who tries to escape from the dystopian machine-driven society described in the novel: the reason why the system needs to have Sandmen such as himself is precisely to prevent all 'runners' from reaching the Sanctuary, a place where they can live free from their society's restrictions. Sawyer, who appears in chapter 10, encapsulates the complex situation that Logan subsequently finds himself in: Sawyer ruminates that 'the system is right. … World can only support so much life. Got to be a way to keep the population down' (2015: 13). While this suggests that the character may have internalized the propaganda of the state, at the same time he seems to interrogate the state's system of eugenic control, especially as he highlights the feeling people commonly have when faced with their Lastday: 'Nobody feels like he's done it *all*. All the traveling, all the girls, all the living' (2015: 12). What the novel intriguingly explores through both characters is a complex division of loyalties: on the one hand, loyalty to the state and its preservation and, on the other hand, loyalty to the self and the individual's notion of self-preservation. What are the limits of each and to what extent is the former tenable when the individual is faced with a state that makes constant encroachments on the right to live and reduces the value of human life to a financial estimate? In calling attention to these questions, *Logan's Run* invites us to interrogate some of the most profound issues regarding ageing, biopolitics and population control. At the same time, in presenting us with a dystopic world in which the value of human life is essentially compromised, the novel also invites us to consider a fundamental set of questions about human life and what makes a life well lived.

Christopher Buckley's *Boomsday* and 'voluntary transitioning'

Unlike Nolan and Johnson's *Logan's Run* and unlike the literary precedents discussed earlier on, Christopher Buckley's *Boomsday* does not engage with the idea of age-based extermination as a *compulsory* process. Neither does it present such an extreme version of age-based extinction as Nolan and Johnson's *Logan's Run*. However, the text offers a profound interrogation of the subject as it engages with the idea of offering governmental incentives to people at the age of seventy to commit suicide, in order to help the younger generations cope with the ever-growing social security debt. Situating the plot within an early twenty-first-century context, the novel engages more specifically with the economic challenges posed due to the retirement of the 'Baby Boomers': having grown old, the generation that had once fostered the 1960s 'cult of youth' now comes to be seen as an economic burden that must be borne by the younger generation. As in Trollope's *The Fixed Term*, where the euphemistic term 'deposition' is used to refer to the termination of old people's lives, in Buckley's novel the idea of encouraging old people to kill themselves is euphemistically referred to by the term 'voluntary transitioning'. Presenting the ways in which this idea gets caught up in the tentacles of politics, being discussed and manipulated by politicians who have no interest in the issue or in saving the social security system, *Boomsday* offers a humorous but scathing satire of American politics. At the same time, though, the novel turns its satirical gaze on the broader society it presents, a large part of which, especially the young, welcomes the idea of mass suicide for older people. In doing so, *Boomsday* not only engages with a set of negative stereotypes about older age but also invites us to imagine a society in which cynicism finds so much ground that the idea of the mass extermination of certain parts of the population is embraced as a social mandate.

First published in 2007, *Boomsday* starts with a brief prologue that presents the reader with a news report about an attack launched by hundreds of young people, in their twenties, against a gated retirement community in Florida – an incident that is cited as one out of a number of such attacks. The news broadcast instantly introduces one of the main ideas with which the book and its protagonist, Cassandra Devine, engage: namely the young generation's fury at the fact that they have to pay ever-increasing taxes to fund the mounting social security debt and the social security benefits enjoyed by the baby boomers. The dire economic consequences suffered by the younger generation due to the retirement benefits of baby boomers are said to have caused a great divide between the two generations. The young demonstrators' fury in this instance is targeted at an apparently luxurious retirement community where old people are found idly enjoying their time playing golf – an idea and an image that the young people who launch the attack presumably find infuriating, given their perspective on the national debt issue. During the attack, the demonstrators write the message 'Boomsday Now!' onto the golf course green: as the newscaster explains, 'The word refers to the term economists use for the date this year when the first of the nation's seventy-seven million so-called Baby Boomers began to retire with full Social Security benefits' (2008: 1).

As the newscaster further comments, the retirement of the baby boomers 'has put a tremendous strain on the system that in turn has sent shock waves through the entire U.S. economy' (2008: 1). The significance of this reference to the disconcerting developments in the economy of the country is rather humorously diffused by the lightness of the statement made by a golf course maintenance employee that 'it might be ... weeks before residents were able to play golf' (2008: 1). Despite the lightness of this comment (that jocosely presents the playing of golf as a priority for the retirement community residents), the employee's response involves an alarming ambiguity: is the residents' inability to play golf due to the damage caused to the golf course or to the injuries they have suffered during the attack? Indeed, as the newscaster's earlier description of the incident clearly notes, the demonstrators not only vandalized the golf course – 'seiz[ing] carts and driv[ing] them into water hazards and bunkers,' 'spray[ing] paint and garden implements to write slogans on the greens' – but also physically attacked the residents of the retirement community, who 'were assaulted as they played golf' (2008: 1).

The description of these assaults introduces an issue that is of central significance in the entire novel: that of violence against older people. While the incident described in the prologue involves physical violence, *Boomsday* at large engages with other, non-physical forms of violence as well: first and foremost, the violence of being seen or being reduced to a body not worthy of life, a body that should be exterminated for the common good and the well-being of society at large. This issue is indeed central in the proposal for 'voluntary transitioning' that is brought forth by Cassandra Devine, the novel's young protagonist, who suggests that a range of governmental incentives – such as tax reductions or, rather paradoxically, free medical care – should be given to people at age seventy, or even sixty-five, to undergo euthanasia. Based on the perception that old people are a mere burden to the economy, the idea of 'voluntary transitioning' reduces the value of human life to an economic estimate, thereby rendering this group of people useless and expendable. As I will suggest, while leading to an amusing and corrosive satire of American politics, Cassandra Devine's idea also comes to function as a social experiment in the novel, bringing to the fore various social attitudes towards old age and inviting us to reflect on a range of 'what ifs' that align *Boomsday* with the genre of speculative fiction: What if an idea such as 'voluntary transitioning' came to be seriously debated in public and political fora? What if the idea that old people are a burden to society and that human life should have a specific timespan came to be normalized? What if society rose to such levels of cynicism that different types of violence against those considered to be unworthy of life became embedded in social life?

Boomsday's young protagonist makes her appearance in chapter 1 of the book as the talented employee of a media training company as well as an influential blogger. Her relation to the incidents narrated in the prologue is established when it is revealed that Cassandra – the name also chosen for her blog, where it is tellingly used as an acronym for 'Concerned Americans for Social Security Amendment Now, Debt Reduction and Accountability' (2008: 7) – has incited the attacks through her blog posts concerning the mounting social security debt and the unfairness of raising taxes on her generation. Having been arrested and subsequently released by the FBI for this reason, and in the meantime having managed to attract considerable media attention, Cassandra then proceeds to introduce her idea of 'voluntary transitioning' – initially to her employer Terry and then to her friend, Senator Randy Jepperson – as what she calls a 'meta-issue', an issue that would 'force the debate' (2008: 91). As she suggests in response to the initial reaction of her two friends, who are apparently taken aback by the idea, 'while I realize that it would never in a thousand years fly, there's evidence to suggest that it's a debate people are eager to have' (2008: 91).

Cassandra, who is clearly a well-read as well as a talented young woman,[8] cites the publication of Jonathan Swift's 'A Modest Proposal' as a forerunner to her own attempt to force a public debate by advancing an outrageous idea – Swift's text being one of *Boomsday*'s numerous direct literary allusions. As she explains to her two friends about the text written by 'The *Gulliver's Travels* guy': 'In 1729, Swift published an article proposing that the way to solve poverty in Ireland was for the poor Irish to sell their children for food' (2008: 92). As she further comments, 'the whole point' behind Swift's 'completely insane' proposal was that 'it got people's attention. It got them debating the Irish hunger problem. He was a minister. He was on the side of the poor' (2008: 92). Indeed, Swift managed to shock many of his readers with his treatise by proposing the cannibalistic consumption of the children of poor people as a means of 'preventing [them] from Being a Burthen to their Parents or Country, and for Making them Beneficial to the Publick' ([1729] 2009: 230).[9] Of course, as has long been suggested, from the very first sentence in the text, through subtle rhetorical techniques, Swift's reader is 'initiated into the satirical purpose of the work and warned away from any form of identification with the proposer' (Smith 1968: 135), with whom the author himself may in fact be understood to clearly disagree.[10] Thus, far from being intended to be taken seriously, the suggestion in Swift's treatise aims not only to invite readers to recognize the perversity of the idea but also to reflect on the possible targets of the author's satire – which, as has frequently been asserted, include English colonialism and landlordism and their devastating effects for the Irish population.

In citing the publication of Swift's text as a forerunner to her proposal of 'voluntary transitioning', Cassandra clearly indicates that her own purpose too is to shock people and force them into a public debate about the national debt rather than for them to take her idea at face value. However, 'voluntary transitioning' – in Senator Jepperson's words, the 'best euphemism I've heard since "ethnic cleansing"' (2008: 98) – comes to be seriously discussed and ends up being officially proposed as a bill to the US Senate. Therefore – nodding to the literary tradition established by Rowley, Middleton and Heywood's 'An/The Old Law', where the Duke's plan for the extermination of old people functions as a test of the citizens' responses – Cassandra's idea of 'voluntary transitioning' functions as a social and political experiment that reveals as much, or even more, about the country's political system and the society's attitudes towards old age as about the national debt issue. Highlighting the disconcerting connection between the media and political decision-making, the novel refers to the role Jepperson's successful media campaign has in preparing the ground for the discussion of the idea at the highest level of political debate:

> Within a week of Randy's TV blitz, the media was treating Voluntary Transitioning, if not with respect, with less reflexive derision. Adjectives such as 'outrageous' and 'despicable' and 'unthinkable' that had been initially Velcroed to the phrase were now replaced by 'bold' and 'revolutionary' and 'dire yet deserving of discussion.' (2008: 124)

At the Senate, the bill finds a much greater number of supporters than apparently expected by Jepperson or Cassandra herself – who ponders if they are 'actually expecting Transitioning to' pass (2008: 149). The vote and final decision-making on the matter are deferred when the White House appoints a 'commission on Transitioning' (2008: 170) – part of a secret deal between Jepperson and the president, who starts to feel threatened by Jepperson's growing political success and promises him the vice presidency in the next election.

The actual purpose of the commission is acknowledged by Cassandra herself when she asks Jepperson: 'Didn't you tell me that presidential commissions were what they appointed when they didn't want to do anything about something, while giving the illusion that they do?' (2008: 170). While serving as a political device to promote the president's political machinations, the commission involves the participation of 'several dozen commissioners, roughly the number required to satisfy every special interest group clamouring to have "input" into the question of whether Americans should be allowed to kill themselves in return for a tax break' (2008: 185). The commission includes various groups that advocate the interests of baby boomers, such as the ABBA (the 'Associate of Baby Boomer Advocates'), and the pro-life lobby with the hilarious acronym SPERM – and the equally ridiculous name 'Society for the Protection of Every Ribonucleic Molecule' (2008: 107) – represented by 'Mr. Life' Gideon Payne (2008: 185). The 'important personages ... appointed to the commission' are given 'instructions to – by all means – study the problem in all its complexity, get to the root of it and report back to the very highest levels of government' (2008: 191). Indeed, the issue of 'transitioning' is vigorously debated by the various groups and the proceedings involve, besides numerous meetings, the conducting of a study by the chairman of the President's Council of Economic Advisers on the economic consequences of the transitioning proposal on the US Treasury. However, the commission ends up doing nothing as, in reporting its findings, the chairman states 'with a clarity and concision all too rare in Washington' that 'further study is needed' (2008: 251). The whole process ends up being more of a travesty – an element highlighted by the live broadcasting of the proceedings as 'a new kind of reality TV show, where instead of being voted off the island, you were voting to kill the contestants' (2008: 192) – and, ultimately, a complete waste of economic and human resources; ironically so, as the purpose of Cassandra's idea for baby boomers' 'voluntary transitioning' was to save the country's resources for the benefit of the younger generation.

Buckley's presentation of this process – that conveniently, as in 'An/The Old Law' and *The Fixed Period*, also serves to defer the dystopic scenario of age-based extinction – no doubt serves to satirize the absurdities of real-life politics, over which the novel seems to hold a magnifying glass. At the same time, though, the novel speculates and invites the reader to reflect on the kind of social responses the idea of inviting old people to terminate their lives might elicit. Inconclusive as the 'commission on Transitioning' may be, its proceedings nevertheless reveal the main terms of the debate concerning the idea. Unsurprisingly, some of the most forceful arguments are presented by the pro-life groups that participate in the commission, especially by Gideon Payne, who castigates Cassandra for 'this miasma of moral degradation to which you have led us' and does not hesitate to suggest a link between the idea of 'transitioning' and the extermination practices of Hitler's Nazi regime (2008: 195). In response, Cassandra insistently draws a distinction between the two, pointing out that 'transitioning' involves the *voluntary* rather than *enforced* extermination of older people:

This isn't the Wannsee Conference, Mr. Payne. We're not talking about exterminating six million Jews, Gypsies, homosexuals, Catholic priests, and mentally disabled. We are talking about a voluntary program by which Americans could opt to do something altruistic, even noble, on behalf of their children, in the face of intractable irresponsibility by the federal government. (2008: 195)

As is clear from the above quotation, Cassandra's defence of the idea of 'transitioning' involves a discourse of nobility, which presents self-extermination as an altruistic act and an ethical duty towards the younger generation and the country at large.

What Buckley's protagonist seems to be oblivious to is how dangerous this discourse of ethical responsibility may be in establishing the idea that certain lives are not worth living or do not have the right to live and, ultimately, in inciting the direct physical violence against these lives that the proposal for 'transitioning' repudiates, especially in the part of the population that proves to welcome it. Indeed, while the idea of 'transitioning' may be met with repugnance by pro-life advocates, it is in fact embraced by an ever-growing part of the population, mostly the under-thirties who, as the presidential advisor Bucky Trumble informs the president, send so many e-mails to the White House in support of Jepperson's bill on the legalization of suicide for older people in return for tax reliefs that their servers end up crashing (2008: 113). As things progress and the issue of 'transitioning' is discussed by the ad hoc commission, it is revealed that 'a surprising 38 percent of the American public now favored having the option of being legally euthanized in return for huge tax breaks and subsidies'. So, 'posters were going up: UNCLE SAM WANTS TO KILL *YOU!*' (2008: 192). Drawing a parallel between enlisting oneself in warfare for the defence of one's country and being killed for the improvement of the country's economy, this chilling appropriation of the familiar Uncle Sam recruitment poster does not simply highlight the idea of voluntary suicide as an ethical duty. For rather than just interpellating, in the Althusserian sense, baby boomers to commit suicide, the motto 'Uncle Sam Wants to Kill *You!*' suggests a more aggressive stance that expresses the desire to actively terminate their unwanted lives. This relates to the creation of an increasingly negative set of stereotypes about old age in the text and to a mounting set of social pressures that would establish 'transitioning' as an indirectly compulsory rather than voluntary decision for old people. The continuum from Cassandra's idea about 'transitioning' to Senator Jepperson's relevant bill and the circulation of the Uncle Sam posters further points to the fine line between these different forms of violence: on the one hand, the more indirect violence of prompting certain parts of the population to 'voluntarily' commit suicide and, on the other hand, the more direct violence of inciting brutality against them.

The link between the discourse found in the proposal for 'transitioning' concerning the ethical responsibility of old people to die and the incitement to violence is suggested in *Boomsday* when it is revealed that a young nursing home attendant, who apparently drew inspiration from Cassandra's views, has been charged with having murdered thirty-six elderly residents over a period of six months. As noted in the text, 'this might have been just another one of those self-appointed avenging angel stories, only the police found his somewhat unkempt apartment plastered with photographs and clippings of – Cassandra Devine', while a police search on his computer revealed that his internet search engine was crammed with views of Cassandra's blog and sites linked to it (2008: 196). Tellingly, the nurse is said not only to have shown no remorse for the multiple murders but also to have repeatedly used terms such as 'Wrinklies' and 'resource hogs' to refer to his victims during his police interrogation (2008: 196) – terms used by Cassandra herself in her 'television and Internet advertising campaign to stigmatize old people' (2008: 136). Cassandra may be utterly dismayed when she finds out that her views became a source of inspiration for a self-appointed angel of death, but the novel reveals the sinister connections between the idea of branding certain parts of the population a burden to society and the possibility of inciting direct violence against them (a possibility that the protagonist seems to be blind about).

If the social experiment of the 'transitioning' idea in *Boomsday* reveals the cynical dimensions of a society in which a large number of people embrace the idea of exterminating old people, the novel also refers to how technological advancement might be ruthlessly used for the purpose of profiteering at the expense of this group. Borrowing from the devices of science fiction and the genre's engagement with the possible impact of science on society and human life, the novel refers to the discovery of a software program called 'Bio-Actuarial Dyna-Metric Age Predicator (BADMAP)' (nicknamed 'RIP-ware') that can predict with near-perfect accuracy the age at which a person will die, by processing the person's DNA, family history and various other variables (2008: 119). As one would expect, such a software would be particularly appealing to insurance companies as well as to nursing homes which 'typically … demanded that a prospective resident turn over his or her entire net worth in return for perpetual care. You could live two years or twenty years; that was their gamble' (2008: 119). However, if a retirement facility could know with any degree of accuracy their prospective customers' remaining time until their death, they could easily maximize their profits by accepting only those with a limited time to live. While insurance companies are said to have been trying to develop such a program for years, RIP-ware, 'the ultimate "killer app."' (2008: 119), is successfully developed by a company belonging to Frank Cohane, Cassandra Devine's estranged father, whose hypocrisy is highlighted when he denounces publicly his daughter's 'transitioning' idea as morally repugnant. Equally ironically, the 'killer app.' is sold to Elderheaven, a large chain of retirement homes whose majority of shares belong to the ardent pro-life advocate, 'Mr. Life' Gideon Payne (2008: 120).

Here, as in various other places in *Boomsday*, Buckley's distinctly humorous approach cannot entirely dispel the dark overtones found in the cynical treatment of old age. Likewise, these disconcerting overtones of cynicism cannot be dispelled by the ultimate deferral of the dystopic scenario of legislating age-based extinction either. As in Rowley, Middleton and Heywood's 'An/The Old Law', what Cassandra Devine's social and political experiment of 'transitioning' effectively does is to expose the wide range of sinister approaches to old age that are found in society – especially in the younger generation, that is referred to as 'the most cynical generation in American history' (2008: 264) – and to suggest how dystopia may be already here, in the way in which society violently reduces certain lives to the status of unworthy existence.

Conclusion

Nodding to their literary precedents, Nolan and Johnson's *Logan's Run* and Buckley's *Boomsday* both provide powerful explorations of age-based extinction that highlight the centrality of this issue within the realm of biopolitics in the twentieth and early twenty-first centuries. As I have shown, the question of ageing and age-based extermination acquired special currency within the context of the twentieth century's exponential increase in the global population and the interrelated issue of population control. Using the devices of speculative and science fiction (that prove particularly apt for this purpose as they enable the bold exploration of the subject), the authors in each case highlight the precariousness of old age when the value of human life is measured on the basis of a strictly economic set of factors. In stretching the limits of age-based extinction to the extreme idea of killing people at the age of twenty-one, Nolan and Johnson's *Logan's Run* calls attention to how unstable the meaning of 'old age' is when it is defined in biopolitical terms. Significantly, this not only indicates how easily the threshold of 'old age' may shift but also highlights how the category may be extended to include all those who are considered to be an economic burden to society. The text includes a number of chilling allusions to the extermination methods of the Nazis in the Second World War. However, in presenting us with the dystopic scenario of an age-based extinction plan that covers the entire population, *Logan's Run* reminds us how biopolitics, the power of the state to control and regulate the bodies and the lives of its citizens, ultimately concerns us all. What Buckley's *Boomsday* invites us to reflect on through Cassandra Devine's social and political experiment of 'voluntary transitioning', though, is that dystopia may not necessarily be located in state-imposed age-based extinction, but in the normalization of ageism within society at large. Indeed, what Buckley's biting satire effectively exposes is not simply the absurdity of a social and political system that is largely driven by the mass media and social media, but the violence of society's cynical approach towards old age: as this reminds us, dystopia may in fact be found in the here and now.

Notes

1 Indeed, more broadly, Buckley's *Boomsday* has a more tenuous relation to the genre of speculative and science fiction than texts like *Logan's Run*. However, as I will be suggesting, it may be read within the context of speculative fiction and also borrows certain elements from science fiction.
2 The play was written around the years 1618–19 but was published in 1656 (in an edition that offers the only printed version of the text from the seventeenth century).
3 See Foucault's *Society Must Be Defended* (2003) *Security, Territory, Population* (2004) and *The Birth of Biopolitics* (2008).
4 As Jeffrey Masten (Rowley et al. 2007) notes in his editorial comments to the text, this method of execution is highly reminiscent of the way in which older people are said to kill themselves in Montaigne's essay on voluntary suicide ('A Custom of the Isle of Cea'), but it also provides a reversed-by-age parallel of the executions of 'unfit children' in Lycurgus' Sparta, as described in Plutarch's *Lives* (2007: 1350). Given the enforced hurling of older people in 'An/The Old Law', the latter example may, despite the age reversal, be said to provide a closer parallel to the executions in the play.
5 For another discussion of gerontocide in 'An/The Old Law', see Schotland (2013).
6 As Mohan Rao notes, during this period, Moore's World Population Emergency Campaign and the Population Council (founded by the Rockefeller Foundation) 'began a systematic and powerful campaign to influence US policymakers to include population control as a component of US aid to Third World countries'. This was

an apparently successful campaign as, by the end of the decade, the US government had massively increased the amounts of funds it gave for population control, both at home and abroad (2004: 110–11). For another discussion of this campaign against overpopulation, see Kasun (1999: 218).

7   The chapter numbering offers a suspenseful countdown to Logan's eventual escape to the place called 'Sanctuary'.
8   The character's learning and educational background are highlighted in the text, especially in the description of how she managed to get accepted into Yale – though she had to discontinue her studies there due to the fact that her father invested her college tuition fund in his business enterprise (see chapter 2, 12–17).
9   Even though Swift's treatment of children's cannibalistic consumption might have shocked (at least some of) his readers, the idea of infanticide was in fact not unfamiliar in the canon of Western philosophical thought, with a well-known classical example in Plato's *The Republic*, where death by exposure is prescribed for 'the children of inferior parents … or any deformed specimen' (2000: 156–8) – this being part of a broader set of eugenic policies described in the text as a means of ensuring the production of the 'best' or a 'pure' breed in the ideal city.
10 On Swift's 'A Modest Proposal', see also Wittkowsky (1943), Phiddian (1996) and Moore (2007).

References

Achilleos, S. (2017), 'Old Age, Biopolitics, and Utopia: Geronticide in Middleton, Rowley and Heywood's *The Old Law*', in K. Bronk (ed.), *Autumnal Faces: Old Age in British and Irish Dramatic Narratives*, 109–34, Oxford: Peter Lang.

Buckley, C. (2008), *Boomsday*, London: Allison & Busby.

Charise, A. (2002), *The Aesthetics of Senescence: Aging, Population, and the Nineteenth-Century British Novel*, Albany: State University of New York Press.

Foucault, M. (2003), *'Society Must Be Defended': Lectures at the Collège de France, 1975–1976*, ed. M. Bertani and A. Fontana, trans. D. Macey, New York: Picador.

Foucault, M. (2004), *Security, Territory, Population: Lectures at the Collège de France, 1977–1978*, ed. M. Senellart, trans. G. Burchell, New York: Picador.

Foucault, M. (2008), *The Birth of Biopolitics: Lectures at the Collège de France, 1978–1979*, ed. M. Senellart, trans. G. Burchell, New York: Picador.

Kasun, J. (1999), *The War against Population: The Economics and Ideology of World Population Control*, San Francisco: Ignatius.

Moody, H. R. (2006), *Aging: Concepts and Controversies*, London: Pine Forge.

Moore, S. (2007), 'Devouring Posterity: "A Modest Proposal", Empire, and Ireland's "Debt of the Nation"', *PMLA*, 122(3): 679–95.

Nolan, W. F., and G. C. Johnson (2015), *Logan's Run*, New York: Vintage Books.

Ojakangas, M. (2016), *On the Greek Origins of Biopolitics: A Reinterpretation of the History of Biopower*, London: Routledge.

Owram, D. (1996), *Born at the Right Time: A History of the Baby Boom Generation*, Toronto: University of Toronto Press.

Phiddian, R. (1996), 'Have You Eaten Yet? The Reader in "A Modest Proposal"', *Studies in English Literature, 1500–1900*, 36(3): 603–21.

Plato (2000), *The Republic*, ed. G. R. G. Ferrari, trans. T. Griffith, Cambridge Texts in the History of Political Thought, Cambridge: Cambridge University Press.

Rao, M. (2004), *From Population Control to Reproductive Health: Maltusian Arithmetic*, New Delhi: Sage.

Rowley, W., T. Middleton and T. Heywood ([1656] 2007), 'An/The Old Law', in J. Masten, G. Taylor and J. Lavagnino (eds), *Thomas Middleton: The Collected Works*, 1331–96, New York: Oxford University Press.

Schotland, S. D. (2013), 'Forced Execution of the Elderly: *Old Law*, Dystopia, and the Utilitarian Argument', *Humanities*, 2: 160–75.

Smith, C. K. (1968), 'Toward a "Participatory Rhetoric": Teaching Swift's *Modest Proposal*', *College English*, 30: 135–49.

Swift, J. ([1729] 2009), 'A Modest Proposal', ed. C. Fabricant, A *Modest Proposal and Other Writings*, 230–39, London: Penguin.

Theis, M. E. (2009), *Mothers and Masters in Contemporary Utopian and Dystopian Literature*, New York: Peter Lang.

Trollope, A. (2008), *The Fixed Period*, Project Gutenberg. Available online: https://www.gutenberg.org/cache/epub/27067/pg27067-images.html (accessed 24 October 2021).

United Nations, Department of Economic and Social Affairs, Population Division (1999), *The World at Six Billion*, New York: United Nations.

Wittkowsky, G. (1943), 'Swift's *Modest Proposal*: The Biography of an Early Georgian Pamphlet', *Journal of the History of Ideas*, 4(1): 75–104.

7

'Whatever comes after human progress': Transhumanism, antihumanism and the absence of queer ecology in Lidia Yuknavitch's *The Book of Joan*

Sean Seeger

Introduction

Published in 2017, Lidia Yuknavitch's critically acclaimed science fiction novel *The Book of Joan* describes an apocalyptic future in which a combination of global warming and resource wars has left the earth largely uninhabitable. In the aftermath, the elite of the old world has taken refuge in an orbiting space station called CIEL, while the few survivors left below live underground in order to avoid the high levels of radiation on the planet's surface. CIEL extracts what resources it can from the earth via a series of umbilical cord-like connections known as skylines. The space station is ruled over by the celebrity-turned-dictator Jean de Man, whose authoritarian regime employs state propaganda, mass surveillance and robot enforcers to maintain its grip on power.

During the preceding decades, the human body has undergone significant changes due to radiation levels and other environmental factors, in a process referred to by one character as 'devolution' (Yuknavitch 2017: 151; hereafter cited by page number). With the sole exception of Joan, one of the two protagonists of the novel, the human race is now without hair, fingernails, toenails or skin pigmentation. The process of mutation has likewise left them without sexually functional genitalia, meaning reproduction by conventional means is now an impossibility. Artificial reproduction, including cloning and other techniques, has been attempted aboard CIEL, but the extent of the mutations undergone by humanity causes these to fail in every case. In response, Jean de Man plans to engineer a new species of human which will reproduce asexually, though this plan has thus far been frustrated. De Man remains at war with the rebel faction led by Joan, who de Man previously captured and pretended to kill in a televised execution intended to demoralize his opponents. He has since learnt that, as the one person resistant to the process of devolution, Joan may hold the key to overcoming the barriers to his scientists' research, leading him to pursue and attempt to recapture her during the course of the novel.

In an influential statement on the science fiction genre, Fredric Jameson has argued that 'the most characteristic science fiction does not seriously attempt to imagine the "real" future of our social system. Rather, its multiple mock futures serve the quite different function of transforming our own present into the determinate past of something yet to come' (Jameson 2005: 217). According to Jameson, science fiction is not an attempt to predict or anticipate the future, but rather an attempt to historicize the author's own moment by viewing it as if it belonged to the past rather than the present, thereby opening up a critical vantage point which, on Jameson's account, science fiction is especially well-positioned to provide. In light of this, it is illuminating to consider how Yuknavitch's novel addresses a number of pressing contemporary social and cultural issues from the estranging perspective made available by science fiction.

The argument of this chapter is as follows. Firstly, *The Book of Joan* is situated in relation to Anglo-American science fiction's long-standing engagement with the modern ideal of progress and some of the literary tropes commonly associated with it, most notably that of ageing. Secondly, the novel is read as mapping two sharply contrasting potential trajectories for humanity: the acceleration of progress along humanist lines in the form of transhumanism, on the one hand, and the rejection of such progress and a turn towards antihumanism, on the other. While these terms each have multiple, sometimes contradictory meanings, and so will need to be defined carefully below, vivid fictionalized images of each of them are to be found in Yuknavitch's novel. Thirdly, it is argued that some of the tensions and anomalies present in the novel are best explained by the absence from Yuknavitch's imaginative schema of a third possibility not encompassed by either transhumanism or antihumanism, namely, queer ecology. One main reason for Yuknavitch's opposition to transhumanism is its view of embodiment and finitude as representing limitations on human power, a stance she portrays as ecologically ruinous. Yet the alternative put forward in *The Book of Joan* – a rejection of all forms of humanism combined with an unsentimental attempt to renaturalize humanity and resituate it in the natural world – arguably depends upon the same dualism as the humanism it is directed against, raising a number of related problems. In this way, the two opposing poles between which Yuknavitch situates the war for the future can be seen to resemble one another, at least in regard to their underlying orientation. Posthumanism is considered as an alternative critical paradigm here, but it is found to be unsatisfactory on a number of grounds. Drawing on recent queer theory, the chapter concludes by arguing that queer ecology may be able to avoid the conflict between nature and culture, which compromises Yuknavitch's attempt to think ecologically, while at the same time refusing the drive to overcome embodiment and finitude, which Yuknavitch correctly locates at the heart of contemporary transhumanism.

Science fiction, progress and ageing

The modern ideal of progress as formulated during the Enlightenment period has been profoundly influential within Anglo-American science fiction. During the nineteenth and especially the twentieth century, science fiction in Britain and the United States was deeply informed by a conception of progress built on the Enlightenment model. This way of thinking about material, intellectual and social development could take more or less explicit and more or less ambitious forms, but whatever form it took, it was clearly one of the main organizing principles and sources of narrative motivation for a great many texts in this tradition, including the work of some of modern science fiction's most celebrated and influential authors.

Sometimes, as in the case of Isaac Asimov's *I, Robot* stories, for instance, progress is present merely as the steady improvement of technical devices and gadgetry ([1950] 2018). At others, as in Olaf Stapledon's monumental 'history of the future', *Last and First Men*, progress takes the form of the evolution of civilization in all its respects over the course of billions of years ([1930] 1999). Elsewhere, progress takes place in the form of a sudden, dramatic shift from the familiar to the utopian, as in the case of Arthur C. Clarke's *Childhood's End*, in which a race of alien beings takes charge of human affairs and administers a prosperous and peaceful new age in world history ([1953] 2010). In other cases, humanity as it currently exists is rendered obsolescent by some new form of life representing a higher stage of development. This scenario can play out in a utopian guise, as in the case of the evolution of humanity into the immortal Star Child at the end of Arthur C. Clarke's *2001: A Space Odyssey* (1968), or take a more dystopian turn, as in Philip K. Dick's *Do Androids Dream of Electric Sheep?* ([1968] 2010), in which synthetic life forms indistinguishable from human beings yet lacking many of their limitations are implied to be the natural successors to their flawed creators. Even in the case of the latter text, which offers a generally bleak view of the future and is typically seen as an expression of the 1960s counterculture, the Enlightenment principle of rational advancement through an increase in knowledge is implicitly retained in the form of technology that promises to overcome human frailties.

The homogeneity of this line of authors – as exclusively white, male, heterosexual and educated in the natural sciences – was highlighted by some of the science fiction produced during the late 1960s and 1970s. As Tom Moylan has shown, writers of science fiction who participated in and contributed to the counterculture as it developed over the following decade – most notably Ursula K. Le Guin, Marge Piercy, Joanna Russ, Samuel R. Delany and, slightly later, Octavia E. Butler – helped to diversify Anglo-American science fiction and reorient the genre around new perspectives, subject positions and political projects (Moylan 2010). In doing so, these authors explicitly contested the foregoing emphasis on the hard sciences, militarism, empire building and 'masculine' values. This important development was relatively short-lived, however, and was followed by a return to more conservative forms as exemplified by William Gibson's work in the 1980s and to a more conventional, Enlightenment-inspired outlook as exemplified by Kim Stanley Robinson's work in the 1990s. To this extent, Yuknavitch's *The Book of Joan* bears more of a resemblance to the science fiction identified by Moylan as belonging to the oppositional political moment of the 1970s than it does to the majority of Anglo-American science fiction on either side of it.

Lying behind much of the Anglo-American science fiction written between the 1920s and the 1960s is the work of H. G. Wells, whose own commitment to progress and to the belief in the transformative power of science and technology in particular animates much of his extensive corpus, in both his fictional and non-fictional writings. In novels like *A Modern Utopia* ([1905] 2005), Wells articulated perhaps the most influential image of a techno-utopian future, where virtually every social and economic problem confronting humanity had been solved, in large part through the application of advanced technologies and modern social engineering. Such was the familiarity of this image thirty years after its initial appearance that Aldous Huxley was able to parody Well's vision of an antiseptic, brightly lit future in *Brave New World* ([1932] 2007) and count on his readers knowing which social prophet he was lampooning. Huxley's choice of the term 'World State' for his anti-utopia takes on further significance in light of recent scholarly work on Wells. In her insightful study, *Inventing*

Tomorrow: H. G. Wells and the Twentieth Century (2019), Sara Cole has shown that Wells held to a very specific understanding of the route out of the difficulties that beset the world during the early decades of the century, including the two world wars, nationalist chauvinism, colonial violence, the Great Depression and the rise of totalitarian regimes. Wells vigorously opposed nationalism and made a passionate case for the need for unity in the face of the divisions of his time. He held that the only alternative to the decline or self-destruction of the human race – something anticipated at points in his dystopian novellas – was a universal, cosmopolitan world state, planned and directed by a single source of governmental authority (Cole 2019: 37). Cole argues that Wells possessed a prescient grasp of the interconnectedness of the modern world and of its links to the condition of total war, leading him to formulate a view of humanity as a collective subject by way of an alternative (2019: 39–40).

The connection between the idea of a world government or world state and that of a single, collective human subject is not unique to Wells, however. There are anticipations of this linkage in earlier works of science fiction, and it continues down to the present day, as Seo-Young Chu has explored (2010: 88–93). As Chu notes, both Wells and Olaf Stapledon, one of Wells's most notable epigones, strongly favoured the unification of humanity and the overcoming of tribal differences (2010: 88). This view was likewise prefigured in the work of various nineteenth-century writers and intellectuals, including Percival Lowell, a US astronomer whose work was an influence on Wells, Stapledon, Asimov, Clarke and other key figures in Anglo-American science fiction (Chu 2010: 90). Especially important here was Lowell's concept of 'planetary subjectivity', a kind of world spirit in which humanity's differences would be transcended through recognition of a single, underlying species mind. This widely shared, quasi-Hegelian idea is important for our purposes as it helps to fill out the picture sketched above of science fiction's relationship to the ideal of progress. As Gary Westfahl has observed, works of science fiction have long had 'an international aura, routinely positing the future emergence of a world government' (2005: 2). Planetary subjectivity, however, while often presupposing the institution of a world government, need not necessarily do so. Planetary subjectivity can take various forms, from Clarke's Star Child, which stands for the entirety of human progress focused to a single point, through to the more general underlying assumption – common to works by Wells, Stapledon, Asimov, Clarke and many others – that there *is* such a thing as a necessary next or even final stage of human development and that this will entail universal agreement on the values and goals proper to that stage. Cole has observed that Wells's nonfiction writings embody this same ideal (2019: 37–40, 87). Wells's popular multivolume history of the world, *The Outline of History*, first published in 1919, for example, switches from traditional history to 'future history' in its final section, casting the First World War as the prelude to a harmonious world state in which international divisions are healed once and for all. As Robert Crossley suggests in his biography of Olaf Stapledon, the narrative structure of Wells's *Outline* was one of the main sources of inspiration for Stapledon's own history of the future, *Last and First Men*, which begins in the fraught decades of the early twentieth century and culminates with the hyper-advanced civilization of the so-called Eighteenth Men in the distant future (Crossley 1994: 155). Progress, as conceived by Stapledon, is progress on the part of humanity understood as a collective agent. *Last and First Men* was itself to prove a key influence on many other writers of science fiction in the twentieth century, including Arthur C. Clarke, Brian Aldiss and Kim Stanley Robinson. There is a genealogy that can be traced, then, from Wells's ideas about progress and unity through the work of Stapledon and then through subsequent waves of Anglo-American science fiction.

An important dimension to the planetary subjectivity which informs such writing is its association of progress with a process of maturation and ageing. If progress as it is understood and represented in Anglo-American science fiction can be traced back to the Enlightenment period, then it may be understood in light of Immanuel Kant's epochal formulation, 'Dare to know!' (*Sapere aude*). If, for Kant, enlightenment meant emerging from self-imposed immaturity, then this implied a view of progress as a linear progression from ignorance to knowledge, from darkness to light and from childhood to a condition more fully approximating adulthood. For H. G. Wells, in both fictional works like *A Modern Utopia* and non-fictional works like *The Outline of History*, the history of humanity follows exactly this pattern: as a linear if halting movement away from an immature, irrational past toward a mature, rational future. For Olaf Stapledon in *Last and First Men*, the final iteration of the human species, the Eighteenth Men, are inconceivably wise beings who stand in relation to earlier human groups as adults to infants and whose minds contain the entirety of human experience heretofore in a manner analogous to an individual's recollection of childhood. In the case of Arthur C. Clarke's aptly titled *Childhood's End*, progress is explicitly figured in terms of ageing and maturation. With the arrival of the alien Overlords and the dawning of the global utopia, earlier stages of human culture are reframed as a condition of childhood, which must now be relinquished along with the childish beliefs and habits that accompanied them.

The case of the Star Child in *2001: A Space Odyssey* would initially appear to be an exception to this trend: in this case, the final stage of human development takes the form of a mysterious cosmic child, in an apparent subversion of the traditional linear pattern. Taken in context, however, the implied meaning of this sequence is seemingly not that there has been a reversion to an earlier stage of development, but rather that every earlier stage has been so vastly superseded that some new symbolism is required to convey the magnitude of the transformation involved. It is noteworthy that, in Stanley Kubrick's film version of the novel, to which Clarke contributed, the protagonist of the story is portrayed, immediately prior to his metamorphosis into the Star Child, as rapidly ageing, appearing in the penultimate stage as an elderly man. Once again, then, human progress is figured via the process of individual ageing; even if this culminates in something so radically new, it must be portrayed in terms of the Star Child's symbolic infancy. A further question worth asking here is whether this sequence ought to be read as incorporating an element of decline as well as progress. The fact that the protagonist is portrayed as infirm and bedridden before his final transformation may point to the former. Whether or not old age carries an additional association with decline, however, the broader narrative of the maturation of the human species in which the sequence is embedded – the evolutionary path from the early hominids at the start of the story to the Star Child at its end – remains linear and cumulative, in keeping with the texts previously considered.

Having seen how progress, maturation and ageing are explored in some representative works of the lineage of twentieth-century Anglo-American science fiction that descends from H. G. Wells, we shall now turn to *The Book of Joan* to see to what extent Yuknavitch repeats, subverts or leaves behind these familiar tropes and themes.

Transhumanism, materiality and stagnation

One facet of contemporary culture which *The Book of Joan* may be seen as responding to is a cluster of tendencies that can for convenience be brought under the heading of 'transhumanism'. This term has been defined by scholars and theorists in a variety of ways and considered from a range of perspectives, from the laudatory (Bostrom 2016; Lovelock 2019) to the critical (Gray 2016; Mason 2019). Perhaps the most instructive brief definition is that of Katherine Hayles, for whom transhumanism is a mode of thought that 'privileges informational pattern over material instantiation, so that embodiment in a biological substrate is seen as an accident of history rather than an inevitability of life' (1999: 2). Published in the same year as Yuknavitch's novel, Mark O'Connell's *To Be a Machine* (2017) offers an illuminating account of transhumanism through interviews conducted with prominent members of the international transhumanist movement, for whom the human mind and body are obsolete technologies awaiting replacement. As O'Connell shows, the epicentre of transhumanist thought is Silicon Valley, but the ideology is increasingly making inroads into mainstream culture and politics. In the eyes of some of its adherents, transhumanism represents the next stage in the evolution of capitalism, often understood in terms of the eclipse of the human. The ruthless logic of this position is that as technology begins to realize possibilities previously confined to science fiction, the human contribution to the functioning of the capitalist system will become increasingly irrelevant, raising the prospect of a world with no obvious role for the majority of people. The latter is a minority view, however, with the majority of transhumanists allowing for the continued existence of human beings, albeit in a post-biological form. One variant of this is dataism, whereby the concept of data is elevated to an ontological principle and the human mind is seen as nothing but a quantity of information capable, in principle, of existing in a wholly digital environment. As Yuval Noah Harari shows in his book *Homo Deus: A Brief History of Tomorrow*, current exponents of dataism look forward to a future in which, as in Hayles's account of transhumanism, biology has been transcended and mind is no longer constrained by materiality or embodiment (2017). A further important variant is that of the futurist Ray Kurzweil, for whom, in a clear rehearsal of the familiar science fiction trope of planetary subjectivity, the next stage of human progress is expected to take the form of the emergence of a near-omniscient superintelligence or 'singularity' destined to take charge of global affairs (2005). Lastly, there is the work of Zoltan Istvan, an American transhumanist political candidate and theorist of technology who, in line with billionaire venture capitalists such as Paul Allen and Peter Thiel, has argued in a series of books and articles that transhumanism ought to be understood as a moral crusade for radical life extension that is specifically directed against ageing and mortality (2013; 2020; 2021). One thing that Istvan's work highlights is the extent to which the transhumanist movement's attitude towards embodiment is motivated by its recoil from the ageing body, which is viewed by Istvan and some of the transhumanists interviewed by Mark O'Connell as the result of an oversight or 'bug' in the 'programming' of the human machine.

Following Jameson's guidance about how to approach science fiction, *The Book of Joan* is not best read as an attempt to intervene directly in debates about transhumanism and the techno-capitalist worldview associated with it. Rather, the novel projects an extreme, hyperbolically imagined future in which we may recognize facets of contemporary life reflected back to us in a distorted yet suggestive form. What Yuknavitch encourages us to think about through her fiction is the role and status not just of the human body but also of materiality more generally in the transhumanist imaginary, that is, not so much its explicit content but its guiding assumptions and values. In the words of Christine, one of the novel's narrators, 'After we tired of television, after we tired of films, after social media failed to feed our hungers, after holograms and virtual realities and pharmaceuticals and ever more mind-boggling altered states of being, someone somewhere looked down in despair at the sad skin of his or her own arm and noticed, for the first time, a frontier' (16). Passages like this draw our attention to the attitude towards material embodiment implied by some variants of transhumanism. As Christine also informs us, sexual acts of any kind are prohibited aboard the CIEL space station: 'Our bodies are meant to be read and consumed, debated, exchanged, or transformed only cerebrally. Any version of the act itself is an affront to social order, not to mention a brutal reminder of our impotency as a nonprocreating group' (34). As she crucially adds, however, 'Unlike those in power here on CIEL, reproduction wasn't what we mourned. We mourned the carnal. Societies may be organized around procreation, but individuals are animals' (49–50). It is this animal dimension of the human – and, by extension, the human participation in nature – which is portrayed as imperilled by Jean de Man's drive to 'perfect' the human species. One of the main implications of the increasing disembodiment of humanity which Yuknavitch's novel makes us aware of is thus the elimination of the visceral and somatic basis of much of our experience.

As its name implies, transhumanism is generally understood as an extension of the humanist project initiated during the Enlightenment. As Cary Wolfe has observed, on a transhumanist picture of the future of the human species, '"the human" is achieved by escaping or repressing not just its animal origins in nature, the biological, and the evolutionary, but more generally transcending the bonds of materiality and embodiment altogether', meaning that 'transhumanism should be seen as an *intensification* of humanism' rather than as a departure from it (2010: xv). Echoing the terms of Katherine Hayle's own critique of transhumanism, Wolfe therefore agrees with those who view transhumanism as an extension of the liberal subject's power into new domains (2010: xv).

In Yuknavitch's novel, the transhumanist conjuncture of progress, power and promethean humanism is strongly evoked by the oratory of Jean de Man, who in one of his holographic propaganda speeches tells the citizens of CIEL, 'Your life is not for them, not for the putrid detritus resisting the future, clinging to Earth for a life that cannot be sustained. Earth was but an early host for our future ascension. Your life can have meaning and justification if you but turn your sights toward a higher truth' (14). In de Man's view and that of the faction he represents, human life as it has been lived up until his own moment has been the product of a persistent error, now recognized as such: the mistake of having been unduly wedded to material embodiment. Although at the stage of development depicted by Yuknavitch, de Man's experiments primarily take the form of alterations made to the human body, the logic of his discourse throughout the novel points to a strong mind–body dualism, the fulfilment of which would be the triumph of the former over the latter through the untethering of mind from body. To this extent, the transhumanism practised on CIEL, while being a step beyond that of the early twenty-first century, is arguably only a transitional moment on the way towards the final realization of the transhumanist ideal of emancipation from our remaining links to the material world.

As John Gray has shown, there are clear parallels between transhumanism and ancient Gnostic traditions, in which a fatal cosmic 'fall' was involved in the movement from purely spiritual being to the deplorable condition of embodied, physical existence (2016). The loathing expressed at points by Jean de Man for humanity's persisting relationship with the earth may be read as a quasi-Gnostic longing for the overcoming of matter altogether. Looking back to the period immediately prior to the wars that have resulted in the apocalyptic circumstances of the main narrative, Christine observes that it had then 'seemed that technology and evolution were on the cusp of a strange bright magnificence. Technology had made houses smart, and cars, and employment centers, and education. The physical world seemed only a membrane between humans and the speed and hum of information' (75). The subsequent devastation of the planet obviously represents a major break in the history of progress, but the powerful strand of transhumanism aboard CIEL means the seeds of the future implicit in the old world are merely awaiting activation at a later date. The physical world, as Christine here recalls, had once come close to being little more than a 'membrane' between humanity and information. The rhetoric and ambitions of de Man imply that this remains the dominant vision of a liberated future among the new elite – both in the context of *The Book of Joan* and in today's transhumanist culture as explored by O'Connell, Harari, Gray and others.

As we have seen, a major strand of twentieth-century Anglo-American science fiction was informed by the Enlightenment ideal of progress, often figured via the trope of ageing. As shall be explored in the following section, *The Book of Joan* may be read as subverting elements of this tradition. At the same time, however, other elements of it are taken over and extended by Yuknavitch. The humanist ideal of writers like Wells, Stapledon, Asimov, Clarke and their inheritors, for instance, morphs into the transhumanism of Jean de Man. The trope of ageing likewise recurs, though it is developed in a number of ways. Firstly, the possibility of ageing, at least beyond a certain point, has been eliminated among the population of CIEL. As a result of material scarcity, no one is allowed to live beyond the age of fifty, at which point they submit to assisted suicide and the water and other elements from their bodies are efficiently recycled in what Christine calls 'a finite, closed system' (7). The explanation given for this practice in the novel is the need to conserve resources, yet it surely lends itself to being understood in relation to the turn against ageing taken by contemporary transhumanists. Although the link is never made in the novel, de Man's decision to cap ageing at fifty could be read as a frustrated response to the same bodily processes lamented by Zoltan Istvan and the Silicon Valley transhumanists: if radical life extension proves unattainable, then ageing can at least be made impossible by preventing anyone from living beyond their fiftieth year.

On a second level, the capping of ageing at fifty is treated as symbolic of the social and cultural stagnation of CIEL. Whereas in novels like Wells's *A Modern Utopia*, Stapledon's *Last and First Men* and Clarke's *Childhood's End*, old age is associated with the culmination of the long journey of the species, in *The Book of Joan*, the impossibility of reaching old age aboard CIEL stands for the blocked road to the future. Here, however, a distinction needs to be drawn between the novel's narration of the lives of individual characters, on the one hand, and its narration of the history of the human species, on the other. While the passage from youth to old age *at the level of the species* was represented as a linear path of development in the Anglo-American science fiction surveyed above, ageing *at the level of the individual* could, as in the case of the ambiguous concluding sequence of *2001*, potentially signify decline as well. In Yuknavitch's novel, by contrast, history has fallen frustratingly short of the transhumanist aspirations of de Man and his followers. Scientific and technological progress nevertheless remains the preeminent goal, despite prevailing conditions meaning that society is trapped at a specific stage of development, as is attested to by de Man's many botched experiments in remaking the human form. One conclusion that might be drawn from all this is that the apparent contradiction implied by regarding old age as *both* completion or fulfilment *and* something to be avoided or engineered out of existence is, from the point of view of a character like de Man or a transhumanist like Istvan, not a contradiction after all. The compatibility of the two views might be expressed as follows: while the historical evolution of *humanity* is best understood symbolically according to one familiar picture of the ageing of an individual human being (the passage from guileless infancy to sagacious old age), part of the promise of such evolution is the eradication of the empirical conditions which constitute ageing in the life of *the individual*. In this regard, de Man is an inheritor of a set of assumptions and a view of ageing that runs back through more than a century of humanist/transhumanist science fiction.

Antihumanism, nature and culture

The Book of Joan, it is important to note, takes place against a backdrop of ecological themes and concerns. The teachings of Joan herself, provided in brief instalments throughout the novel and then condensed into a letter to her partner at the end of the book, emphasize the human continuity with nature against the alienated condition personified by the inhabitants of CIEL, 'fast becoming pure representations of themselves', in Christine's words (63). By contrast with this, the relationship to nature embodied by Joan is framed as a return to humanity's authentic origins: 'You are giving them back their sacred relationship to the planet and the very cosmos they came from', a resistance fighter says to Joan (227). As the title of the book suggests, Yuknavitch's novel clearly takes sides in the conflict it portrays, aligning itself *with* Joan and *against* Jean de Man, her nemesis and narrative counter-principle. This conflict may be read on at least three levels: there is the war between Joan and de Man themselves, there is the ideological conflict over the destiny of the human species and there is the more abstract opposition of nature and culture, which is shown to encompass the other two. If de Man's transhumanism may be understood as the end stage of the humanist progress narrative, Joan's prophetic teachings embody an antihumanist worldview running exactly contrary to the former.

In her letter to her partner, Joan writes, 'You deserve a world better than this. You deserve whatever comes after human progress and its puny failures' (266). Joan identifies what has been called progress with the brutal subjugation of nature, including humanity itself through its participation in nature. In opposition to this, Joan's resistance movement represents an antithetical, antihumanist version of the human story. As Joan puts it, 'What if being human did not mean to discover, to conquer. What if it meant rejoining everything we are made from' (227). Returning to 'everything we are made from' is Joan's radical alternative to de Man's longing for the elimination of matter and corporeality. Whereas de Man is convinced that the ultimate human purpose is to transcend the material world, Joan is no less convinced that humanity's true end lies in reversing course and immersing itself once again in the raw, lawless stream of natural processes. If de Man's vision stands for the triumph of control, Joan's represents a relinquishing of control in favour of a deferral to nature in its nonhuman otherness. From Joan's point of view, in a clear echo of deep ecological thought, the humanist conception of progress and its transhumanist progeny inevitably result in the destruction of the earth due to its inherent anthropocentrism, treating the planet as little more than a set of resources for human projects.

Joan's antihumanism needs to be distinguished on this point, however, from a dominant current within critical theory which offers a comparable critique of the dominance of techno-scientific rationality. In a helpful essay on the politics of posthuman and transhuman technologies, Luciana Parisi has identified a line of thought within critical theory descending from the Frankfurt School and running through to the present day according to which 'technoscientific epistemology – or knowledge generated through technoscientific rationalisation or conceptualisation of the real – determines the ontological condition of thought, thus reducing the possible configurations of political subjectivity mainly to what can be known, measured, [or] calculated' (2017: 215). Set against this, there is what Parisi calls the 'anti-technoscientific view' which, as she puts it, 'works to preserve the ontological condition of thought (that is, of political thought autonomous from the technoenvironment in which it operates)' and which 'necessarily identifies technology with power on the one hand and separates the sacredness of human thought from the mechanical and automated systems invented by humans on the other' (2017: 215–16). Despite the affinities between this anti-technoscientific stance and Joan's antihumanism, there is also a crucial difference, which is arguably decisive for the overall import of Yuknavitch's novel. This is that the critique of technoscientific rationality on the part of critical theory remains humanist in its guiding ethical orientation: as Parisi observes, it attempts to establish a bulwark between human political rationality and the encroachments of technoscience. Joan's antihumanism, on the other hand, is a repudiation of the entire humanist legacy, radically decentring humanity and stripping it of any claim to uniqueness. For her, the human animal is simply a species among other species, equally a part of nature and equally dependent upon it: 'We always look up. What if everything that mattered was always down? Where things are base and lowly. Where worms and shit and beetles bore their way along' (147). Later, in her letter to her partner, she writes:

> There is no longer any reason to further a philosophy. There is only being. 'Knowing' has one use-value that I can see: Does it extend survival and promote a thriving species, plant or animal? If not, it's just the life of the mind, and the life of the mind has no telos without relationships to every other alive thing. (263)

Here and elsewhere, Joan's denunciation of reason and progress is not presented by Yuknavitch as a prelude to a proposal for alternative modes of reason and progress, but as a rejection of any attempt to transcend our common animal existence.

The question of the relation of Joan's antihumanism to the trope of ageing in twentieth-century science fiction and the role played by ageing aboard CIEL discussed in the previous two sections is relevant here. Aside from occasional references made to the immense age of the earth, the topic of ageing is only engaged obliquely in the Joan strands of the narrative. Nevertheless, Joan's rhetoric of 'everything that mattered' lying at our feet all along is surely suggestive. Maybe, she implies, *our* new beginning will take the form of a return to *the* beginning. Perhaps, that is to say, the fresh start sought by an exhausted human species lies in a recovery of its earliest origins rather than in further onwards movement towards a future coordinate on a linear timeline. Breaking with established science fiction convention, infancy and old age would then seem to be oddly conjoined, with the 'new' life of humanity being marked by its dissolution into the primeval life of nature. This way of construing Joan's antihumanism may help to explain why the trope of ageing is less explicit in these sections of the novel: her ideal implies a timeless condition that is beyond the contrast between youth and old age.

The picture of nature implied by Joan's antihumanism can also be contrasted with that of ecological theory, to which it stands in a complex relationship. The 'return' to nature envisaged in *The Book of Joan*, it should be noted, does not depend on a conservative or nostalgic image of the natural world. The idea of a pristine, unspoiled nature supposedly in 'equilibrium' with itself has been powerfully criticized by, among others, Timothy Morton, beginning with his major study *Ecology without Nature* (2007). At the same time, however, Joan evidently adheres to a binary opposition between nature and culture, albeit with the former taking priority. Rather than pointing towards the triumph of culture over nature, as in the case of de Man's transhumanism, Joan looks forward to a time when culture will be seen for what it is: a regrettable detour taken by nature in its chaotic striving for life. As the following thoughts on the part of Christine indicate, this view is not confined to Joan but is shared by those aligned with her:

> I've been thinking about how our desires and fears manifest in our bodies, and how our bodies, carrying these stories, resist the narratives our culture places on top of us, starting the moment we are born. It's our idiotic minds that overwrite everything. But the body has a point of view. It keeps its secrets. Makes its own stories. By any means necessary. (71)

Passages like this suggest a sharp dichotomy between nature and culture as well as between body and mind. To this extent, Christine, the earth resistance fighters and Joan herself share a common outlook, according to which there has been a fateful 'fall' from nature into culture – a fall redolent of de Man's quasi-Gnostic sense of embodied life as the fallen condition of pure mind, but this time in reverse. The fact that Christine goes on to speak of the body as carrying stories, suggesting that it too is possessed of a kind of narrative sense, might seem to spell difficulties for this reading, blurring as it does the line between nature and culture. This difficulty is defused, however, by recalling that the stories Christine has in mind are not ones *authored* by her body, but rather ones she has manually *inscribed* on herself, and which therefore still take the form of culturally authorized symbols. In the world anticipated by the resistance's antihumanism, in which humanity's animality is fully embraced and 'our idiotic minds' are no longer permitted to overwrite our bodies, there will presumably be no such symbols. Having built such a stark opposition between nature and culture into the narrative and thematic framework of her novel, Yuknavitch is forced to choose between the only two options on offer: transhumanism *or* antihumanism. Presented with this choice, she opts for the latter, accepting whatever tensions and anomalies this may give rise to in the text.

The absence of queer ecology

As we have seen, *The Book of Joan* portrays a future in which two possibilities are set against one another: transhumanism and the triumph of culture over nature or antihumanism and a turn back toward nature, understood as the true source of all life. As a courageous, noble, inspiring figure, Joan is unambiguously cast as the hero of Yuknavitch's story, while the cruel, sadistic, malevolent figure of Jean de Man is unambiguously the villain of the piece. Insofar as the novel may be read as an indirect reflection on the possibilities open to humanity in the early twenty-first century, confronted by ecological, technological and political threats of multiple kinds, however, this dichotomous thinking is liable to seem reductive and may occlude other valuable options. One such option would be posthumanism, of the sort formulated by Katherine Hayles (1999) or Cary Wolfe (2010). Posthumanism is more suited than either transhumanism or antihumanism to think the imbrications of nature and culture and to make allowance for the presence of nonhuman forces within the human. There may in fact be intimations of the posthuman in some of the passages of the novel focusing on the narrative carried by Christine's body of the sort we saw above, which perhaps accord with Wolfe's observation that posthumanism calls for much greater attention to how materiality shapes mind and thought (2010: 120). This strand is not, however, sufficiently developed by Yuknavitch to stand as a fully-fledged alternative to the positions represented by Joan and de Man. The prefix 'post' in the term posthumanism, meanwhile, may entail its own difficulties in the present context. Despite Wolfe's insistence that 'posthumanism comes both *before* and *after* humanism' (2010: xv), it is hard to avoid the sense of an implied historical teleology of the sort that *The Book of Joan* is clearly directed against and which has in any case come to seem dubious in light of the dystopian conjuncture which late modernity has brought us to. To this extent, posthumanism may present problems it is incapable of resolving, whatever its appeal in other regards.

Another, potentially more fruitful approach to the issues of materiality, ecology and temporality raised by *The Book of Joan* is that of queer theory and specifically queer ecology. Morton has argued that queer theory has 'a strange friend in nonessentialist biology', according to which 'life-forms themselves undermine distinctions between Natural and non-Natural' (2010: 277). An alliance between queer theory and ecology 'would suppose a multiplication of differences at as many levels and on as many scales as possible' (Morton 2010: 275), contradicting views of gender and sexual variability as a 'cultural' imposition on a given set of 'natural' binaries. Indeed, the absence of queer ecological thought of this sort may help to explain another of the novel's anomalies. At the climax of the story, during the defeat of Jean de Man, it is unexpectedly revealed that de Man 'is not a man but what is left of a woman' (245), with evidence of multiple gender reassignment surgeries, including 'several dangling attempts at half-formed penises' (245). It is very unclear how this scene ought to be interpreted or how it might be integrated with everything else in the novel, and no critic to date has offered a satisfying explanation of it. It could be argued that the seemingly transphobic implications of the exposure of de Man in this way are a further consequence of the novel's nature/culture binary. Whatever Yuknavitch may have intended by making de Man transgender, the framing of her novel in terms of an opposition between 'raw' nature and 'artificial' culture means that she cannot avoid coding him as an 'unnatural' figure, as is implied by the use of the word 'attempts' with reference to his genitalia, which establishes a clear continuity with the many earlier references to the failed attempts to create a new human species aboard CIEL. The limitations of the novel's reimagining of nature and of the position of human beings within it are perhaps nowhere more apparent than in its treatment of gender.

In his book *No Future: Queer Theory and the Death Drive*, Lee Edelman has influentially criticized what he terms 'reproductive futurism', which places heteronormativity outside contestation and renders queer resistance to the status quo unthinkable through a culturally embedded understanding of the future oriented toward reproduction (2004). During the course of his argument, Edelman puts forward an interpretation of P. D. James's *The Children of Men* (1992), a dystopian novel focusing on a sterility crisis, which Edelman sees as an especially clear illustration of the logic of reproductive futurism (2004: 12–13). On Edelman's reading, the novel reiterates the heteronormative trope of achieving symbolic immortality and maintaining the social order through reproduction, while childlessness is coded as antisocial, narcissistic enjoyment or jouissance. In the case of Yuknavitch's novel, the rebel faction could perhaps be seen as following Edelman in preferring the 'anti-social' option of refusing the future as represented by CIEL's attempts to restart the human race, thereby potentially fulfilling the role of the queer who 'comes to figure the bar to every realization of futurity, the resistance, internal to the social, to every social structure or form' (Edelman 2004: 30). The radical negativism of Edelman's project is not the only queer theoretical paradigm available to us, however.

While Edelman's stance, like Joan's own antihumanism, represents a rejection of humanist teleologies, Elizabeth Freeman's book *Time Binds: Queer Temporalities, Queer Histories* is concerned with thinking history otherwise and with non-teleological ways of relating to time in which nonnormative gender and sexuality play a central role. On Freeman's account, queerness is a site from which to contest modern Western conceptions of time. 'Queer time', she writes, 'overtakes both secular and millennial time', displacing linear chronologies and pointing to nonlinear modes of temporal experience (Freeman 2010: x–xi). It is noteworthy that for Freeman, 'Moments of participation in queer time are often grounded in *bodily* experiences/pleasures' (2010: xi), meaning they transcend the nature/culture binary: queer time is simultaneously natural *and* cultural. Although Freeman does not explicitly forge connections with ecological thought, the parallels between her understanding of queer time and Morton's reflections on the queer potential of ecology and developments in the life sciences are clear. A further parallel, this time with work in age studies, may also be noted here. Cynthia Port has drawn attention to some of the commonalities between queer subjectivity and the condition of old age: 'No longer employed, not reproducing, perhaps technologically illiterate, and frequently without disposable income, the old are often, like queers, figured by the cultural imagination as being outside mainstream temporalities and standing in the way of, rather than contributing to, the promise of the future' (2012: 3). Obviously, the fact that queers and the old often do not participate in conventional modes of temporality does not mean that they exist outside of time. Rather, as Port shows, they inhabit what Freeman calls in a related context 'structures of belonging and duration that may be invisible to the historicist eye' and which cannot be subordinated to teleological and normative temporal frames (Freeman 2010: xi). As in the case of gender, then, *The Book of Joan*'s handling of temporality is arguably constrained by a forced choice between linear progress and its refusal. Queer theory may have much to offer here.

Displacing and implicitly critiquing the tendency within Anglo-American science fiction to rely on a humanist conception of progress modelled on the development of the individual from infancy to maturity, Yuknavitch instead advances an antihumanist agenda in which historicity would seem to be suspended in favour of a return to a nonhuman, precultural condition. The role of age and ageing here is ambiguous, and varies depending on which level of the text one focuses on. At the level of the individual, *The Book of Joan* recapitulates by way of the designs of Jean de Man the generic tendency to associate technological progress with the elimination of bodily shortcomings, including ageing and ultimately embodiment itself. At the level of the species, however, where the novel takes Joan's side against de Man, the trope of ageing is either replaced by ecological metaphors – such as returning to 'everything we are made from' (227) – or gives way to the timeless present of the nonhuman where, as Joan says, 'There is only being' (263). In this way, Yuknavitch simultaneously contests the humanist/transhumanist conception of progress while reproducing its guiding opposition between the historicity of culture and the timelessness of nature. By contrast, queer ecology's contestation of the dominant nature/culture binary, combined with its ability to forego historical teleology without foreclosing the possibility of historical existence, arguably makes it a more promising candidate for beginning to articulate 'whatever comes after human progress'.

References

2001: A Space Odyssey (1968), [Film] Dir. Stanley Kubrick, USA: Metro-Goldwyn-Mayer.
Asimov, I. (2018), *I, Robot*, New York: HarperVoyager.
Bostrom, N. (2016), *Superintelligence: Paths, Dangers, Strategies*, Oxford: Oxford University Press.
Chu, S. (2010), *Do Metaphors Dream of Literal Sleep?*, Cambridge, MA: Harvard University Press.
Clarke, A. C. (2010), *Childhood's End*, London: Pan.
Clarke, A. C. (2018), *2001: A Space Odyssey*, London: Orbit.
Cole, S. (2019), *Inventing Tomorrow: H. G. Wells and the Twentieth Century*, New York: Columbia University Press.
Crossley, R. (1994), *Olaf Stapledon: Speaking for the Future*, New York: Syracuse University Press.
Dick, P. K. (2010), *Do Androids Dream of Electric Sheep?*, London: Gollancz.
Edelman, L. (2004), *No Future: Queer Theory and the Death Drive*, Durham: Duke University Press.
Freeman E. (2010), *Time Binds: Queer Temporalities, Queer Histories*, Durham: Duke University Press.
Gray, J. (2016), *The Soul of the Marionette: A Short Enquiry into Human Freedom*, London: Penguin.
Harari, Y. N. (2017), *Homo Deus: A Brief History of Tomorrow*, London: Vintage.
Hayles, N. K. (1999), *How We Became Posthuman*, Chicago: University of Chicago Press.
Howe, I. (1970), *Decline of the New*, New York: Harcourt, Brace, and World.
Huxley, A. (2007), *Brave New World*, London: Vintage.
Istvan, Z. (2013), *The Transhumanist Wager*, Nevada: Futurity Imagine Media.
Istvan, Z. (2020), *The Anti-Deathist: Writings of a Radical Longevity Activist*, Nevada: Futurity Imagine Media.
Istvan, Z. (2021), *A Transhumanist Journal: Writings That Launched the Transhumanist Movement*, Nevada: Futurity Imagine Media.
Jameson, F. (2005), *Archaeologies of the Future*, London: Verso.
Kurzweil, R. (2005), *The Singularity Is Near: When Humans Transcend Biology*, London: Duckworth.
Lovelock, J. (2019), *Novacene: The Coming Age of Hyperintelligence*, London: Allan Lane.
Mason, P. (2019), *Clear Bright Future: A Radical Defence of the Human Being*, London: Allan Lane.

Morton, T. (2007), *Ecology without Nature*, Cambridge, MA: Harvard University Press.

Morton, T. (2010), 'Queer Ecology', *PMLA*, 125(2): 273–82.

Moylan, T. (2010), *Demand the Impossible: Science Fiction and the Utopian Imagination*, Bern: Peter Lang.

O'Connell, M. (2017), *To Be a Machine*, London: Granta.

Parisi, L. (2017), 'Automate Sex: Xenofeminism, Hyperstition, and Alienation,' in H. Gunkel, A. Hameed and S. O'Sullivan (eds), *Futures and Fictions*, 213–30, London: Repeater.

Port, C. (2012), 'No Future? Aging, Temporality, History, and Reverse Chronologies', *Occasion: Interdisciplinary Studies in the Humanities*, 4, available online: http://occasion.stanford.edu/node/98.

Stapledon, O. (1999), *Last and First Men*, London: Gollancz.

Wells, H. G. (2005), *A Modern Utopia*, London: Penguin.

Westfahl, G. (2005), 'Introduction,' in W. Kin Yuen, G. Westfahl and A. Kit-sze Chan (eds), *World Weavers: Globalization, Science Fiction, and the Cybernetic Revolution*, 1–18, Hong Kong: Hong Kong University Press.

Wolfe, C. (2010), *What Is Posthumanism?*, Minneapolis: University of Minnesota Press.

Yuknavitch, L. (2017), *The Book of Joan*, London: Canongate.

8

A spectral future: Dementia and the nonhuman in *Marjorie Prime*

Michael S. D. Hooper

In *The Haunted Stage: The Theatre as Memory Machine*, Marvin Carlson insists that the theatre is haunted on several different levels. Infrastructurally, individual performance sites may, according to long-held superstitions, be haunted by previous owners, actors or their associates. Beyond this, though, earlier productions, their casts and scripts are an undeniable point of reference and departure for those that succeed them. Greater than just intertextuality, this recycling of earlier theatrical performances is labelled by Carlson 'ghosting' (2003: 7) and amounts to an experience the audience has had before now which has been transplanted into a new context. As a result, theatre is closely allied to memory, both individual and cultural. What we witness on stage, or the act of merely entering a particular theatre, triggers various associations, consciously or subconsciously. Like the process of remembering itself, the theatre, then, reimagines what has gone before, even when the performance conditions are apparently the same; accordingly, it is, in the words of Carlson's title, a 'memory machine'.

Carlson's holistic approach – he considers texts, actors, productions and performance sites – means that he does not dwell on ghosts in specific plays for long and that haunting as a primeval fear tends to be assumed. Yet, though it is barely mentioned specifically, our sense of the uncanny is connected to the very recycling with which Carlson is concerned. As Sigmund Freud's influential 1919 essay makes clear, the uncanny is our sense of the familiar within the strange; it is what we have repressed or kept secret, 'concealed and kept hidden' (2003: 132). Carlson's definition of ghosting may not arouse 'fear and dread' (Freud 2003: 123), but it does represent a meeting between what is known to us in the present, the theatrical performances that we experience as new and possibly innovative, and what we have forgotten or relegated to a subconscious level.

Within this broad theatrical context, this 'ghostly tapestry' (Carlson 2003: 165), plays about old age and specifically dementia, seem to multiply the sense of haunting, while they also appear to present their own internal doubling: the split self that signals the discontinuity of selfhood. Consistent with a cultural discourse in which 'the media frequently adopts a Gothic and apocalyptic perspective on Alzheimer's disease' (Goldman 2017: 4), mainstream American plays that tackle dementia emphasize decline and loss, the seemingly incontrovertible truth that the individual living with the condition is a shadow of his/her earlier self, inclined to act unpredictably or speak nonsensically and behave monstrously. The devastation at what he/she can no longer be or do is, in turn, compounded by the reactions of friends and carers unable to distance themselves from the impact of dementia and cope with the burden of care. The familiarity of long acquaintance, the memory of intimate connections, meets the strangeness of absence, or at least of uncertainty.

Though Freud does not expound on this himself, there is another notable sense in which the uncanny purportedly operates: the way in which artificial creations – lifelike dolls and automata, for example – have an animacy and degree of verisimilitude that is disturbing because it is perceived as undermining. Freud's ideas on the uncanny are strongly directed (at least initially) by fellow psychologist Ernst Jentsch, who comments on the deliberate use of the phenomenon in literature. Leaving the reader in doubt as to whether a character is human or nonhuman is a successful technique that can engage narrative interest and prolong suspense if 'his [the reader's] attention is not focused directly on the uncertainty' (qtd. in Freud 2003: 135). The unnerving quality of robots, in particular, has been a subject of debate since the delayed critical response to Masahiro Mori's theory of the 'Uncanny Valley' appeared in 1970. In this, at a mathematically worked out point, the valley of Mori's title, artificial life forms are poised between familiarity and strangeness. They create uncanniness precisely because their engineered appearance is just short of an exact human likeness but close enough to suggest it.

It is these aspects of the uncanny – its presence within a specifically theatrical context closely linked to memory, its application to ageing and dementia and its relevance to the authenticity and sentience of nonhuman life forms used as caregivers – that I wish to explore within this chapter. In particular, I will use Jordan Harrison's 2014 play, *Marjorie Prime*, to examine the ways in which the person living with dementia and suffering 'a most extreme instance of ruptured selfhood' (DeFalco 2009: 14), which manifests itself in doubling and otherness, interfaces with technology amidst debates about memory, narrative and posthuman care. Drawing on Harrison's stated inspirations for the play, the chapter will consider if reimagining old age and dementia in a future setting creates fresh perspectives, releasing the affected individual and her family from a ghostly sense of displacement, and whether the use of hologrammatic carers constitutes a meaningful engagement with the posthuman or merely an attempt to create a human legacy through the transhuman.

Shortlisted for the Pulitzer Prize for drama, *Marjorie Prime* is set in an unspecified future apparently very similar to the present.[1] Its defining characteristic or, to use science fiction terminology, its *novum* or new concept, is the use of holograms, known as Primes, in care settings. These are essentially pixelated recreations of loved ones that can be programmed by their owners with personal information that gradually gives the illusion that they are becoming the person they visually resemble. Though the first Prime we meet in the play, Walter, is essentially a companion and aide-memoire for his wife, Marjorie, now living with dementia, others can have slightly different functions depending on the needs of the person for whom they are designed. When Marjorie dies, for instance, her daughter Tess, with whom she has had a somewhat fractious relationship, is deemed to require Marjorie Prime to ease her grief and talk through former differences, and when Tess herself commits suicide, Jon, her husband, acquires Tess Prime to deal with the trauma. The adding of further Primes after the characters' deaths leads us to a point, part three, where the play takes us much further into the future and a time in which the Primes, now the only characters, seem to have achieved independence; their conversation, though, merely seems to highlight their continuing dependence on their creators, dominated as it is by the narrative fragments they have learnt.

Jordan Harrison has spoken at length about the genesis of the play, explaining his motivation in emotional and intellectual terms (Harrison, Kauffman and Christian 2015). Affected by his own grandmother's dementia, he was troubled by her exhaustion and, in particular, her inability to record daily experiences in a journal. Fascinated by the analogue to digital switchover and having read Brian Christian's book *The Most Human Human* (2011) about the Turing Test, and no doubt aware of the increasing use of AI in caregiving, Harrison uses the frustrations of memory loss as a springboard into questions about technology's functionality, its potential humanness. Also relevant, and mentioned separately (George 2015), is *The Electric Grandmother* (1982), a film based on Ray Bradbury's short story 'I Sing the Body Electric' (1969) about a family that initially purchases a robot as a replacement for a dead wife and mother and then later reacquires her when the children, having reached old age and still living in the family home, need live-in care. A brief scene towards the end of the film, in which the eponymous grandmother sits in a semicircle with similar robots talking about her earlier experiences with the family, would seem to have given Harrison the idea for part three of *Marjorie Prime*.

Putting the uncanny on stage

None of these inspirations quite prepares us for what I consider to be the play's overriding eeriness, its lurking supernaturalism, a quality alluded to, but not fully stated, in reviews of the first American productions. Premiering at the Mark Taper Forum theatre in Los Angeles in September 2014, the play was given a rather mixed review by Charles McNulty for the *Los Angeles Times*. While the acting was praised, the play itself was found to be 'ultimately more conceptually intriguing than dramatically satisfying', 'smart' but with 'an abstract quality … that stems from ideas being more highly valued than their personal embodiment' (McNulty 2014). Moreover, McNulty felt that the performance gave him 'the kind of experience that keeps unfolding in the mind' (2014) long after its completion. In this last respect, Ben Brantley's reaction to the New York premiere at Playwrights Horizons in December 2015 was remarkably similar. He found the play a 'quietly unsettling drama' and noted that 'this production keeps developing in your head, like a photographic negative, long after you've seen it' (Brantley 2015).

These observations may point to a number of factors, but what lingers most is surely the idea that machines which are creating the illusion of humanness are actually being represented by human actors: the normal boundaries between the two are transgressed and re-transgressed, and in the case of the appearance of the last two Primes, there is a rather abrupt transition from the human character to its hologrammatic likeness that is also unsettling. Joking about his tendency to create plays with lavish production costs, Harrison himself has talked about his use of actors in place of special effects, a policy that makes the Primes both more credible and disturbing for the audience: 'We're basically, like, putting the uncanny on stage is how I think of it. … They're [the Primes] familiar and unfamiliar, seductive and repellent at the same time' (Harrison, Kauffman and Christian 2015). These contrasting reactions, which, echoing Freud, are closer than we might think (since the German words for canny and uncanny, *heimlich* and *unheimlich*, can be used interchangeably – see Freud 2003: 132), attest to our discomfort with technology when we cannot separate or distinguish it from the human, when we succumb to illusion. It is, as Harrison's comment insinuates, a deliberate choice that stems from the playwright's attitude towards science fiction, at least in this play.

The 'Author's Note on Primes' that accompanies the published text is very telling in this respect. Alongside a qualified denial of SF – 'I don't think of it as science fiction – at least not the predictive sort' (Harrison 2016: 65) – Harrison implies at several points that he is creating illusion (over and above Naturalistic imitation or theatricality) or deliberately withholding information from the audience: we should be able to forget the artificiality of the Primes; 'the audience should catch on' (2016: 65) that the play is set in the future, and 'the less the audience is put in mind of how the technology works, the better' (2016: 65). In other words, the concept of the play, transmitted through both the set and the characters, is one that probes familiarity and strangeness. It is both science fiction and not science fiction, a drama set in the future that constantly revisits and mulls over the past.

To make the illusion more pronounced and to underline the idea that we all, humans and nonhumans alike, gradually shape identities through our everyday performances, Harrison makes several metatheatrical references to role play and character development. Marjorie, for example, opens the play with a sense of dramatic responsibility: 'I feel like I have to perform around you' (Harrison 2016: 7), she confides to Walter, which, as Shelby Brewster points out, anticipates the Prime's 'excessive and unexpected humanness' (2017: 18), something Marjorie feels obliged to replicate. It also alludes, perhaps, to the striking and ghostly visual dissonance the audience must immediately accept: that Walter, Marjorie's former husband, is some fifty years younger than her because she has chosen to remember him as a young man. The reasons for this are not immediately clear, but it would seem that Marjorie, who can be playful, even suggestive, at times, either wants to be reminded of her youth with a once-handsome companion or is constrained by the greater limitations of her short-term memory. Regardless, Marjorie has been conditioned to perform the role of wife and hostess ('I used to entertain a lot', she tells Walter; Harrison 2016: 7) in spite of the physical and mental frailty of her advanced age that would appear to make this unlikely.

Akin to the preparatory work usually carried out in the rehearsal room, the Primes' absorption of information helps them to build parts that are false but have the appearance of being natural, until they, the Primes, 'incriminate themselves' (Harrison 2016: 65). Responses like 'I'll remember that fact' (2016: 12) or 'Tell me more about your mother' (2016:10) are accompanied by the stage directions *'generic'* (2016: 12) or *'faintly generic'* (2016: 10) that highlight unnaturalness, a slipping of the role. Because they are infrequent, these moments are all the more noticeable, and combined with the suggestion that the Primes '*might remain at the perimeter of the stage*' (2016: 14) when they are not directly involved in a scene, they remind us that these characters are ghostly extras, imperfect understudies not quite adjusted to human conversations or fully able to impersonate the deceased figures they shadow. Harrison's 'Author's Note' justifies this teleologically: the Primes' lurking presence points to their immortality. Yet we surely cannot dismiss the idea that they continue to listen and absorb information not directed at them or that, like our memories, the Primes remain dormant until activated in the context of the present moment.

Michael Almereyda's 2017 film adaptation takes a slightly different approach that, while losing this eerie sense that the technology we have created cannot be got rid of, conveys more directly the idea of spectres. The Primes vanish or appear unannounced just before the camera turns from or back to them, making them seem not just phantoms but also almost figments of the imagination. And towards the end of the play's first scene, the camera is very deliberately focused on Walter Prime's feet at the point where Marjorie walks through them. A visual clue for any viewer who has not grasped Walter's status, this instantly shows that he is no more than an 'imagistic embodiment' (Brewster 2017: 18), a fact recognized by the periodically confused Marjorie.

The haunted mind

The fear that dementia both possesses the individual and has a stranglehold over society of epidemic proportions is a widespread one, permeating the media, literature and film. Marlene Goldman, drawing on Susan Sontag's observations about major diseases like cancer and AIDS, suggests that Alzheimer's has been similarly 'transported into the territory of the Gothic' (2017: 4) where it can easily be branded an evil or a curse. This 'inflated rhetoric' (Goldman 2017: 6) is also noted by Anne Davis Basting, who traces it back to alarmist news coverage from the 1980s. One of the tragic stories to emerge from this is that of the 'inspiring person ... slowly emptied out by a devastating illness' (Basting 2009: 33).

In *Marjorie Prime*, Marjorie's dementia does not appear to be acute. Indeed, Elinor Fuchs (2017) has commented wryly that if the character really had the condition, she would not even recognize her husband in the Prime. While she seems to have forgotten her grandchildren, partly because they visit infrequently, Marjorie recognizes other people and can distinguish between Walter Prime and her deceased husband. She understands the purpose of the Primes, that companionship is intended to improve mental health or at least arrest decline, and even comprehends that Walter's power is increasing commensurate with her own ebbing faculties. She speaks coherently and without hesitation, and her responses to statements and questions indicate that she can still arrive at her own judgements, disarm with her wit and appreciate that some of her linguistic and cultural references might have slipped from current use. Nonetheless, Marjorie is confused about certain key aspects of her life. With prompting, she remembers going to the movies frequently with Walter but not the experience of seeing *My Best Friend's Wedding* the night that Walter proposed to her. She asks if her son, Damian, who committed suicide years before, is still asleep. And certain episodes explain why she needs supervision: she does not eat properly, blaming her suppressed appetite on the medication she receives; she has a bad fall in the night, has to be rushed to hospital but, in the morning, remembers nothing of the incident; and, finally, in the last moments we see her, she involuntarily urinates.

This last instance of personal shame, not necessarily linked to dementia, hardly suggests a haunted figure on the brink of death. In truth, we do not know how long after this Marjorie dies because, consistent with the play's avoidance of public grief, there is no immediate statement about what has happened to her, just her unannounced replacement by the more presentable Marjorie Prime.[2] And it is this substitution that suggests one of the ways in which Marjorie is haunted. Though she never refers to it herself, she is always in the process of becoming Marjorie Prime, as the title of the play would intimate. This transitional status underscores the way in which her dementia will continue to isolate her to a point where, in Marjorie's more lucid moments, living will become a contemplation of further decline, an incompleteness that places her on the margins, like the Primes themselves. Her hologrammatic double is a pivotal figure combining Harrison's original inspirations – his grandmother and the potential of technology – and one that postulates both the proliferation of Primes and their application outside of age-related illness.

But Marjorie's uncanniness is insisted upon in other ways, too. In the play's second scene, there are two instances where she addresses '*no one in particular*' (Harrison 2016: 20, 21) and experiences memories or visions she cannot fathom: one, expressed tautologically, of a 'figure in my mind. I'm trying to figure out' (2016: 20) and the second of the improbable experience of 'waking up on a bridge with a lot of people around' (2016: 21). In both cases, apparently familiar behaviour, responding normally to both Jon and Tess, is interrupted by moments of detachment, even absence. Slightly later, in scene three, Jon leaves Marjorie listening to a recording of the Winter section of Vivaldi's *Four Seasons*, a piece she formerly played when part of an orchestra. Consistent with the popular belief that music can both calm those living with dementia and unlock memories, this moment shows Marjorie reminiscing about the technique needed to play the piece and '*lost ... in the memory of her supporting part*' (2016: 25).³ Her pleasant reverie – a comforting familiarity that the audience is encouraged to share ('*we are lost, with her*'; 2016: 25) – is, however, immediately juxtaposed with a cry for help: an invocation to her dead husband that is a reminder of his ghost lurking behind Walter Prime and the dread of her own spectral purposelessness: 'Walter I'm scared. This is *it* – there isn't anything after' (2016: 26).

These examples are not atypical. People living with dementia may transition quickly from lucidity to hallucination, mental withdrawal and/or incoherence and then back again. When performed, though, the moments of disorientation and insecurity in *Marjorie Prime* are heightened by the semi-invisible presence of Walter Prime at the edge of the set who is both Marjorie's prompt and her always incomplete memories, her only reason to be hopeful and a reminder of what she cannot access. Like other mainstream American dementia plays – *Dot* (2015) by Colman Domingo or the adaptation of *Still Alice* (2013) by Christine Mary Dunford, for example – *Marjorie Prime* traces an arc of decline in which Marjorie is only too aware of her failings, and those around her, Tess and Jon, have polarized attitudes regarding her care. Unlike these plays, Harrison's text foregrounds narrativization as a possible (but not altogether successful) means of salvaging a sense of self, of embellishing Marjorie's autobiography to a point where it seems purposeful.

Given that the person living with dementia is often only capable of constructing narrative fragments that 'become increasingly opaque to listeners' (DeFalco 2009: 58), storytelling necessarily falls to a witness who is partially responsible for creating a testimony that is not just the 'emplotment of memory' (2009: 55) but also 'review and interpretation' (2009: 57). Usually a family member, the witness becomes a collaborator, a role that has ethical and political implications related to the 'careful balance of empathy and respect' (2009: 61). The very act of ordering and clarifying parts of the subject's life is uncanny: a project in which certain experiences may appear familiar to either/both witness and subject and in which others remain stubbornly hidden. Furthermore, for the caregiving witness, the strangeness of the person living with dementia may be accompanied by a new and unsettling awareness of his/her own otherness (2009: 60).

American plays tackling dementia mostly make sense of the subject's life and situation through the conversations of the other characters, and at times, these may be conducted in that person's presence, as if he/she cannot comprehend what is being said. In these moments, needless to say, the subject is treated as a ghost, deemed unable to articulate a point of view and affect proceedings. *The Waverly Gallery* (1999) by Kenneth Lonergan supplements this type of (usually negative) commentary with interspersed monologues delivered directly to the audience by, appropriately enough, a speechwriter, Daniel Reed, the grandson of Gladys Green who develops dementia. These do not attempt to create a fuller biography; rather, they chronicle Gladys's deterioration and its impact on the family and specifically on Daniel himself, who is torn between being grateful that he is 'out of it now' and being driven 'to remember every detail, because it really happened to her, and it seems like somebody should remember it' (Lonergan 2000: 108). In *Still Alice*, an extra level of commentary is provided by 'Herself', essentially the protagonist's double or conscience that permits 'a wider window into Alice's mind' ('Author's Note', Dunford 2018: 6) and functions as an occasional narrator.

Because Marjorie is the recipient of care designed to stimulate her memories, especially those that are episodic in nature, and because the Primes rely on the inputting of information, *Marjorie Prime* is, in no small part, a play about narrative, information giving and correction. Walter Prime recognizes Marjorie's fondness for stories – 'I could tell you a story. You liked that the last time' (Harrison 2016: 8) – but he also has to accept her occasional preference for silent companionship, a concession to the exhaustion that Harrison noticed in his own grandmother. More interestingly, it is the uncanny nature of these narratives, their familiar but strange resurrection of past events, that fleetingly exorcises Marjorie's haunting. Though Jon clings to the belief that the retention of autobiographical narrative – 'Just to have eight or nine stories to hold onto. New things are already coming to the surface' (2016: 18) – is of paramount importance, it is Marjorie's awareness of narrative form and her playful participation that are more important than what she actually continues to remember. For example, when Walter Prime starts the requested account of how the family acquired a dog, Toni, Marjorie objects that 'it sounds like a fairy tale when you tell it' (2016: 10) – childlike and told too simply. Marjorie may feel that she is being infantilized or that the memory is being trivialized; at the same time, she is obliged to accept '*an uncomfortable truth*' (2016: 11): that, when reconstructed, some memories can be told only using broad brushstrokes. Equally, she is alert to embellishment, points where Walter is adding extraneous detail that serves no purpose other than showing off his knowledge.

Most significant, though, is Marjorie's willingness to collaborate and invent. In the story about Walter's marriage proposal, she suggests substituting *Casablanca* and 'an old theater with velvet seats' (Harrison 2016: 9) for (what must have been at the time) the less glamorous modern experience of watching *My Best Friend's Wedding*. Knowing, at this point, the importance of the event, Marjorie reclaims ownership of the memory and, further, sees the possibility of enriching it through fiction, a fiction that can become truth: 'Then, by the next time we talk, it will be true' (2016: 9). This deliberate fictionalizing is a rebellion against Tess and Jon, who are both under the misapprehension that memory needs to be mined, brought intact to a metaphorical surface. More than this, though, it reveals that Marjorie, apparently tormented by memory loss and a consequent inability to find sustained comfort, intuitively understands that memory's 'truth' is an illusion and that all memories are reshaped in the present. As DeFalco helpfully analogizes it, memory is a palimpsest, a 'process of endless substitution' (2009: 55) and modified connections in which we cannot expect a 'correlation between one's memory of a thing and the thing itself' (2009: 55). The memory that Marjorie proposes embellishing is already a version of what happened – probably a composite of Marjorie's memory on one of her 'good days' (Harrison 2016: 12) and that which has filtered down to Tess and Jon (the Primes absorb information from various people, not just those for whom they are created) – and consequently altering details to romanticize the event should be immaterial. Walter makes the expected demur, but at the start of part three, he has taken back the story with Marjorie's changes and added details of his own. Performing it to the other Primes suggests his final approval and co-authoring of a past he is expected to know, not treat as a game. And exceeding the boundaries of his initial programming, Walter demonstrates a freedom with memory that renders him more human – fallible and creative at the same time.

Though brief, this moment highlights how Marjorie can very occasionally slip away from her haunted self, from the daily oppression of forgetting, and enjoy a collaborative inventiveness that proves, in a very limited way, her continuing appreciation of rudimentary narrative elements like plot and setting, what amounts to a 'coherence without facticity' (McLean 2006: 157).[4] And programmed to assimilate verifiable facts, Walter Prime learns, over time, the pleasure of not just repeating information but also manipulating it for the purpose of entertainment; he appreciates the value of being an accomplice, not simply a prompt and technological replacement for Marjorie's real husband.

Uncanny authenticity

The easy way in which Marjorie and Walter interact and the former's understanding of the functionality of the Primes hardly suggest an atmosphere of menace. However, as the play's chief sceptic, Tess voices concerns reminiscent of Sherry Turkle's critical view of technology initially published some three years before *Marjorie Prime* was first produced. *Alone Together: Why We Expect More from Technology and Less from Each Other* talks of the way in which we find ourselves in a 'robotic moment', a 'state of emotional ... philosophical – readiness' to accept machines in a variety of (normally human) roles that offer just a 'performance of connection' (Turkle 2017: 9). Tess shares this sense of vulnerability, which she sees as aggravated by the layperson's ignorance, in her first duologue with Jon: 'We buy these things that already know our moods ... we tell them our deepest secrets, even though we have no earthly idea how they work. We treat them like our loved ones' (Harrison 2016: 16). The blurring of technological possibility and future potential (Tess adds that 'every *day* is science fiction'; Harrison 2016: 16) means that we can no longer defer our anxieties, pin them on a future we may never reach. Tess is unnerved by an invisible cyber network, one that, as her repeated use of the first-person plural pronoun indicates, she, too, is guilty of blithely accepting. As she realizes, the Primes need information to function, but there is no way of knowing who, what or how many have access to that information and whether it will be used responsibly. Provided by Senior Serenity, presumably an approved private enterprise, these computer programs are tailored to individual requirements, yet their creation remains murky and their indefinite lifespan means they continue to function independently beyond their original purpose. In this respect, Harrison plays not only on our concerns about privacy in a digital age but also on what are now clichéd SF fears about a hostile robot takeover or the obsolescence of humankind in a purely technological future, a dystopian vision that extends back to the very first mention of robots in Karel Čapek's play, *RUR* (1921). *Marjorie Prime*'s evolutionary politics are not alarmist, however; they merely confirm a transhuman preoccupation with reproducing versions of both ourselves and our life stories, journeys perpetuated and memorialized in ghostly pixels. The play's references to sound and sound producers confirm this. Tess and Jon liken Walter to a ventriloquizing parrot that lives forever, and Jon later confirms Tess's view that talking to a Prime is no more than talking to yourself, the machine's sound being an echoey backboard.

For Jon, the advocate of Prime technology, this conclusion that the uploading of data merely reproduces our own voice, not a simulacrum of the loved one, seems an admission that he cannot find solace for his grief in technology, that the promise of artificially generated ethical care has failed, leaving him more alone than ever. Similarly, Jordan Harrison realized, after his initial idea that he might be able to create a play centred on the responses of a chatbot, that a computer was not yet advanced enough to provide the requisite emotional engagement (Harrison, Kauffman and Christian 2015). Does this mean, by extension, that the Primes fail to empathize, that they are ultimately incapable of emotional engagement? Is Jon's concurrence with Tess merely motivated by grief, his frustration that Tess Prime needs time to become a convincing version of Tess? Or does it signify that the work of the Primes is invalid, that their status is always inferior to that of humans?

The question of authenticity, of whether robots in particular, but other forms of technology too, can impersonate humans to such a high degree that they feel, or have the semblance of feeling, recognizable emotions is one which has gained urgency, not least for fiction writers. Ian McEwan's *Machines Like Me and People Like You* (2019) and Kazuo Ishiguro's *Klara and the Sun* (2021) are examples of two recent novels that probe the humanness of androids, their respective abilities to express sexual and romantic love, compassion and a loyalty that seems to exceed their programmed remit. Naturally, texts like these raise questions not just about the potentiality of machines and their ontology but also about our own assumptions as humans. Do we admit roles beyond functionality and servitude, and do these generate uncanniness outside of that provoked by physical resemblance?

Masahiro Mori's 'uncanny valley' theory, formulated as long ago as 1970, suggests that our 'heightened sense of affinity' (2012: 98) for robots made to look like humans dissipates when our minds are deceived twice: initially into thinking that the machine is human and then into realizing that it, or a part of it, like a prosthetic hand, is artificial. The resulting dip or valley on a graph measuring affinity against human likeness steepens when the machine moves. Mori goes on to theorize that we are 'equipped with this eerie sensation' (2012: 100) to protect us instinctively from 'proximal sources of danger': 'corpses, members of different species and other entities we can closely approach' (2012: 100). McEwan gives us a sense of this biological defence mechanism in *Machines Like Me* when his protagonist, Charlie Friend, 'disliked the too-solid feel' (2019: 128) of his robot, Adam, and 'begins to feel unhinged, uncertain' (2019: 129) when he looks the machine in the eye, conscious of both a 'clean divide' (2019: 129) between them and the familiarity of 'the same physical laws' (2019: 129).

Unlike Adam, the holograms in *Marjorie Prime* have been deliberately created as imitations of people familiar to the living characters. Though these same characters comment on their looks and responses, there is no clear suggestion that they are unnerved by seeing copies of their relations in a disembodied form. For the audience, however, the situation is different. Their status incrementally revealed through the dialogue, the Primes unsettle because they are so plausible, because, as Harrison says, we 'should be able to forget that they aren't real' ('Author's Note', Harrison 2016: 65). When we become aware of their artificiality through a stilted, unnatural remark or the slight ways in which substitution is communicated – indicated in stage directions like '*more smartly dressed and made up than before*' (2016: 35) and '*herself on a good day*' (2016: 54) – we are disturbed rather than reassured. This requires a subtle balance since exaggerating difference in performance, 'broadcasting their [the Primes'] inhumanness' ('Author's Note', 2016: 65) through overly mechanical movements and voice patterns, would defuse the play's necessary uncanniness, making it difficult to view the already vaguely conceived technology seriously. Indeed, the Primes move very infrequently – counter to Mori's claim about motion and its heightening of eeriness – their omnipresence and intangibility being sufficient to transmit their irreducible strangeness.

These divergent responses, those of the characters and those anticipated of an audience, are partly determined by Jordan Harrison's adoption of the science fiction mode, since what appears routine in the play's future actually treads 'a very fine line between the realistic and the marvellous' (Brewster 2017: 14), constituting 'cognitive estrangement' (2017: 14) to the audience/reader, and it is another instance of Freud's familiar/strange split. Brewster specifically locates cognitive estrangement within 'memory technics' (2017: 14) or any form of memory inscription, but it can equally have implications for future caregiving and, therefore, the status of nonhuman life forms. The use of machine technology in care scenarios is, of course, realistic. Various robots – anything from more conventional-looking androids with recognizably human torsos and limbs, to seals and other animals, to voice AIs and video screens controlled by smartphone apps – are routinely employed to carry out assistive tasks like cleaning and lifting, as well as to provide companionship and mental stimulation. In Harrison's future world, there is an unacknowledged tiering, a presumptive hierarchy of caregivers: the limitations of the Primes mean that a human nurse, the shadowy offstage Julie (another ghost in that she does not appear in the play) referred to several times by the characters, attends to Marjorie's physical needs. The choice of holograms, made both by consumers in the imagined world of the play and ultimately by Harrison, determines that at the highest, and presumably most expensive, level, care is verbal and intended to be visually affecting, not haptic. This is entirely consistent with the commonplace view that ageing and cognitive impairment are virtually inseparable, that retaining and even restoring memories perpetuating a nostalgic view of the subject's earlier life is crucial to well-being. Yet this does not mean that the concerns commonly voiced today – about the isolation, privacy and deception of both old and young people in their interactions with robots – do not apply.[5] Though, outwardly, she might not appear lonely, Marjorie spends sustained periods of time with what is essentially a projection, a being that offers only a semblance of physical presence. And while she understands the concept of the Primes and can distinguish a Prime from a human being, Marjorie cannot remember what she has told Walter or attribute significance to it, leaving her especially vulnerable to the ethical issues referred to above.

The play's denouement makes plain that the only material benefit the Primes have assuredly gained is the art of recycling stories, a narrative repertoire that Jon had hoped Marjorie would be able to use to preserve her selfhood. On account of the humans' absence, we assume that the Primes have outlasted their masters or that they have come to prefer each other's company. Either way, we do not witness the legacy of care that Tess speculated about earlier ('Like will Mitchell be talking to a Prime of me some day?', Harrison 2016: 49) or any sense of posthuman diversity. Nudging us much further into the future (*'centuries maybe'*, 2016: 59), part three invites not only the obvious question about whether the Primes have, in the intervening period, developed the ability to emote rather than just learn feelings but also whether they are/have become a species in their own right and not simply a tool/memory technic or ghostly echo amidst a depopulated planet.

Following Mark Coeckelbergh's argument that virtual robots/technology can be viewed or treated in the same way as embodied ones 'given a sufficient degree of immersion' (2011: 201), it seems clear by part three of *Marjorie Prime* that Harrison is still unsure about the Primes' precise status. The restatement of human exceptionality by Tess and then Jon – the realization that the Primes merely repeat rather than engage and so devalue their primary function as caregivers – is both undercut and reinforced. By now so faithful, the Primes' uncanny impersonation of humanness is initially *'not robotic'* (Harrison 2016: 59), their flow of speech being natural and collaborative, more so than it had been with their human interlocutors. But Harrison supplies a footnote in the printed text explaining that the three pauses indicated in the stage directions for this final scene are to be much longer than previous ones and 'far too long to be natural' (2016: 61). Moreover, there is no awkwardness betrayed by the speakers, who remain 'placid' (2016: 61) throughout the prolonged gaps. These silences, apparently normal to the Primes, have a by-now-familiar eeriness for the audience that is surely suggestive of those final stages of Marjorie's Alzheimer's that we do not witness. The inability of the Primes to respond with verbal spontaneity, to follow the unstated rules of social interaction, forces us back to the pejorative configuration of Alzheimer's as Gothic horror identified by Goldman, the ultimate imperfection of these human replicas implicitly reinscribing the regrettably dominant metaphor of the haunted, absent, even monstrous body living with the condition.

Like actors who have momentarily forgotten their lines or who are waiting for a cue, the Primes inadvertently signal their unreadiness to be humans, even after all the years that have passed since their initial programming. Perhaps they have become an imperfect memorial to humanity, vocalizers of autobiographical snippets once thought so integral to selfhood but now meaningless, still further out of context. Alternatively, perhaps their emergence from anthropocentrism has freed them from servitude – the burden of listening and assimilating. Either way, the play's last sentence, spoken by an already wistful Marjorie Prime, seems to convey a surprising sincerity, changing the original Marjorie's reported tribute to her husband into one to both human memories and humans themselves: 'How nice that we could love somebody' (Harrison 2016: 64).

Conclusion: Ghosting ourselves

Marjorie Prime is not so much a play about dementia as occasioned by it. In Jordan Harrison's future, there is still no prospect of a cure for a condition that continues to have a profound and far-reaching impact, and in a society that is even more guided by a hypercognitive imperative, care is centred on memory – its restimulation and reinstallation. In this obsession with recall and its imagined lifelines, the ghost of dementia persists, even after the passing of the only person living with it in the play: Marjorie. It is joined, though, by the spectral images we create and summon to offset our increasingly angst-ridden and isolated lives, the buffers we place between ourselves and personal failure, and ultimately extinction. The Primes, part of the 'spook-house' (Savran 2000: 583) of an industrialized world that has spawned 'new media and new industrial and social technologies … virtual realities, inspiring fear, and offering intimations of the sublime' (2000: 583), double our disquiet: our uncertainty over whether human networks can stem, or make more bearable, cognitive and physical decline, the sense that technology has become so sophisticated and arcane that few of us can understand, and therefore trust, its workings. Two of the several meanings of the word 'prime' – to prepare someone for a situation by supplying them with relevant information and to be of first importance – indicate the way in which the Primes' quiet succession, their presumed deposition of the humans, is an inevitability, programmed into their very pixels. Yet, this new species is configured ambivalently as hollow approximations of ourselves, voice boxes that keep our individual and shared pasts alive, machines given no point of termination that endlessly recycle stories in a timeless, denuded living-room made '*more spare somehow*' (Harrison 2016: 59).

In interview comments, Jordan Harrison has insisted on a more positive reading than this, pointing to the Primes' likely ability to continue to scrutinize the memory narratives they have already altered and supplemented. They are, he states, 'trying to be human' (George 2015), the proof being their ability to empathize beyond mere recitation. Whether we accept this or not – and I find the final exchanges between Walter and Marjorie Prime at best ambiguous – the ghostliness of the play (and film, 'creepy without being horrible', Erickson 2017: 52) persists, culminating with the reprise of Vivaldi's 'Winter', '*violins plucking high notes like icicles*' (Harrison 2016: 64). This is a fitting elegy, perhaps, for a family reduced to echoes in time – stand-ins on the haunted stage.

Notes

1 Given that Margaret is eighty-five and, we later find out, was born in 1977, we can work out that the play is set in 2062. There is no direct reference to this date, though.
2 In his review of the film adaptation, Steve Erickson talks about director Michael Almereyda's 'fondness for narrative ellipsis, particularly when deaths occur' (2017: 51).
3 See, for example, an article entitled 'Dementia and Music' on the Age UK website, https://www.ageuk.org.uk/information-advice/health-wellbeing/conditions-illnesses/dementia/dementia-and-music/ (accessed 30 June 2021).
4 Athena Helen McLean's (2006) study of a nursing-home resident, Mrs Fine, indicates that even when a person living with dementia re-stories part of her life to cope with trauma, she can maintain narrative coherence and preserve her identity.
5 Amanda and Noel Sharkey list 'six major issues that need to be considered before deploying robot technology fully in eldercare' (2012: 37).

References

Basting, A. D. (2009), *Forget Memory: Creating Better Lives for People with Dementia*, Baltimore: Johns Hopkins University Press.

Brantley, B. (2015), 'Review: In *Marjorie Prime*, Lois Smith Connects with the Past', *New York Times*, 14 December. Available online: https://www.nytimes.com/2015/12/15/theater/review-in-marjorie-prime-lois-smith-connects-with-the-past.html (accessed 30 June 2021).

Brewster, S. (2017), 'Performing Cognitive Estrangement: Future Memory Technics in Jordan Harrison's *Marjorie Prime*', *Foundation*, 46(128): 13–25.

Carlson, M. (2003), *The Haunted Stage: The Theatre as Memory Machine*, Ann Arbor: University of Michigan Press.

Coeckelbergh, M. (2011), 'Humans, Animals, and Robots: A Phenomenological Approach to Human-Robot Relations', *International Journal of Social Robotics*, 3(2): 197–204.

DeFalco, A. (2009), *Uncanny Subjects: Aging in Contemporary Narrative*, Columbus: Ohio State University Press.

Dunford, C. M. (2018), *Still Alice*, London: Samuel French.

Erickson, S. (2017), '*Marjorie Prime*', *Cineaste*, 43(1): 51–3.

Freud, S. (2003), *The Uncanny*, London: Penguin.

Fuchs, E. (2017), 'Dementia: The Theater Season's "In" Disease Part 1', *Theatre Times*, 16 January. Available online: https://thetheatretimes.com/dementia-theater-seasons-disease-part-1/ (accessed 18 January 2021).

George, M. (2015), 'The Future of the Past in Jordan Harrison's *Marjorie Prime*', *American Theatre*, 9 July. Available online: https://www.americantheatre.org/2015/07/09/the-future-of-the-past-in-jordan-harrisons-marjorie-prime/ (accessed 28 January 2021).

Goldman, M. (2017), *Forgotten: Narratives of Age-Related Dementia and Alzheimer's Disease in Canada*, Montreal: McGill-Queen's University Press.

Harrison, J. (2016), *Marjorie Prime*, London: Samuel French.

Harrison, J., A. Kauffman and B. Christian (2015), 'Playwrights Horizons: *Marjorie Prime* with Jordan Harrison', *Works & Process at the Guggenheim*, 9 November. Available online: https://www.youtube.com/watch?v=wyq5i9NJnis (accessed 30 January 2021).

Lonergan, K. (2000), *The Waverly Gallery*, New York: Grove.

McEwan, I. (2019), *Machines Like Me and People Like You*, London: Jonathan Cape.

McLean, A. H. (2006), 'Coherence without Facticity in Dementia: The Case of Mrs Fine', in A. Leibing and L. Cohen (eds), *Thinking about Dementia: Culture Loss, and the Anthropology of Senility*, 157–79, New Jersey: Rutgers University Press.

McNulty, C. (2014), 'Review: Playing with Memory in *Marjorie Prime*', *Los Angeles Times*, 22 September. Available online: https://www.latimes.com/entertainment/arts/la-et-0923-marjorie-prime-review-20140923-story.html (accessed 30 June 2021).

Mori, M. (2012), 'The Uncanny Valley', trans. K. F. MacDorman and N. Kageki, *IEEE Spectrum*, 19(2): 98–100.
Savran, D. (2000), 'The Haunted Houses of Modernity', *Modern Drama*, 43(4): 583–94.
Sharkey, A., and N. Sharkey (2012), 'Granny and the Robots: Ethical Issues in Robot Care for the Elderly', *Ethics and Information Technology*, 14(1): 27–40.
Turkle, S. (2017), *Alone Together: Why We Expect More from Technology and Less from Each Other*, New York: Basic Books.

9

A cure for ageing: Digital cloning as utopian end-of-life care in the 'San Junipero' episode of *Black Mirror*

Eszter Ureczky

Several recent feature films and television series have problematized the socio-psychological, biotechnological and bioethical aspects of the contemporary Western culture of healthism and rejuvenation. These works could be generically identified as clinical film dystopias and include texts like *Youth* (Paolo Sorrentino 2015), *A Cure for Wellness* (Gore Verbinski 2016), *I, Daniel Blake* (Ken Loach 2016), *The Father* (Florian Zeller 2020) and *I Care a Lot* (J. Blakeson 2020),[1] addressing what has been theorized as the twentieth- to twenty-first-century 'crisis of care'. Susan B. Phillips, for instance, claims that 'increasingly in the helping professions, personhood and caring have been eclipsed by the depersonalizing procedures of justice distribution, technological problem-solving, and the techniques and relations of the marketplace' (1996: 2), while Nancy Fraser defines the 'crisis of care' as 'a more or less acute expression of the social reproductive contradictions of financialized capitalism' (2016: 99). Most citizens of the Global North today live and die in medicalized, biopolitically monitored somatocracies, where old age, especially when it is accompanied by disability, qualifies as an economic and biological malfunction – a disease to be cured.[2]

It seems that the dominant 'period illness' (Spackman 1989: 5) of the twenty-first century can be paradoxically identified as health itself, that is, the ideology and practices of healthism and eternal youthfulness. Health as a *condition*, in both senses of the word as a state of being and a pathological process, in many ways appears to be the result of Western discourses on health and self-care in the past three centuries. As Michel Foucault points out, with the disappearance of bedside medicine and the 'sick man' after the eighteenth century, which was followed by the emergence of hospital medicine and the patient in the nineteenth century (1963: 17), new social frameworks of care and welfare came into being in the twentieth century. It seems that by the early twenty-first century the wellness hotel guest and the care-home resident have become crucial figures in the history of Western care systems. In literature, Thomas Mann's *The Magic Mountain* (first published in 1924) can be read as an early twentieth-century, seemingly utopian predecessor and mid-war hypotext of present-day clinical dystopias, as this novel depicts the institutional space of the hospital/sanatorium/hotel as the technological and medical space of care, connecting the lives of the characters amidst the modernist, capitalist craze of fast-paced production. But in the present late-modern era, almost a hundred years later, is the real or virtual space of the caring institution an escapist utopia of wellness and health or more a dystopia of chronic stagnation and death denial?

Black Mirror (2011–19), a dystopic British anthology TV series, addresses the ongoing social crisis of death denial and the prospect of eternal digital afterlife by projecting the controversial aspects of technological enhancement into the near future. As there is no consistent plot that continues from episode to episode, the series' individual stories are rather interconnected by their inherently dystopic and sci-fi themes, focusing on recurring bioethical questions. The episode 'San Junipero' (season 3, episode 4; Harris 2016) explores ageing, euthanasia and digital cloning, as well as the idea of digital consciousness. Moreover, 'San Junipero' combines its critique of present-day biopolitical practices concerning ageing with LGBTQIA love by depicting two older, institutionalized, terminally ill women who meet in the virtual reality of the utopian seaside resort called San Junipero and eventually decide to stay there together, up in the cloud, ever after. The episode puts special emphasis on both the somatic and spatial experiences of the couple's transition from life to death (i.e. eternal digital life) and from repressed homosexuality to a 'lived' queer experience, and thus, the concepts of passing through and coming out appear as doubly transgressive gestures, central to the dystopic logic of this critically acclaimed, Emmy-award-winning episode.

Lauded as '2016's most life-affirming piece of television' (Drage 2018: 62), 'San Junipero' also seems to be the 'most optimistic episode' (Daraiseh 2019: 151) of *Black Mirror*'s first five series, suggesting the ability of technology to not merely improve but also elevate human experience – a sharp contrast with the overwhelmingly dark tone of the rest of the series. But how do the already rather dystopic discourses of care and ageism transform into a utopia of disembodied, ever-lasting digital youthfulness and free love? Is the virtual reality of San Junipero the ultimate realization and celebration of post-human empowerment, self-care and agency, or a high-tech deferral of the 'crises' of care and ageing? In the era of 'time poverty' (Fraser 2016: 115) for most middle-class Global North citizens, where quality time and quality life appear to be basic yet unachievable human rights, do services like San Junipero mean that youth and bliss can and will have to be postponed to the timelessness of the afterlife? To offer a potential answer to these hypothetical questions, the chapter first contextualizes the episode as a representation of the current 'crisis of care' by relying on care ethics and age(ing) studies, then it examines the representation of end-of-life care in relation to digital cloning and finally it focuses on San Junipero as a virtual space of interracial queer utopia that potentially disguises the eerily dystopic dimensions of digital afterlife. In my reading, the parodistically picture-perfect happy ending of 'San Junipero' only seems to transcend the ideologies of ageism, ableism and heteronormativity, and even though it does contribute to queer visibility, it rather confirms the currently dominant visual regime of eroticized, youthful and healthy bodies.

The 'crisis of care' and the silvering screen

San Junipero as a technological service supporting end-of-life care (and afterlife care in the fictional universe of the episode, too) could also be understood as an emerging form of the long-standing tradition of institutional care in the West. Thus, it seems necessary to clarify what can be meant by the notion of care in an early twenty-first-century cultural context. By defining care, still often commonly described in a clichéd but telling manner as the 'labour of love', Dragojlovic and Broom see it as essentially a 'relational practice' and emphasize the intersubjective element of home care, in particular. They claim that 'relations of care need to be approached as assemblages of affective intensities of attention, love, compassion, tensions, discrepancies, contradictions, disappointment, loss, sadness, and (at times) psychological and physical harm' (Dragojlovic and Broom 2018: 154). However, care has become an increasingly institutionalized practice in late modernity, rewriting pre-existing notions of familial responsibility and emotional bonding. The field of care ethics today consequently aims at interpreting both home and institutional care as social-bioethical issues, as 'care ethics can and should offer a comprehensive account of both individual and political morality' (Slote 2007: xiii).

During the second half of the twentieth century, a major shift came about in the relationship of these two forms of care (home and institutional) in many countries of the Global North due to the development of the welfare state. Before the arrival of hospital medicine in the late nineteenth and early twentieth centuries, informal, family-level 'kin care' was the traditional, normalized framework of care. Current care practices are still largely rooted in the ethical insight that care is ideally a personalized, voluntary act, but it has also become a collective, demographically necessitated duty. While home care has never fully lost its morally (but not economically) valorized role, the increasing institutionalization, professionalization and marketization of care in the past decades have transformed it into a basic duty of the welfare state and a booming branch of business, despite significant differences in care funding and organization in different national and cultural contexts. Care is an inalienable part of the 'foundational economy', the essential services on which day-to-day life depends, both material and social (Bunting 2020: 227). Thus, the phenomenon of the 'crisis of care' as the central bioethical dilemma lurking behind the romantic plot of 'San Junipero' and a part of the global phenomenon characterized as the 'greying of societies' uncovers elementary questions about contemporary challenges of human rights and citizen rights.

While there have been several calls 'to de-institutionalise care' recently, the fictional world of 'San Junipero' focuses on several impressive, yet disturbing aspects of the future of high-tech institutional care that can also be understood as the extreme and/or logical outcome of current neoliberal processes. The episode provides several panoramic shots of the protagonists' respective nursing homes, which are located in rural, scenic settings but are still equipped with cutting-edge medical infrastructure – suggesting that this level of care might not be affordable for just anyone, even though the episode does not make any references to the protagonists' class standing as opposed to their race, gender and age signifiers. The above-mentioned neoliberal processes are currently 'changing market relations, changing the role of the state and [placing] an increasing emphasis on individual responsibility' (Dragojlovic and Broom 2018: 2); that is neoliberalism changes the state and market relationship and leads to the extension of competitive markets. While citizenship today means having access to certain central resources, such as economic security, health and education, where 'a person's right exists irrespective of their standing in the market' (Neysmith 2003: 13), the growing responsibilization of the individual and the privatization of risk threaten this ideal of citizenship. As a result, the current frameworks of care offer citizens a previously unknown freedom of choice while also putting an unparalleled amount of pressure on them to make the 'right' choice in the end, as the life and death questions of the episode demonstrate. In 'San Junipero', Kelly, who has terminal cancer, has to choose between dying 'naturally' in the care home or passing through to San Junipero and staying there with Yorkie forever. Visually, the moral as well as emotional weight of this decision is symbolized by two shots appearing in the middle and near the end of the episode. When we see the old, ill Kelly for the first time, we see a close-up of the extended hand of her nurse helping her climb the stairs of the 'assisted living' institution she is a resident of in the state of Nevada. At the end, when she is about to choose to stay in San Junipero, we see Yorkie similarly extending her hand to Kelly after a car accident in the virtual reality, where such injuries come without any physical pain or wounds. Thus, the episode shows the viewer that Kelly accepts both kinds of care, institutional and personal, but eventually chooses the virtual touch of her lover, not the 'real' support of her flesh-and-blood professional caretaker.

Earlier in the episode, Kelly also has an argument with Wes, a clingy man she has briefly hooked up with in a San Junipero bar called Tucker's, and the man tries to reassure her that what he wants from her is real romance and not to 'put us in a retirement home deal', suspecting that Kelly dislikes conventional, business-like and institutional forms of care, where the individual, in a consumerist fashion, can simply choose to use a service from the market – which, in the case of San Junipero, ultimately means becoming digitally disembodied. In this respect, the episode asks important questions about citizenship, consumerism and personal as well as collective rights when it comes to end-of-life care and care for the disabled older body. It interrogates the idea of personal responsibility for one's own quality of life: 'the notion of "quality-of-life" was traditionally used to measure environmental conditions that either improved or impaired the quality of a person's life. ... Now, rather than measuring conditions that improve life, the notion of quality-of-life has increasingly come to signify the very worth of a person's life' (Paterson 2008: 106). If the changing notion of quality of life increasingly decides the very worth of a person's life, one could argue that caring services like San Junipero also foreground the biopolitics of ageing in greying societies.

This focus on ageing sheds light on a real-life sociological issue, as in the twenty-first century, 'demographers estimate that, worldwide, by 2050, one out of five persons will be over 60' (Neysmith 2003: 3). Care and ageing are closely connected in the episode, refuting several traditional stereotypes of ageing as an unavoidable descent into helplessness, pain and death. In reaction to the unquestionable social reality of global ageing, 'San Junipero' offers both an affirmative and a darker reading of old age, just as contemporary cultural and social narratives of ageing show radically divergent approaches to the question. On the one hand, we can talk about 'the abjection of old age' interpreting the process of ageing as a universal, non-reversible process of decline, where 'old people are simply "in the way", excessive or illegible within contemporary society' (Chivers 2011: 8). Today, old age and disability increasingly qualify as a threat to the ethos of the sexually and economically productive individual as the model self of modernity and late capitalism, sometimes leading to the social isolation and dehumanizing treatment of older people in care homes. The very fact that both protagonists live in remote institutions seems to confirm this view: the segregation and pathologizing of the old. According to the predominantly capitalistic logic of late modernity, older people are expendable as they are biologically and economically unproductive yet need an increasing amount of care due to generally improving life expectancies. However, the same capitalistic logic can also recognize them as the ideal consumers and target population of life-enhancing products and services, usually meant to make intersubjective care unnecessary and keep them as self-reliant (which often simply translates into lonely) as possible. This double-edged cultural narrative of ageing calls for action in the sense that 'old age' requires disability to be 'legible within an "efficient" capitalist society' (Chivers 2011: 8), and the episode does contribute to this visual legibility and social discourse of old-age disability by showing the physical and emotional struggles of the protagonists (Kelly has cancer; Yorkie is quadriplegic). However, the episode also makes the often demonized and underrated system of institutional care somewhat likeable, as it markedly humanizes care home workers, too, by depicting them as kind, caring individuals. Greg, Yorkie's committed, emotionally invested male nurse, is willing to marry her to make euthanasia a legally available option for her, while Kelly's nurse, who remains unnamed, appears as a serene, patient but less three-dimensional and somewhat blank presence by her side, more like a perfect nursing robot than a real caring companion.

We can also witness, however, the paradigm of 'successful ageing' (Gilleard and Higgs 2013: 80) today, propagating 'the busy ethic' of the third age (2013: 46). In this paradigm, where old age is 'no longer viewed as a process through which the subject becomes an object to be managed by others, bodily ageing has emerged as (another) arena for self-care, for lifestyle fashioning' (2013: xi). Moreover, there is a phenomenon identified as the 'silver tsunami' (Ciafone 2017: 165) taking place in Western societies in business, health care and public policy today. The increasing number of films addressing such questions are identified by Chivers as the 'silvering screen' (Chivers 2011: xvi), a process she interprets as a positive one in terms of increasing the general cultural visibility of older people. But is 'San Junipero' also silvering the screen? Is it actually making old age and its implications more visible and culturally legible? Considering the screen time of the young and the older versions of the protagonists, it does not seem to do that at all: in the sixty-minute episode, the older Yorkie and Kelly get about ten minutes of screen time only. Their older, present selves appear only thirty-nine minutes into the show, and the extended end scene features their younger avatars in the virtual reality. If, in contemporary Global North consumerism, 'first and most publicly evident is the use made of and engagement with "anti-ageing" consumerism and the "pursuit of somatic enhancement"' (Gilleard and Higgs 2013: 45), San Junipero can be interpreted as an extreme form of somatic enhancement – precisely on account of getting rid of the failing, ailing physical body and perpetually simulating an incorruptible, customizable, virtual one instead. What Catherine Mills identifies as 'the contemporary neoliberal and biopolitical order of able-nationalism' (2018: 175) is thus also reproduced by the episode's depiction of exclusively young and healthy, sexual bodies in its utopian virtual reality.

Euthanasia as digital cloning

'San Junipero' seems to construct an intentionally questionable utopia of pro-death choice, where the characters appear to be in full control of their end-of-life decisions, but the story also implies that there is a spiritual emptiness behind the technological genius of the system. In this sense, the episode's treatment of death also epitomizes the history and denial of death in today's Western culture. As Ariés argues, after the Middle Ages, death 'became a place where the individual traits of each life, of each biography, appeared in the bright light of the clear conscience, a place where everything was weighed, counted, written down, where everything could be changed, lost, or saved', while in the modern period, especially after the eighteenth century, 'death became the unaccepted separation' and in the nineteenth century 'became unnameable' (1974: 105–6), and today we are facing the 'the cruelty of solitary death' (1974: 102). Hans Georg Gadamer similarly talks about 'an almost systematic repression of death' (1996: 63), and Norbert Elias argues that 'never before in the history of humanity have the dying been removed so hygienically behind the scenes of social life' (2001: 23). Since 'in the developed world, death is now very largely in the province of old age and this in turn has changed, in an equally dramatic way, the ways in which societies provide for and attach meanings to the end of life' (Seale 2005: 378), the episode's joint depiction of chronic/terminal illness and old age is central to its treatment of the bioethical dilemmas concerning institutional forms of care and death in the age of digital cloning. End-of-life decisions and ageing are also a joint dilemma in today's societies, because 'the shift from infectious to degenerative disease involves a lengthening of dying trajectories' (Seale 2005: 378), as Kelly's extended struggle with cancer and Yorkie's long-term quadriplegic condition in the episode both show.

In 'San Junipero', the signs of modern death denial are apparent. No one (neither staff nor patients) even uses the word 'death', except for the scene when Kelly tells Greg, Yorkie's nurse, that they should call the passing through dying, but Greg immediately corrects her by saying, 'if you can call it dying'. Moreover, all the phenomena connected to death are also described euphemistically: the care home where Kelly lives is described as 'assisted living', and San Junipero itself is advertised as 'immersive nostalgia therapy' for residents, as opposed to 'full-timers', those who have actually died and decided to get their consciousness digitally cloned and uploaded to the virtual reality. The non-dead visitors of the virtual city are called 'tourists', who can have a 'trial run', while someone waiting for euthanasia is 'scheduled to pass', and finally, the message 'all systems suspended' on the screens means the actual death of the patient's biological body, suggesting a kind of temporariness to this event. Moreover, the fact that the choice residents can make is merely a digital one makes the solution especially bittersweet, as at the end of the episode, the celebratory soundtrack contrasts with the large, sinister rooms of computers where the chips are connected – called TCK Systems, evoking the name of Tucker's bar in San Junipero. Ultimately, 'San Junipero' seems to represent passing through to the digital afterlife as a consumer choice for Kelly and Yorkie rather than the satisfying of an anthropological, spiritual need or a fulfilling psychological compensation for ageing, illness and death in the era of medicalized, hygienic end-of life care and death denial.

At the same time, the highly understated language and lavish virtual spaces of 'San Junipero' can also be read in a more progressive way as a means of futuristic palliative care, which is meant to alleviate physical and psychological suffering, not to prevent, treat or cure death. What Catherine Mills calls the 'immortality imperative in modern medical sciences' often goes against the principle of 'right to die' and 'assisted dying', where death is but 'a symptom of techno-scientific failure' (2018: 127).[3] According to the World Health Organization, 'palliative medicine attends to the assessment and treatment of pain and other problems, physical, psychosocial and spiritual' (Morris 2017: 130), and in this respect, San

Junipero might be interpreted as the perfect form of palliative care, which can at least virtually extend healthy life expectancy as opposed to disability-adjusted life expectancy (Seale 2005: 379). The etymology of the word 'palliative' is telling as well: 'the Latin root *palla* does refer to an outer cloak or covering, but cloaks in earlier eras – before sidewalks and paved roads – had a job to do: offering protection against the assault of dirt, mud, rain, and sleet. Palliative medicine might be described as protecting patients against the assault of symptoms' (Morris 2017: 130). The virtual reality of San Junipero in this sense is a part of care, not cure, insofar as the nostalgia therapy literally takes patients' minds off their physical bodies, covering up their suffering by creating a transitory, protective phase between embodiment and the disembodied afterlife they might choose.

But San Junipero is not only represented in the episode as a means of end-of-life or palliative care but also connected to the controversial issue of voluntary active euthanasia in the case of both protagonists. On the one hand, this practice can be a way to 'embrace assisted death as justified killing, a form of taking ownership for one's death' (Bishop 2011: 198). However, some critics are suspicious about cinematic depictions of disabled characters practising their right to euthanasia and claim that 'films such as *Million Dollar Baby* and *Mar Adentro* implicitly promote euthanasia for the disabled' (Bishop 2011: 10). Kelly and Yorkie, even though they end up making the same choice (undergoing euthanasia and becoming full-time residents of San Junipero), embody two different narratives of illness and euthanasia. Kelly is terminally ill with metastatic cancer and obviously in growing, debilitating physical pain; in her case the episode seems to suggest that it is relatively easier to refute the argument against euthanasia, 'the view that life is a "super good" that must be preserved at all costs' (Paterson 2008: 108). Nevertheless, Kelly's initial view of death is that 'when I'm done, I'm done'; she does not want to enjoy the digital pleasures of San Junipero as her late husband and daughter could not make or did not have that choice. Nevertheless, the issues of consent and social pressures remain relevant factors in her final decision, as the episode seems to emphasize. That is Kelly seems to make a fully informed and considered decision, driven by her own agency and choice.

In contrast, Yorkie's agency is fully technologized due to her long-term comatose condition (she had a car crash forty years before, at the age of twenty). On the one hand, Greg explains to Kelly that he and Yorkie talk 'through the comm box', which means that Yorkie can communicate with the help of a technological device, translating her thoughts into readable messages for the outside world, and thus, her technology-dependent agency empowers her to connect with the outside world. On the other hand, Greg also tells Kelly that if Yorkie wants to request euthanasia, then a 'triple sign-off' is needed from a doctor, the patient and a family member as there is 'triple lockdown on euthanasia' in the state of California, where her care home is located. Thus, her agency is not accepted in this biopolitical matter as a reliable source of end-of-life decisions. Yorkie's privacy in relation to her agency is also problematized by the scene where in the hospital cafeteria Greg casually tells Kelly Yorkie's background story about her teenage suicide attempt and car accident after coming out to her family and being rejected for her Otherness. At that point in the story, Yorkie has not told Kelly this herself in their conversations in San Junipero. Despite the two protagonists' radically different motivations, the episode suggests an overall pro-euthanasia approach, where this practice is a normalized part of end-of-life care and self-care, maybe even the ultimate form of death with dignity.

While the whole *Black Mirror* series can be interpreted within a sinister bioethical framework – the episodes 'existing both as philosophical thought experiments and as socially conservative, technophobic cautionary tales, these texts serve a distinct political agenda when invoked in bioethics literature' (Kendal 2015: 90) – the issues of digital cloning and euthanasia as basic bioethical problems are handled quite differently in the various episodes. Digital cloning is a recurring motif of all *Black Mirror* seasons with a somewhat didactic, morally charged, awareness-raising purpose, unlike euthanasia, which is not specifically discussed in any other episode. There is, moreover, a major difference between the episodes' addressing of the issue of digital copies:

> In all episodes featuring cookies [a small file that is sent by a website to your computer and that contains information about how you use the site, so that this information is available the next time you use the site], with the possible exception of 'San Junipero' and 'Black Museum', the cookie is a digital double rather than a digital transference or extension of the physical self, and thus its experience is not a direct continuation of the experience of the original, who must still eventually die'. (Carden 2021: 145)

'San Junipero' does appear to be an exception within the *Black Mirror* universe in terms of the problem of the double as well, as in most episodes featuring a digital double, the copy is a repetition of the original, often serving as a means of torture or punishment, a secular, high-tech private hell, while the original survives and sometimes remains unaware of the existence of the copy. In 'San Junipero', however, digital cloning only temporarily coexists with the biological life form of the original, emphasizing the act of voluntary transitioning between the two, based on an informed decision. 'San Junipero' thus shows these issues up in their larger context of transhumanism, which 'seeks to advance humanity by integrating humans with technology through self-directed evolution that effectively creates computer-human hybrids, offer[ing] the most significant debate on the role of technology with regard to mortality' (Perez 2020: 306). By problematizing the significance of the flesh-and-blood human body in these matters, 'San Junipero' depicts the current problem of embodiment being increasingly separated from the notion of self-identity.

This hybridity of humanity and technology is primarily connected to the episode's representation of personhood and the essential split involved in computer-based somatic enhancement devices. In the scene where we witness Kelly's burial and her subsequent re-emergence as now a full-time resident of San Junipero, 'this duo of graveyards can be interpreted as the ultimate realization of a Cartesian mind-body dialectic, the achievement of the masculinist fantasy of control over the self, the separation of extended, imperfect body from the infinite, disembodied and unextended mind' (Drage 2018: 70). When Kelly tells the suicidal Yorkie in the virtual reality that she hopes her 'pain slider is set to zero', or when she says 'sorry for killing you' in their first scene together, as she is trying to get rid of Wes and lies that she has to talk to Yorkie as she has only six months to live, she ironically emphasizes the split nature of body and mind in the San Junipero experience. Also, when Kelly discusses the situation with Greg, she explains that time in San Junipero is rationed out for patients, as there is a risk that 'you dissociate body from mind', and she sarcastically adds, 'like that doesn't happen in every senior home already'. Kelly here voices her own anxieties about ageing and digital consciousness through common stereotypes about old age and also the institutional explanation for the limits set on patients' usage of the system. Namely, that it might cause addiction and the long-term damaging of the unity of body and mind – which proves that the Cartesian duality of body and mind is still regarded as the dominant norm of humanity in the 'real' world of the episode outside of San Junipero. The virtual reality implies the denial of the physical body through technological means – with the mind seen as the location of identity – but once they leave San Junipero, they are back to a world where they are still primarily treated and cared for as physical bodies, as patients, not as cookies. Kelly's comment is thus a kind of metafictional or self-reflexive one that draws attention to the issue at the heart of digital cloning.

Technology appears to kill and separate as well as bind and perpetuate bodies and subjectivities in the episode. The whole show includes several subtle visual allusions to the Cartesian split between the mind/body or body/subjectivity along with doubleness. For example, the opening image features the city lights of San Junipero being reflected on the rippling waves of the sea, producing a necessarily distorted version of the 'original', which is of course just a simulation of a real beach. A few seconds later we see Yorkie's glasses also reflecting the street lights of the virtual city. Yorkie later admits to Kelly that 'the lenses don't do anything' and they are just a 'comfort thing', so the glasses are yet another illusion, symbolizing the freedom of choice and doubling. Furthermore, the glasses are the first thing Kelly notices and likes about Yorkie, saying, 'You're authentically you' – an example of dramatic irony as Kelly at this point can have no idea of the authentic Yorkie. Yorkie's avatar also steps into a puddle during her first visit to San Junipero, which shows a muddled reflection of the moon – a heavenly body without its own light, only reflecting back the light of the sun, and thus known as an age-old symbol of illusions, irrationality and femininity. It is also Yorkie who looks at a shop window, yet another reflective surface, and the TV screen within says, 'Could you please stop it? I just wanna have some fun!', which foreshadows Yorkie's anxieties about sexuality and embodiment. Kelly is also consistently associated with images of doubleness in the episode: when she is upset after her first fight with Yorkie, she smashes the bathroom mirror in the bar toilet but immediately notices that no blood on her hand or crack in the mirror (the logo of the whole series) is visible – her body and the world around her are equally unreal and thus without any real material or moral stakes. Last but not least, a shy man who wants to pick Yorkie up by the video games arcade describes one of the games as having 'two different endings', just like their own life stories, depending on their afterlife choices.

Images of doubles and reflections are ultimately a metaphor or even mastertrope of the whole series: 'Throughout the *Black Mirror* series, the mirror often materializes as a metaphor for disciplinary power (such as in "Nosedive") and punishment (such as in "White Bear"); however, in "San Junipero", the mirror emblemizes emancipation from the limits of the human body and from the judgment of society' (Constant 2018: 353). On the whole, the central bioethical message of 'San Junipero' seems to be that technology is capable of creating the illusion of intersubjective bonds all too perfectly, even without the involvement of the material body, offering this experience as a compensation for the loss of 'real' tactile connections and at the same time disturbingly calling the authenticity and reliability of our biological, 'lived', material somatic reality as the foundation of the self into question – leaving behind the duality of the body and mind as the sources of subjectivity and locating the source of humanity in the potentially disembodied, free-floating consciousness of the already-dead but still-consuming client.

Spaces of queer utopia

In his essay 'Of Other Spaces', Foucault identifies the space of the cemetery as the heterotopic Other City (1984: 6), especially when it was moved from the churchyard to the margins of the city at the beginning of modernity and with the spread of industrialization and urbanization. Following this train of thought, the digitally doubled virtual reality of San Junipero can be read as a post-human cemetery, which is moving the dead not to the margins of the city per se but to a digital city on the margins of human consciousness. The space of this city, which could be discussed as a utopia, dystopia or heterotopia of digital afterlife, is strongly determined by the fact that the episode is a queer love story with a happy ending. I believe Gilleard and Higgs's insight is crucial here, as according to them, gender studies, critical race theory, disability studies and queer theory 'have all struggled with the contradictions that arise from rejecting the biological essentialism that dominated the categorical thinking of classical modernity, while seeming to replace it with an equally unsustainable cultural essentialism that treats the body's corporeality as a source for unreal yet highly referential signs and signifiers' (2013: 2). By relying on this insight, the final section of the chapter focuses on the genre- and gender-related questions of the episode, claiming that even though San Junipero, the 'party town', as Kelly puts it early on in the episode, could be superficially read as a gay utopia, finally providing a story of a lived and happy queer (and interracial) relationship, it is still a dystopic deferral of queer desire rather than a dystopic deferral of biopsychosocial totalitarianism. In the light of the whole episode, the romantic aspect of the story appears to be intentionally idealized in its depiction, cloning and thus exposing the empty clichés of the heterosexual Hollywood happy ending.

The notion of utopia is defined by Gordin as 'places of future or distant past' (2010: 4), while dystopia 'bears the aspect of lived experience' (2010: 2) – but as most critics agree, fictional worlds are usually both, just like San Junipero. In the scene when Yorkie and Kelly are having their big fight and Yorkie is desperately trying to convince Kelly to become a full-timer and join her in San Junipero for good, Kelly argues that she cannot do so as her late husband and disabled daughter did not have a similar chance. 'I believe they are nowhere',

Kelly says desperately to explain her initial refusal to join San Junipero for ever, suggesting that the city is a utopian non-place and as such not really the alternative to the actual nothingness of 'traditional' death her own family chose. According to Daraiseh, there are 'both utopian and dystopian energies, placed in dialectical opposition even within the episode' (2019: 153), which complicates the common reading of this episode as the only optimistic *Black Mirror* story. While Daraiseh also claims that 'San Junipero' 'seems primarily to be a utopian exploration of the potential of technology to create a post-human future that is better than our present and possibly even more authentically human' (2019: 156), the episode does more than that in depicting the hidden risks of such a post-human world, and San Junipero can primarily be read as a heterotopic space within the dystopic world of the episode. According to Constant's reading of *Black Mirror*, 'heterotopia is a mirroring site of both utopia and dystopia' (2018: 357), and there are four planes to it: 'topos: everyday life (normal-real), heterotopia: retirement and rest homes (other-real), mirror: server room (heterotopia-utopia), and San Junipero (other-real) – a heterotopia inside another heterotopia, formed when the dichotomy between real and unreal space collapses when Yorkie and Kelly's bodies are no longer split by the mirror' (2018: 363). San Junipero as a nostalgic digital space of old-age heterotopia, with its own inner rules, is an externalized and objectified image of contemporary death anxiety and death denial, an attempt to reassuringly contain and distance the experience of death, and as such, it can be identified as a heterotopic city of the (digitally) living dead.

The urban spaces and natural landscapes of San Junipero seem to underline this point. The metaphorical landscapes of old age have often been imagined as either unknown or dark: 'in a manner reminiscent of Victorian exploration, social researchers have characterised the sociology of later life as uncharted territory awaiting their discovery – a dark continent like Victorian Africa' (Blaikie 2005: 165), a symbolic landscape with a powerful metaphorical association between chronology, place and space. If there is any dynamism in this metaphorical landscape, it is typically a downward spiral: 'life is pictured as the journey of life; the life course is seen as a river, taking many bends and turns; life stages are pictured as a flight of steps ascending towards the zenith of early adulthood, levelling out, then descending after retirement; our days become a downhill slalom ride' (2005: 164). As opposed to this, the previously mentioned opening image of 'San Junipero' offers a close-up of the waves of the sea, which, apart from producing a necessarily distorted version of the 'original', may also evoke the waters of Lethe, the Greek mythological site of forgetting, death, the non-place of non-identity, and this immediately signifies how the episode sets out to move beyond traditional boundaries of decline and progress. But the city's name is also a part of this metaphorical realm, evoking conventional metaphors of ageing despite its visual originality: 'the town is presumably named after Saint Juniper, a Franciscan priest who is said to have given a meal of trotters to a dying man. Like Juniper, San Junipero grants the moribund one last request: to be young again' (Cook 2020: 116). The episode thus does not cinematically evoke the conventional visual metaphors of ageing, but it does capitalize on escapist, nostalgic images of youth. Overall, it both employs and rejects conventional metaphors of ageing.

Parallel with the problem of space, the representation of time in the episode is central to the understanding of San Junipero as a virtual reality, as Yorkie and Kelly move through the nostalgically rendered pop culture of the twentieth century from the 1970s to the early 2000s. The protagonists' attitudes towards technology also become a means of characterization, as the socially awkward Yorkie is immediately attracted to technology, the arcade in the bar, while Kelly is all about the 'party town' experience. The indoor scenes of the bar feature a game arcade, a nostalgic reminder from the very real 1980s, the heyday of late capitalism and the increasing routinization of life in the United States, as 'virtual reality, like dystopian thinking, was part of the zeitgeist of the Reagan-Thatcher 1980s' (Daraiseh 2019: 154). The arcade with the games which 'got different endings' also serves a 'metafictional function' (2019: 156), the forerunner of later technology, especially Multi-Player Online Role Playing Games. This postmodern, self-reflexive gesture is all the more important as Fredric Jameson defines postmodernism as the cultural logic of late capitalism, featuring 'an enfeebling of the ability to imagine alternatives to capitalism' (2019: 160). The episode itself is strongly self-reflexive and metafictional and critically interrogates the historical past. When it comes to the 1980s as the dominant historical backdrop to the story and how they consciously planned 'a retro episode' (Brooker and Jones 2018: 257), director Owen Harris describes the setting as follows: 'it was the 80s setting that excited me. If you look back to a lot of films from that decade … the mood was far more optimistic, almost to the point where you could classify it as a genre. The genre of eternal optimism! *Black Mirror* comes from a background of satire, which is by nature somewhat cynical' (2018: 261). As San Junipero scenes are predominantly set in the 1980s, it seems that this is the decade preferred by most visitors as their ideal retro period of eternal youth and love. It is strange, however, that there is absolutely no mention of the AIDS pandemic in this era, which initially struck the gay community; the repression of AIDS death is thus yet another layer of general death denial in the episode.

Within this nostalgic utopia and/or escapist dystopia, the fact that the protagonists are a same-sex couple appears to be crucial, even though Brooker and Jones deny this: 'at some point, the thought arrived of making this a same sex couple. Rather than that feeling like a gimmick, it became both relevant and irrelevant to the story' (2018: 260). Mackenzie Davis, the actress playing Yorkie, admits that 'the reception of the episode has been such an education on my own blind spots as a straight white woman' (2018: 278). The episode's treatment of medical and sexual taboos (euthanasia and homosexuality) thus appears to be equally important. Benjamin Noys starts his book *The Culture of Death* by drawing a parallel between the sexual liberation of the 1960s, which challenged the taboos around sex, and the 1990s, the era of death liberation (2005: 1). These two types of liberation, queer love and death denial, thus chronologically followed each other in real life in the second half of the twentieth century. It is true that 'the show radically upends the "Bury Your Gays" trope' (Drage 2018: 62), that is, the representational tradition that gay characters tend to die or be unhappy in mainstream cinema. However, when Kelly says about her lifelong bisexual urges that she 'never acted on any of it', she speaks for a generation of closeted lesbians. Yorkie is also anxious about 'two girls dancing' and others watching and potentially judging this. A further irony is that the pop song 'Girlfriend in Coma' can refer to the transforming geek Yorkie, her dis/ability and affective rebirth in death, as well as to Kelly's repression of her own queerness. Ultimately, the biggest achievement of the episode seems to be the 'queering of death' (2018: 62), the linking of the bioethical dilemmas of later-life decisions to the exploration of queer identity. Kelly and Yorkie do get their happily ever after as they drive off in their scarlet red sports car in the seaside sunset; still, the ending is so blatantly happy that one cannot read it but ironically: the gays are now only biologically buried and even married – we even hear the line of the wedding vows when they say 'in sickness and in health' – but can share a life together only when they are on the other side of material reality.

The episode, furthermore, does not only queer death but also represents ageing lesbian love, a highly underrepresented theme both in film and TV, and seems to offer an affirmative narrative for both women's experience of their sexualities. In this sense, the bigger taboo in the fictional world of the episode and in the cultural environment of viewers still appears to be not gay love but later-life sexuality.[4] In Western modernity, 'old age appeared white like winter, drooped like a dying flower, shriven like rotten fruit' (Gilleard and Higgs

2013: 23), and these images also imply withered sexual appetites. The 'gendered double standard of ageing' (Liddy 2017: 170) includes the unwatchability of sexual, eroticized, naked older women, while sexually active older men are more prevalent in both popular and high culture. Even if older female characters are depicted as sexual beings in mainstream visual culture, 'the characters are all white, middle-class, slim women, and sexual relations are still expressed within committed, romanticised and heterosexual relationships' (Liddy 2017: 177). The show consequently appears to be complicit in the consistent youthing of sexuality, even if it does challenge heteronormativity. Although the episode thematizes the questions of both lesbian and later-life sexuality jointly, it represents them only in an essentially split fashion: the coming out takes place, but only the young characters are shown as actively sexual beings.[5] This point can also be supported by the fact that the only example of intimacy we see between the old characters is a kiss on the forehead and a touching of the hands, both of which could be merely friendly gestures, suggesting that old-age sexuality, especially when it is a queer one, is still a taboo sight even in a dystopian series that is famous for hitting all the neuralgic spots of present-day cultural anxieties. In the brave new world of San Junipero, being openly gay is normalized, but not even in the utopia of eternal digital life is it acceptable to look old and still be sexually active. If the 1960s broke the queer taboo and the 1990s the death taboo, the early twenty-first century might bring about the liberation of old-age desire – but not in 'San Junipero'.

Conclusion

At the end of his seminal book on the cultural history of death in the West, Philippe Ariés asks whether it is 'impossible for our technological cultures ever to regain the naïve confidence in Destiny which had for so long been shown by simple men when dying' (1974: 107). Since 1974, the first publication of this book, technological cultures and biomedicine seem to have developed a similarly naïve faith not in destiny but in eternal life through the timelessness and disembodied nature of digitalization, even though there is increasing scepticism around this. While the main dilemma of the late twentieth century was the medicalization and desacralization of death, the early twenty-first century is about to face a crisis posed by the potential digitalization of passing through. But does this mean the perpetuation of the loss of humankind's spiritual relationship with death or the threshold of a new era of the 'soul's' afterlife?

In his last, posthumously published work, *The Agony of Power* (2010), Jean Baudrillard prophetically writes the following about current systems of welfare and care: 'we are not succumbing to oppression or exploitation, but to profusion and unconditional care. From there, revolt has a different meaning: it no longer targets the forbidden, but permissiveness, tolerance, excessive transparency – the Empire of Good. For better or worse. Now you must fight against everything that wants to help you' (2010: 88). This eerie early-twenty-first-century, beyond-the-grave bioethical warning seems to epitomize all the allures and threats of technological enhancement represented by the episodes of *Black Mirror*. As I am finalizing this conclusion, news has just come out about Microsoft releasing a chatbot which can impersonate deceased people, and this new product is already being advertised as 'a Black Mirror episode come true', while a scandal has recently broken out about a university student accidentally finding out that an online course he took consisted of the digitalized lectures of a deceased professor.

While the mistake of making technology or even art responsible for the social ills they represent has been often committed in the reception of dystopic genres, the dialogues such works create concerning burning bioethical dilemmas are unquestionably necessary and constructive. What does it eventually mean to be a citizen of San Junipero? On the one hand, the narrative of 'San Junipero' appears to be a novel way of moving beyond the ideologies of ageism, ableism and heteronormativity, where older, ill or queer people are often denied social and representational space. Near the end of the episode, when a desperate (and already 'passed over') Yorkie tries to convince Kelly to join her in the virtual reality, she passionately argues that 'it's not a trap' – but can we watch Yorkie here as a reliable narrator of her own digitally cloned life story? The intentionally clichéd and metafictional final scene of the episode, when Yorkie and Kelly drive off into the beach sunset in a scarlet red sports car, is rather a parody than a pastiche of the mainstream (straight, white, healthy, young) Hollywood happy ending and ultimately leaves the viewer suspicious of its progressive representational strategy precisely by calling into question the very idea of a meaningful ending.

Notes

Supported by the ÚNKP-20–04 New National Excellence Program of the Ministry for Innovation and Technology from the source of the National Research, Development and Innovation Fund.

1 Other related films on the topic, with special emphasis on the space of the hospital/sanatorium, are *The Road to Wellville* (Alan Parker, 1994), *Hotel Splendide* (Terence Gross, 2000) and *From the Land of the Moon* (Nicole Garcia, 2016). For a comparative study including Eastern European clinical film dystopias, see Ureczky (2018).
2 This idea can be traced back to Seneca's idea: 'senectus morbidus est', that is 'old age is disease' (Achenbaum 2005: 22).
3 Ezekiel Emanuel points out that euthanasia was widely accepted in ancient Greece and Rome, with physicians of the Hippocratic school being the exception. Frequently cited as well in histories of euthanasia is Renaissance English humanist Thomas More's (1478–1535) *Utopia* (1516), which describes 'the ideal hospital as a place where everything is done to cure those who can be cured, and to mitigate the pain of those who cannot be cured' (Thornber 2020: 403).
4 'Throughout the 1930s and 1940s, representations of mature women in American film were dominated by portrayals of motherhood, while female actors over sixty-five years primarily played minor characters such as wives and mothers or "lonely spinsters," projecting "images of decline" ' (Mills 2018: 168).
5 *Supernova* (Harry Macqueen, 2021) could be analysed as a counterexample, for it represents later-life sexuality, queer love, chronic illness as well as end-of-life decisions with staggering clarity, intimacy and complexity.

References

A Cure for Wellness (2016), [Film] Dir. G. Verbinski, USA, Germany: New Regency Productions, Blind Wink Productions.
Achenbaum, W. A. (2005), 'Ageing and Changing: International Historical Perspectives on Ageing', in M. L. Johnson (ed), *The Cambridge Handbook of Age and Ageing*, 21–9, Cambridge: Cambridge University Press.
Ariés, P. (1974), *Western Attitudes towards Death: From the Middle Ages to the Present*, London: Marion Boyars.
Baudrillard, J. (2010), *The Agony of Power*, Los Angeles: Semiotext(e).
Bishop, J. P. (2011), *The Anticipatory Corpse: Medicine, Power, and the Care of the Dying*, Notre Dame: University of Notre Dame Press.
Black Mirror (2011–19), [TV series], Creator: Charlie Brooker, UK: Zeppotron, Channel 4 Television Corporation, Babieka.
Blaikie, A. (2005), 'Imagined Landscapes of Age and Identity', in G. J. Andrews and D. R. Phillips (eds), *Ageing and Place: Perspectives, Policy, Practice*, 165–75, Milton Park, UK: Routledge.
Brooker, C., and A. Jones (2018), 'San Junipero', in *Inside Black Mirror*, 253–79, London: Ebury.

Bunting, M. (2020), *Labours of Love: The Crisis of Care*, London: Granta.

Carden, C., and M. Gibson (2021), 'Living on beyond the Body: The Digital Soul of Black Mirror', in M. Gibson and C. Carden (eds), *The Moral Uncanny in Black Mirror*, 141–52, London: Palgrave Macmillan.

Chivers, S. (2011), *Old Age and Disability in Cinema*, Toronto: University of Toronto Press.

Ciafone, A. (2017), 'The Third Age in the Third World. Outsourcing and Outrunning Old Age to *The Best Exotic Marigold Hotel*', in S. Chivers and U. Kriebernegg (eds), *Care Home Stories. Aging, Disability, and Long-Term Residential Care*, 155–73, Bielefeld: Transcript.

Constant, S. J. (2018), 'Heterotopias and Utopias in Black Mirror', in A. M. Cirucci and B. Vacker (eds), *Black Mirror and Critical Media Theory*, 353–68, Minneapolis: Lexington Books.

Cook, J. (2020), 'San Junipero and the Digital Afterlife: Could Heaven be a Place on Earth?', in D. K. Johnson (ed.), *Black Mirror and Philosophy: Dark Reflections*, 109–17, Hoboken: Wiley Blackwell.

Daraiseh, I., and M. K. Booker (2019), 'Unreal City: Nostalgia, Authenticity, and Posthumanity in "San Junipero"', in T. McSweeney and S. Joy (eds), *Through the Black Mirror: Deconstructing the Side Effects of the Digital Age*, 151–64, London: Palgrave Macmillan.

Drage, E. (2018), 'A Virtual Ever-After', in A. M. Cirucci and B. Vacker (eds), *Black Mirror and Critical Media Theory*, 62–81, Minneapolis: Lexington Books.

Dragojlovic, A., and A. Broom (2018), *Bodies and Suffering: Emotions and Relations of Care*, Milton Park: Routledge.

Elias, N. (2001), *The Loneliness of the Dying*, New York: Continuum.

Foucault, M. (1963), *The Birth of the Clinic: An Archaeology of Medical Perception*, Milton Park: Routledge.

Foucault, M. (1984), 'Of Other Spaces', *Architecture/Mouvement/Continuité*, October: 1–9.

Fraser, N. (2016), 'Contradictions of Capital and Care', *New Left Review*, July/August: 99–117.

Gadamer, H.-G. (1996), *The Enigma of Health*, Stanford: Stanford University Press.

Gilleard, C., and P. Higgs (2013), *Ageing, Corporeality and Embodiment*, Kolkata: Anthem Press.

Gordin, M. D., H. Tilley and G. Prakash (2010), 'Introduction', in M. D. Gordin, H. Tilley and G. Prakash (eds), *Utopia/Dystopia: Conditions of Historical Possibility*, 1–20, Princeton: Princeton University Press.

I Care a Lot (2020) [Film] Dir. J Blakeson, UK, USA: Black Bear Pictures, Crimple Beck, STX Films.

I, Daniel Blake (2016), [Film] Dir. Ken Loach, UK, France, Belgium: Sixteen Films, Why Not Productions, Wild Bunch.

Kendal, E. (2015), 'Utopian Visions of "Making People": Science Fiction and Debates on Cloning, Ectogenesis, Genetic Engineering, and Genetic Discrimination', in P. Stapleton and A. Byers (eds), *Biopolitics and Utopia: An Interdisciplinary Reader*, 89–118, London: Palgrave Macmillan.

Liddy, S. (2017), 'Older Women and Sexuality On-Screen: Euphemism and Evasion?', in C. McGlynn, M. O'Neill and M. Schrage-Früh (eds), *Ageing Women in Literature and Visual Culture: Reflections, Refractions, Reimaginings*, 167–80, London: Palgrave Macmillan.

Mar Adentro (The Sea Inside) (2004), [Film] Dir. Alejandro Amenábar, Spain, France, Italy: Sogepaq, Sogecine, Himenóptero.

Million Dollar Baby (2004), [Film] Dir. Clint Eastwood, USA: Warner Bros, Lakeshore Entertainment, Malpaso Productions.

Mills, C. (2018), *Biopolitics*, Milton Park: Routledge.

Morris, D. B. (2017), *Eros and Illness*, Boston: Harvard University Press.

Neysmith, S. M. (2003), 'Enter the Elderly Woman as Citizen: The Implications of a Feminist Ethics of Care', in J. M. Humber and R. F. Almeder (eds), *Care of the Aged*, 3–26, New York: Springer.

'Nosedive' (2018) [TV episode, *Black Mirror*] Dir. Jake Michels, UK: Legendary Digital Networks.

Noys, B. (2005), *The Culture of Death*, Oxford: Berg.

Paterson, C. (2008), *Assisted Suicide and Euthanasia: A Natural Law Ethics Approach*, Farnham: Ashgate.

Pérez, E., and S. Genovesi (2020), 'Death in Black Mirror: How Should We Deal with Our Mortality?', in D. K. Johnson (ed.), *Black Mirror and Philosophy: Dark Reflections*, 292–300, Hoboken: Wiley Blackwell.

Phillips, S. S. (1996), 'Introduction', in S. S. Phillips and P. Benner (eds), *The Crisis of Care: Affirming and Restoring Caring Practices in the Helping Professions*, 1–16, Washington, DC: Georgetown University Press.

'San Junipero' (2006) [TV episode, *Black Mirror*] Dir. Owen Harris, UK: House of Tomorrow.

Seale, C. (2005), 'The Transformation of Dying in Old Societies', in M. L. Johnson (ed.), *The Cambridge Handbook of Age and Ageing*, 378–87, Cambridge: Cambridge University Press.

Slote, M. (2007), *The Ethics of Care and Empathy*, Milton Park: Routledge.

Spackman, B. (1989), *Decadent Genealogies. The Rhetoric of Sickness from Baudelaire to D'Annunzio*, Ithaca: Cornell University Press.

The Father (2020), [Film] Dir. Florian Zeller, UK, France: Les Films du Cru, Film4Orange Studio.

Thornber, K. L. (2020), *Global Healing: Literature, Advocacy, Care*, Leiden: Brill.

Ureczky, E. (2018), 'Crises of Care: Precarious Bodies in Western and Eastern European Clinical Film Dystopias', *Contact Zones: Studies in Central and Eastern European Film and Literature*, 1. Available online: http://contactzones.elte.hu/journal/20181-2.

Youth (2015), [Film] Dir. Paolo Sorrentino, Italy, France, UK, Switzerland: Indigo Film, Barbary Films, Pathé.

10

Ageing, anachronism and perception in dystopian narrative: The case of Margaret Atwood's 'Torching the Dusties'

Susan Watkins

There can be a certain blindness within dystopian and speculative fiction in relation to questions of ageing and narrative. Domingo argues that demodystopias (dystopias about population change) tend to 'present demographic evolution as a social problem in need of a (usually urgent) solution' (2008: 725). Imagined urgent solutions to the demographic 'problem' of an ageing society vary, but what Margaret Morganroth Gullette has identified as the decline narrative is usually prominent. According to Gullette, most cultural scripts about the life course make use of narratives about the ageing process that correspond to 'decline ideology' (2004: 11). Her ideas can be extended to apply to society more broadly. Decline narratives imagine the future in various ways, from loss of fertility and the apocalyptic care 'burden' of increasing numbers of old people (Chivers and Kriebernegg 2017: 20) to the gothic, apocalyptic narrative of personal and social decline implicit in age-related dementia (Goldman 2017). Margaret Atwood's 'Torching the Dusties', from her *Stone Mattress* (2014) collection, deploys some of these ideas, taking place in an exclusive care home for wealthy older people and ending with the home's horrific destruction by the 'Our Turn' movement, which takes violent action to destroy those 'burdensome', ageing inhabitants who have, according to the protesters, hogged limited resources and are responsible for anthropogenic climate change. Atwood has made clear that she believes the story to be about generational discord and economic inequality:

> It's a story about economic imbalance. … Wonderful though our automatonised [*sic*] world is becoming, there are a lot of people who don't have jobs; and those people are young. When you have a lot of young people who don't have jobs,

you are going to get a lot of energy of an angry kind. Older people have built up resources. … Currency is called 'currency' for a reason: it has to circulate. When you block the circulation you get a stagnant state of affairs. (Wagner 2014: 36)

Despite the clear association between old age and economic privilege here, later in the same interview Atwood admits that understanding the relationship between youth, age and allocation of resources is a matter of *perspective*. Discussing the potential dangers of policies on assisted dying, she comments: 'I understand both *points of view*. Like anything else we do, that kind of choice is subject to abuse' (Wagner 2014: 36, emphasis added).

In the story, vision and perspective are to the fore, because the protagonist, Wilma, suffers from declining vision caused by macular degeneration, accompanied by visual disturbances or illusions, as a result of Charles Bonnet syndrome, in which little people, or 'Chuckies', appear in her peripheral vision. The visions of the Chuckies are noticeably anachronistic; unlimited to historical time period, geographical location or cultural genre, they celebrate pleasure, dancing, singing and even skating. The Chuckies can be used as a lens through which to read the issues raised by the story and as symbols of the broader shifts in perception that the story explores. Their presence insists that we 'look' at new narratives to describe the ageing process, for both the individual and the wider culture or society, and reconsider the dystopian mode as one that is capable of focusing on creative re-perception of older people.

Chuckies

Charles Bonnet syndrome (CBS) was first described in 1760 by the Swiss philosopher of the same name, whose father experienced visual hallucinations associated with sight loss. The main feature of CBS is visual hallucinations accompanying sight loss, without psychiatric problems or cognitive impairment. The hallucinations range from relatively simple patterns and shapes to complicated visions like those experienced by Wilma in the story. According to Best et al., these 'visual hallucinations' are the result of 'de-afferentation of the visual cortex' (de-afferentation meaning the interruption or destruction of the connections of nerve cells) and 'cortical hyperexcitability'. Symptoms are often underreported 'due to patients' fears of being categorised as mentally ill and a relative lack of awareness among the medical profession'. Best et al. conclude that although there is no effective treatment, 'education can help patients feel more in control of CBS, in terms of coping and managing it' (2019: 1).

Wilma's use of the term 'Chucky', suggested by her eye specialist, for her visual disturbances, has interesting connotations. The *Oxford English Dictionary* offers two meanings of the word: the first 'a term of endearment or affectionate form of address for a loved one, esp. a woman or child' dating from 1683, the second a Scottish word for a chicken or any bird, dating from 1724. A more familiar allusion for readers of a certain age is to the *Child's Play* horror film (1988), in which a doll, Chucky, is possessed by the soul of a serial killer. Science fiction aficionados may also recall John Wyndham's ([1968] 2010) novel *Chocky*, in which an alien consciousness, nicknamed Chocky, inhabits a twelve-year-old boy's mind. At the end of Atwood's story, Wilma and her companion Tobias wait in the garden of Ambrosia Manor, the care home where they both live, as it is burnt down by the 'Our Turn' protesters. As they watch, Wilma sees the Chuckies dance and sing as the flames increase. This eerie and disturbing conclusion could be interpreted as celebratory, aligning the Chuckies with the violence of the Our Turn movement and building on an existing popular cultural association between the term 'Chucky' and the horror genre. This is undoubtedly a valid reading; however, I believe their function throughout the story is to generate, via the device of anachronism, a more thoroughgoing disturbance of conventional perceptions of age, ageing, gender and time. Thus, the visions of the Chuckies have the potential to disturb, maybe even counteract, the emphasis in the Our Turn protests (and in much dystopian fiction) on older people as a useless waste of resources. The Chuckies question how we choose to *look* at older people's place in our society and culture and position in the life course.

Ageing and the gaze

It is significant that Wilma describes herself using many of the terms she associates with the Chuckies. As a consequence of her disease, Wilma can only catch glimpses in her peripheral vision of the world around her. She describes her reflection in a mirror as resembling her mother (a common experience for women as they age) but with the distinction that the 'sideways glance' makes her look 'more mischievous. Possibly more malevolent as well, like an elf gone to the bad. That sideways glance lacks the candour of a full frontal gaze, a thing she will never see again' (Atwood 2014: 230). The tangential perspective of the wicked elf, or even Chucky, established here – something that her loss of sight actually allows Wilma to develop – becomes an important alternative to the conventional gaze by which the older person is established either as a threat or as an absence.

Kathleen Woodward's understanding of the mirror stage of old age is both echoed and challenged here. For Woodward, 'old age is thus understood as a state in which the body is in opposition to the self' (1991: 62). Looking at one's ageing body in the mirror is an experience that includes 'strangeness, the uncanny, old age, decrepitude, death, fear, danger' (1991: 68). These feelings are important for Woodward, because in actuality, what she refers to as the experience of 'adaptive repulsion' in response to one's ageing reflection is actually 'a process which is a sign of achieved psychic organization, not failure' (1991: 71). Although Wilma's feelings echo that adaptive repulsion to some extent, 'disconcertingly like her mother … white hair, crumpled tissue-paper skin and all' (Atwood, 2014: 230), the mischievous malevolence and sideways glance actually suggest a kind of liberation from some expectations.

Given Atwood's established interest in perception and ageing in her other work, it is not surprising to find that she focuses again on issues relating to the gaze, gender and age in this story.[1] 'Torching the Dusties' begins by establishing Wilma's reliance because of her poor sight on fellow resident and companion Tobias. The ageing process appears to cement traditional distinctions between men as those who look and women as those who are looked at. However, there is a caveat: older women are less likely to be the objects of *desiring* looks: it is via memory – in his tall tales about his sexual conquests of the past – that Tobias reconstructs conventional gendered distinctions that position women as objects of the gaze. More importantly, in the present of the story, Tobias can provide knowledge and information that Wilma lacks due to her poor vision. He therefore has power, because 'the bottom line is that Tobias can still see' (Atwood 2014: 227). Wilma is significantly disadvantaged by her lack of possession of the gaze, and this disadvantage does have a gendered component. Her reliance on Tobias frustrates her, as she does not trust him to report accurately what is happening outside Ambrosia Manor once the 'Our Turn' protests begin. She would prefer to 'see for herself' (2014: 236) but has to be led to safety in the garden by Tobias once the attack on the care home begins. However, despite this vulnerability, it is also important that as readers we 'view' things from Wilma's perspective. As Snaith suggests: '"Reading" the final tale through the failing eyes of Wilma also becomes critical in engaging with broader issues around an ageist society. … Wilma's failing sight becomes analogous to our own limitations and ability to "see" the potential failures of society in life outside of fiction' (2017: 122).

One of the limitations that Snaith alludes to is the fact that the gaze of the world turns away from older people, except in the spectacular form of destructive othering and scapegoating. In response to the news that care homes for older people are being destroyed, Tobias remarks: 'The whole world has an appetite for ringside seats at such events. Witch-burnings and public hangings were always well attended' (Atwood 2014: 262). The metaphors here associate older people with circus performer, witch and convicted criminal; all significantly reduce agency and position older people as objects of a punitive disciplinary gaze. Towards the end of the story the vulnerability of older people and the vulnerability of women in relation to the gaze coalesce, when Wilma wonders whether Tobias has made up the threat to Ambrosia Manor. Could he be a serial killer attempting to lure her to her death by strangulation, or is the Our Turn movement some sort of 'mass hallucination' (2014: 266)? At the same time, however, Wilma also reflects on her previous passivity in terms that question the association between having the gaze and having power. She recalls commenting to her husband that the word *lurker* would be 'written on her tombstone. Because hadn't she spent most of her life just watching?' (2014: 237). Maybe those that society does not watch are able to watch the most, even if such a 'sideways' gaze is not necessarily associated with empowerment.

Anachronism

In 'Torching the Dusties', the speculative, dystopian mode of looking generates a significant challenge to ideas about ageing, maturation and development, which is furthered by the story's use of anachronism. The obtrusive anachronism of the Chuckies is present from the very beginning of the story, where we are told:

> They have no respect for historical accuracy, these people. It's as if some bored theatrical costume designer got drunk behind the scenes and raided the storage boxes: an early Tudor neckline here, a gondolier's jacket there, a Harlequin outfit over there. Wilma has to admire the slapdash abandon. (Atwood 2014: 225)

The emphasis on costume and performance is relished for its improvisational creation of a grotesque, carnivalesque pleasure that muddles historical period and national costume. The Chuckies wear ribbons, beads, sequins, buckles, plumed hats, high wigs and bright colours. Usually they dance, process, promenade and, on one occasion, skate.

Anachronism is also present in many other places in the story. Tobias, with his glamourous Hungarian ancestry, tells tall stories full of 'archaic' comparisons (Atwood 2014: 226) and 'rococo' details from 'creaky, ornate operettas' (2014: 231). By his own account, he has attended four universities and has three birthplaces. Ersatz objects proliferate, from the coffee grinder that Tobias remembers from his youth, to the replica of the Brussels 'Manneken Pis' or peeing boy statue on Ambrosia Manor's lawn. Antiques such as Wilma's escritoire and dressing table are out of time and place and of limited use in the fake environment of the care home with its 'fraudulent' crest (2014: 242) embossed on menus 'of seventy or eighty years ago' (2014: 244).

I have previously argued that Atwood's use of anachronism in her work about ageing can be understood in relation to Edward Said's concept of 'late style' (Watkins 2013). Said argues that late style abruptly juxtaposes the antiquated with the avant-garde, in an 'untimely' refusal of conventional maturation and development narratives. Much of Atwood's other work on ageing corresponds to what Said terms the 'undiminished power and yet strangely recapitulatory and even backward-looking and abstracted quality' of late style (2006: 25). In this story, however, the speculative, dystopian mode and the device of anachronism generate an even more significant challenge to ideas about maturation and development. Sarah Falcus has argued that generational anachronism, or disorder, is central to many dystopian visions. She claims that 'in these worlds, apocalyptic environmental and social collapse frequently results in, and is often tied to, societies where the life course, progress and the promise of the future are all disrupted by threats to generational continuity' (2020: 65). Falcus builds on Lee Edelman's 2004 discussion of reproductive futurism, or what she terms his 'focus on the child as the figure of futurity' in her discussion of anachronism in dystopian fiction, asking us to consider that, inevitably, the 'shadow side' of reproductive futurism is 'the figure of the old person and the spectre of ageing itself' (2020: 67). Making use of Cynthia Port's 2012 essay on the ways in which 'new approaches to queer temporality suggest intriguing possibilities for reconsidering the temporalities of old age' (2012: 2), she argues that dystopian fictions of ageing are capable of generating a curious, open mixture of 'hope and anxiety' (Falcus 2020: 83) via the deployment of what Mary Russo has referred to as the 'risks' of anachronism (1999).

Atwood deploys anachronism in a similarly 'risky' way in 'Torching the Dusties'. Rather than an *entirely* negative look into the disastrous future, Atwood casts a wicked sideways glance at conventional assumptions about generational continuity. Risk-taking can have both positive and negative results; how one views the outcome of taking a risk depends on one's perspective. The story proves the point that dystopian speculative temporalities and perspectives focused on re-seeing older people can question our assumptions about who the future is for and which metaphors we use to imagine it. Tobias and Wilma take a risk, hiding in the garden to wait out the violence of the Our Turn attack on Ambrosia Manor. They choose not to feel responsible for others, whether those with severe dementia in the Advanced Living wing or their friends from the Early Assisted Living wing. This might be viewed as selfish, or alternatively as an example of creative, improvisational cunning. At least, as examples of anachronistic older people, they will survive the destruction of Ambrosia House. Snaith finds a 'new utopian strategy' in the tales in *Stone Mattress*, arguing that Atwood uses virtual reality and cyberspace to create new spaces for older people within the 'distinctly dystopian' (2017: 116) narratives of the collection. Although this is the case in many of the stories, in 'Torching the Dusties' in particular, other possibilities are imagined. As Tobias and Wilma crunch peanuts and view the spectacular destruction of Ambrosia House from the garden, they persist into a 'real-life' future in the terms of the story, where, according to the logic of the Our Turn movement, they were not supposed to exist at all. The last words of the story, 'Look. Look! They're singing!', refer to the screaming inhabitants burning to death in the home, as well as to the Chuckies dancing, mixed with the flames. Perhaps they also refer to Wilma and Tobias themselves.

Intertexts

Many of the frequent intertextual allusions in the story also engage with ideas about anachronism. Atwood uses such allusions to build a pointed series of cultural references, which emphasize the need for us to re-perceive and reposition older people in our imagining of the future. It could be argued that intertextuality is itself a retrospective process. Atwood remarked in *Negotiating with the Dead* that 'all writers learn from the dead. As long as you continue to write, you continue to explore the work of writers who have preceded you; you also feel judged and held to account by them' (2002: 178). An allusion to an earlier writer or text refers backwards; however, it also does different work in its new environment. Intertexts are therefore anachronisms in themselves. The name of Ambrosia Manor, for example, is an ironic nod to the immortality of the Greek Gods, conferred by ambrosia and nectar, their food and drink (Leeming 2005: n.p.).

A number of allusions in the story make implicit comments on the relatively privileged position of Ambrosia Manor's inhabitants. Early in the story, the Chuckies appear wearing green after Wilma reads the scene in Margaret Mitchell's *Gone with the Wind* (1936), where a desperate Scarlett O'Hara makes a dress out of green curtains. If Wilma is being compared to Scarlett here, then the implications in terms of gender and race are worth unpacking. Initially, Wilma alludes solely to the subversive aspects of the novel's treatment of white femininity in her characterization of Scarlett O'Hara as 'headstrong'. She discusses the scene where she makes curtains into a dress in order to attract and fool Rhett Butler as an attempt at survival based on assuming a veneer of wealth and respectability.

Later in the story, however, Wilma's discussion of Scarlett and the novel as a whole becomes more ambivalent when she calls her an 'idiot' for 'mooning over that wimp' (Ashley Wilkes) while 'destruction is at hand ... Atlanta will burn. Tara will be gutted' (Atwood 2014: 260). The implicit comparison between Tara and Ambrosia Manor is noteworthy. Multiple kinds of inequality are compacted into the space of Ambrosia Manor. The inequalities of ageism are present: Ambrosia Manor is, as Kriebernegg argues, a 'space of exclusion designed to contain the purportedly "burdensome" and "deviant" aspects of old age' (2018: 47). Present also is the financial inequality of a society where only some old people can afford places like Ambrosia Manor. The care home also represents, like Tara, a space which does not acknowledge its own economic dependency on others: the Our Turn movement is fuelled by the resentment in young people created by perceived generational inequality (both economic and environmental).

The legacy of *Gone with the Wind* and its film adaptation makes clear the extent of Scarlett's and Tara's privilege and, by implication, suggests Wilma's and Ambrosia Manor's. Durden discusses Mitchell's 'radical, if equivocal, treatment of gender' (2007: n.p.), one which is pointedly focused solely on White women, with Black women slave characters like Mammy and Prissy described using racist stereotyping. Both Mitchell's novel and the film are full of racist nostalgia for the antebellum Confederate South, containing a problematic exoneration of slavery and plantation culture that left a poisonous legacy in Jim Crow laws at the time of Mitchell's writing. Durden concludes rightly that 'no fair-minded reader can confuse the necessary representation of historical racism with an authorial agenda of racist revisionism' (2007: n.p.). In 1940 Hattie McDaniel was the first African American to win an Oscar for Best Supporting Actress for her role as Mammy in the film of *Gone with the Wind* but was admitted to the awards ceremony at the segregated Ambassador Hotel only after the producer, David O. Selznik, intervened. She was made to sit at a separate table from her co-stars (Coggan 2018: n.p.).

Other fictional allusions make a similar point about other characters' relation to privilege. Things worsen in Ambrosia Manor as the Our Turn protests step up a gear, and Wilma reflects that Tobias has 'dumped his *Scarlet Pimpernel* foppish-aristocrat frippery', supposedly moving into 'Man of Action' mode instead (Atwood 2014: 250). The entry in *The Oxford Companion to Edwardian Fiction* (Kemp et al. 2005) for *The Scarlet Pimpernel* (1905), by Baroness Orczy, is instructive:

> The bestselling story of the League of the Scarlet Pimpernel, a band of young English gentlemen, *dedicated to the rescue of innocent aristocratic victims of the French Revolution and subsequent Reign of Terror*. Their leader, Sir Percy Blakeney, continually outwits the enemy (personified by the cunning intellectual, Chauvelin) not simply through plain courage but also by his use of disguise and his sheer insouciance. Blakeney similarly disguises his identity from his society friends in England (and even, for a while, from his wife), thus establishing a model (which would be widely used by detective and spy story writers) of the effete and ineffectual aristocrat who is, in reality, a dashing, ingenious, and determined man of action. Not surprisingly, *The Scarlet Pimpernel* inspired several sequels and has been regularly adapted for stage, screen, and television. (2005: n.p., emphasis added)

Whether or not there are 'innocent victims' among those who are in a privileged position is the key question Atwood wants readers to consider. The allusions to *Gone with the Wind* and *The Scarlet Pimpernel* set up the idea of a society that is way past its sell-by date. Wilma understands that Ambrosia Manor is privileged (she compares it later to a blockaded Versailles facing the revolutionary mob [Atwood 2014: 254]), but she tries to distance herself from an awareness that she and Tobias are the beneficiaries of that privilege. Are they, however, more than lucky and entitled (Wilma describes them both as 'comfortable') individuals who escape the fate of their peers: the equivalent of the aristocrats rescued by Percy Blakeney or those southern plantation owners who survived the civil war?

If Atwood's intertexts encourage us to become aware of inequality and privilege, they also emphasize the question of perspective and make us conscious of our own attitudes and perceptions. Perhaps, the most telling of all the high cultural intertexual allusions in the story, then, is Wilma's imperfectly remembered reference to the Post-Impressionist painter Pierre Bonnard (1867–1947): she mistakenly substitutes his name for Bonnet's when naming her eye syndrome. Langton argues that 'Bonnard's achievement is to make paint itself and the act of painting parts of the spectator's experience' (2001: n.p.). As with Bonnard's concentration on highlighting formal choices for the viewer, so Atwood's own use of allusion emphasizes the extent to which perception is subjective and also culturally and socially determined.

Film adaptation

Like Atwood's story, Marlene Goldman and Philip McKee's short film adaptation of 'Torching the Dusties' (2019) has a focus on issues of vision, the gaze and perspective, asking us to consider how we might re-view older people. In the medium of film, it is possible to make sight, perspective and the gaze even more central. The film makes a number of significant and interesting changes to her story, which I focus on in the remainder of this chapter. One crucial alteration is the decision to give the male character, Frank, rather than his wife, Wilma (in the film adaptation they are a married couple), the eye disease. Wilma is in fact the glamourous, active and decisive one of the pair, who uses binoculars to view the protests at the gate and is shown moving around the care home actively (see Figure 10.1). She is the one who engineers their escape from Ambrosia Manor. She hides Frank in a laundry hamper, adopting the disguise of baseball caps and overalls (see Figure 10.2).

In Atwood's story, Wilma suggests this option, but Tobias rejects it, so in several ways the film chooses to centre agency and resourcefulness in Wilma rather than Frank. The film thus reverses the conventional gendered dichotomy between the man as the active one who looks and moves the story on and the woman as the passive one who is looked at. If in places that dynamic is

Figure 10.1 Wilma using binoculars, 3.25 min. *Torching the Dusties*, directed by M. Goldman and P. McKee, 2019.

Figure 10.2 Frank hiding in the laundry hamper, 10.16 min. *Torching the Dusties*, directed by M. Goldman and P. McKee, 2019.

questioned in the original story (e.g. in the idea of Wilma as 'lurking' and watching with a sideways glance), it does tend to dominate it. With a towel over his head sitting in the hamper, Frank resembles E.T.: the Extra-Terrestrial in the famous ride-in-the-sky scene (*E.T.* 1982); here the adaptation ironically draws on Steven Spielberg's well-known interest in childhood as a theme and makes a visual parallel between Frank's wrinkles and balding head and the alien E.T., playing with ideas of ageing as a second childhood.

Our perspective as viewers is aligned with Frank for the most part. The film opens with a shot of an eye, as seen via medical imaging equipment (see Figure 10.3), accompanied by the voice-over of a doctor, who discusses macular degeneration and Charles Bonnet syndrome, explaining (ironically) to Frank: 'You'll always know what's real and what isn't'. That medical imaging can only ever give an approximation of reality establishes from the start the issues around perception and subjectivity which continue to be prominent throughout. This point is made on several levels. In casual conversation, for example, the maid, Katya, says to Frank: 'See you after lunch'. He replies: 'If I don't see you first'. When Wilma tells Frank there are no police responding to the protests at the gate, he replies: 'You just didn't see them. That's all'. When they escape from Ambrosia Manor and hide in the garden, she remarks of the protesters: 'I don't think they can see us'.

Connected to the emphasis on vision is the device of abrupt juxtaposition, which has a similar function to the use of anachronism in Atwood's story. The

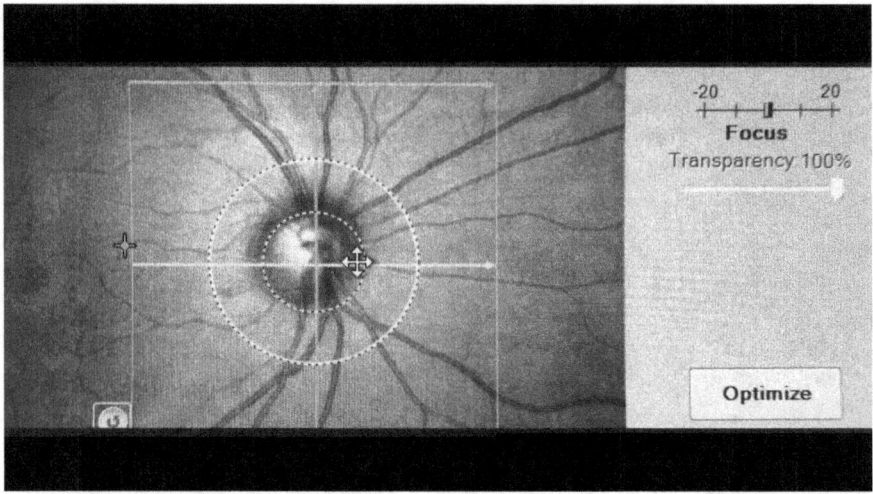

Figure 10.3 Close-up shot of Frank's eye, 00.28 min. *Torching the Dusties*, directed by M. Goldman and P. McKee, 2019.

scenes at the very beginning of the film with the close-up shots of an eyeball and optician's equipment are followed soon after by one of flames burning in darkness and muffled shouting. Later in the film, a shot of a pair of thick-lensed glasses, followed by a book cover with a close-up of an eye and part of the title '… And Vision', is accompanied by audio of a radio phone-in conversation. That conversation includes an economist discussing the risks to society of 'ageing past earning', using key terms such as 'crisis', 'disaster' and 'silver tsunami', which all construct apocalyptic narratives. The fact that the 'Our Turn' movement's actions bring to the fore questions about how we *perceive* older people is emphasized throughout. As Frank listens to the radio phone-in about the protests, we hear a caller say: 'We have a vision for the future: torch the dusties.' This particular phrase – 'We have a vision for the future' – is not present in the story and makes the connection between vision, attitudes to older people and reproductive futurism explicit.

In the film, the Chuckies are not grotesque miniatures but instead life-sized adults engaged in domestic service. They wear the uniforms of nineteenth-century maids and butlers. The butler figure, in particular, looks directly 'back' at Frank, in a reverse shot that supports the emphasis on the question of who sees and looks elsewhere in the film (see Figure 10.4). The nineteenth-century costumes also make an important point about Frank's dependence on domestic service and its racialized history. Marilyn Barber has argued that 'the changing ethnicity of domestics from the 19th century to the present parallels broad

Figure 10.4 Butler figure looking back at Frank, 5.20 min. *Torching the Dusties*, directed by M. Goldman and P. McKee, 2019.

changes in the pattern of immigration to Canada ... the constant scarcity of servants in Canada facilitated female immigration, but, especially in the 20th century, channelled many immigrant women into low status occupation [*sic*] shunned by Canadians' (1991: 3). In the film, Frank is impatient with Katya – his 'real-life' maid – and the film thus makes explicit the kinds of labour involved in caring for privileged older people. The racial politics of this dynamic are also suggested: the actor playing Katya is a woman of colour. The two actors playing the imaginary Victorian maid and butler appear to be White, so the film suggests the historical shift in the history of service as waves of immigration are deployed by the Canadian government over the nineteenth and twentieth centuries to provide a new service class for wealthy White people. The filmmakers' representation of the Chuckies accords with the function of some of the literary allusions and intertexts in the story, which, as we saw earlier, work to make parallels with other societies clinging on to privilege in the face of sweeping change, such as the antebellum South and the aristocracy in revolutionary France.

This point is also made by the musical intertexts in the film. George Gershwin's 'Summertime' from his folk opera, *Porgy and Bess* (1935), features during Wilma and Frank's escape, which is juxtaposed with murky shots of the protesters in baby masks carrying torches and clubs and throwing fuel over the windows of Ambrosia Manor (see Figure 10.5).

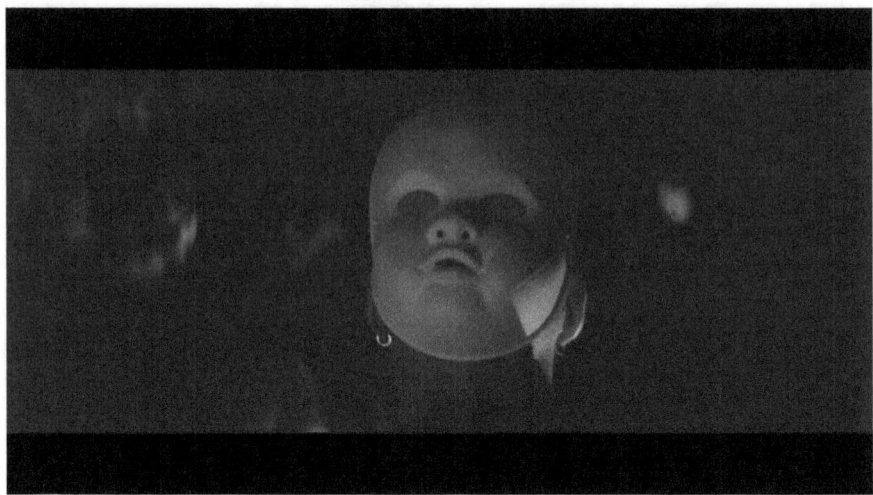

Figure 10.5 Protesters in baby masks, 10.24 min. *Torching the Dusties*, directed by M. Goldman and P. McKee, 2019.

While obviously ironic – Wilma and Frank are actually in the autumn of their lives – it is also true that their lives have been relatively easy, as the song has it. The implicit allusion to death is also apparent in Wagner et al.'s 'The Ride of the Valkyries' (1914), which accompanies the first slow-motion appearance of Wilma, bringing Frank's coffee. The Valkyries, according to Scandinavian mythology, were 'Odin's twelve handmaids who conducted the slain warriors of their choice from the battlefield to Valhalla. The name comes from Old Norse Valkyrja, literally "chooser of the slain"' (Knowles 2005: n.p.). Where the story voices Wilma's fears that Tobias has invented the entire Our Turn movement, with fake radio broadcasts, paid actors and recordings of protests, there is an equivalent in the film in the 'rehearsed' quality to her reactions and decisions. Is it Wilma who is the bringer of death?

The racial histories that the musical intertexts allude to are also important. Richard Crawford remarks on Gershwin's use of the term 'folk' in connection with *Porgy and Bess* as follows:

> Gershwin invoked the word at a time when the concept of 'the folk' as a term denoting respect for 'otherness' was gaining popular acceptance. The US government's public works programmes during the Depression years signalled a growing inclination to preserve, study and value the indigenous practices of different American subcultures, including economically disadvantaged ones. From that perspective, a tale about southern blacks by a white novelist, set to music by a New York-based, Jewish songwriter-lyricist team and played on the

Broadway stage, was easy to criticize on grounds of authenticity. In addition, the opera was about African-Americans, whose lives, long after slavery and emancipation, were still affected by racial stereotyping – by being seen as a feckless but violent people, given to singing or brawling their troubles away. A work like *Porgy and Bess*, which confirmed that stereotype, was seen in some quarters as yet another hindrance to the quest of black Americans for social respect. (2006: n.p.)

'Summertime' is therefore a way to raise concerns not only about conventional narratives of the life course but also about cultural appropriation and racialized histories of labour and servitude as they pertain to the care work of looking after privileged older White people.

Conclusion

Both story and film encourage readers and viewers to 're-view' how we understand older people. Tolan argues that throughout her work, Atwood's treatment of ageing can be seen as an 'essentially ethical attempt to inhabit a phenomenon most commonly seen from without' (2017: 337). In both versions of 'Torching the Dusties', seeing 'from within' means working within the conventions of dystopia, a genre which inevitably involves a process of extrapolation and speculation. However, whereas many dystopian visions of ageing rely on narratives of decline or apocalypse, in both Atwood's story and Goldman and McKee's film, the device of anachronism is used to explore more creative speculative possibilities within the dystopian mode. Anachronistic intertextual allusions and juxtapositions in both texts question conventional modes of looking or gazing at older people and how we perceive them and their place in visions of the future. The Chuckies are at the centre of the story and the film, even though at first glance they might appear to be tangential or adjacent to the primary concerns of both. The Chuckies function to emphasize how societies based on multiple forms of inequality view older people, enabling both versions of 'Torching the Dusties' to ask a series of difficult questions about whether privileged older individuals should survive the destruction of such societies and persist into future worlds. The film adaptation makes more apparent than the story the racialized history of service and care for older people in Canada. It also reverses the gendered aspects of the gaze that are present in Atwood's story. Thus, the film's creative choices allow us to 're-perceive' Atwood's story and its implications in fresh ways.

Note

1 For a useful outline of how ageing is treated in Atwood's other work, see Tolan (2017).

References

Atwood, M. (2002), *Negotiating with the Dead: A Writer on Writing*, Cambridge: Cambridge University Press.

Atwood, M. (2014), 'Torching the Dusties', in *Stone Mattress*, 225–68, London: Bloomsbury.

Barber, M. (1991), 'Immigrant Domestic Servants in Canada', *Canada's Ethnic Groups*, 16, Ottawa: Canadian Historical Association.

Best, J., P. Y. Liu, D. Ffytche, J. Potts and M. Moosajee (2019), 'Think Sight Loss, Think Charles Bonnet Syndrome', *Therapeutic Advances in Ophthalmology*, 11: 1–2.

Child's Play (1988), [Film] Dir. Tom Holland, USA: Warner Home Video.

Chivers, S., and U. Kriebernegg (2017), *Care Home Stories: Aging, Disability, and Long-Term Residential Care*, 14, Aging Studies, Bielefeld: Transcript Verlag. Available online: https://core.ac.uk/download/pdf/80328206.pdf (accessed 22 March 2021).

Coggan, D. (2018), 'Inside the Complicated Legacy of Hattie McDaniel, the First Black Oscar Winner', *Entertainment*, 22 February. Available online: https://ew.com/oscars/2018/02/22/hattie-mcdaniel-first-black-oscar-winner-legacy/ (accessed 22 March 2021).

Crawford, R. (2006), 'Porgy and Bess', *The Grove Book of Operas*, Oxford Reference, Oxford: Oxford University Press. Available online: https://www.oxfordreference.com/view/10.1093/acref/9780195309072.001.0001/acref-9780195309072-e-203 (accessed 19 March 2021).

Domingo, A. (2008), 'Demodystopias: Prospects of Demographic Hell', *Population and Development Review*, 34(4): 725–45.

Durden, P. (2007), 'Mitchell, Margaret, 1900–1949', Ann Arbor: ProQuest. Available online: https://search-proquest-com.ezproxy.leedsbeckett.ac.uk/encyclopedias-reference-works/mitchell-margaret-1900-1949/docview/2137891576/se-2?accountid=12037 (accessed 4 March 2021).

Edelman, L. (2004), *No Future: Queer Theory and the Death Drive*, Durham: Duke University Press.

E.T.: The Extra-Terrestrial (1982), [Film] Dir. Stephen Spielberg, US: Warner.

Falcus, S. (2020), 'Age and Anachronism in Contemporary Dystopian Fiction', in E. Barry with M. V. Skagen (eds), *Literature and Ageing*, vol. 73, 65–86, Essays and Studies, Cambridge: D. S. Brewer.

Gershwin, G. (1935), 'Summertime', *Porgy and Bess*. YouTube. Available online: https://www.youtube.com/watch?v=Sr2AnmNH2b0 (accessed 24 March 2021).

Goldman, M. (2017), *Forgotten: Narratives of Age-Related Dementia and Alzheimer's Disease in Canada*, Montréal: McGill-Queen's University Press.

Gullette, M. M. (2004), *Aged by Culture*, Chicago: University of Chicago Press.

Kemp, S., C. Mitchell and D. Trotter (2005), 'Scarlet Pimpernel, The', *The Oxford Companion to Edwardian Fiction*, Oxford Reference, Oxford: Oxford University Press. Available online: https://www.oxfordreference.com/view/10.1093/acref/9780198117605.001.0001/acref-9780198117605-e-1038 (accessed 4 March 2021)

Knowles, E. (2005), 'Valkyrie', *The Oxford Dictionary of Phrase and Fable*, Oxford Reference, Oxford: Oxford University Press. Available online: https://www.oxfordreference.com/view/10.1093/acref/9780198609810.001.0001/acref-9780198609810-e-7438 (accessed 19 March 2021)

Kriebernegg, U. (2018), ' "Time to go. Fast not slow": Geronticide and the Burden Narrative of Old Age in Margaret Atwood's "Torching the Dusties" ', *European Journal of English Studies*, 22(1): 46–58.

Langton, J. (2001), 'Bonnard, Pierre', in *The Oxford Companion to Western Art*, Oxford Reference, Oxford: Oxford University Press. Available online: https://www.oxfordreference.com/view/10.1093/acref/9780198662037.001.0001/acref-9780198662037-e-321 (accessed 22 March 2021).

Leeming, D. (2005), 'Ambrosia', *The Oxford Companion to World Mythology*, Oxford Reference, Oxford: Oxford University Press. Available online: https://www.oxfordreference.com/view/10.1093/acref/9780195156690.001.0001/acref-9780195156690-e-63 (accessed 22 March 2021).

Mitchell, M. ([1936] 2019), *Gone with the Wind*, London: Vintage.

Port, C. (2012), 'No Future? Aging, Temporality, History and Reverse Chronologies', *Occasion: Interdisciplinary Studies in the Humanities*, 4: 1–19.

Russo, M. (1999), 'Aging and the Scandal of Anachronism', in K. Woodward (ed.), *Figuring Age: Women, Bodies, Generations*, 20–33, Bloomington: Indiana University Press.

Said, E. W. (2006), *On Late Style: Music and Literature Against the Grain*, London: Bloomsbury.

Snaith, H. (2017), 'Dystopia, Gerontology and the Writing of Margaret Atwood', *Feminist Review*, 116: 118–32.

Tolan, F. (2017), 'Aging and Subjectivity in Margaret Atwood's Fiction', *Contemporary Women's Writing*, 11(3): 336–53.

Torching the Dusties (2019), [Film] Dir. M. Goldman and P. McKee, Vimeo, uploaded by Laura Nordin, https://vimeo.com/340526708.

Wagner, E. (2014), ' "Ooooh! Are we Going to Talk about Dying?": The *New Statesman* Interview', 31 October. Available online: https://www.newstatesman.com/cult

ure/2014/10/margaret-atwood-ooooh-are-we-going-talk-about-dying (accessed 22 March 2021).

Wagner, R., Vessella's Italian Band and O. Vessella (1914) 'Ride of the Valkyries', [Audio], Library of Congress. Available online: https://www.loc.gov/item/jukebox-134379/ (accessed 24 March 2021).

Watkins, S. (2013), '"Summoning Your Youth at Will": Memory, Time and Aging in the Work of Penelope Lively, Margaret Atwood and Doris Lessing', *Frontiers: A Journal of Women's Studies*, 34(2): 222–44.

Woodward, K. (1991), 'The Mirror Stage of Old Age', in *Aging and Its Discontents: Freud and Other Fictions*, 53–71, Bloomington: Indiana University Press.

Wyndham, J. ([1968] 2010), *Chocky*, London: Penguin.

11

Playing with possibilities: Ursula Le Guin and speculations on the human condition: An anocritical approach

Roberta Maierhofer

The 'narrative presence' of gender and age

In her article 'Space Ageing: Where Are the Galactic Grandmas? The Lack of Older Women in Sci-Fi Novels Reflects and Reifies Ageism and Sexism', Sylvia Spruck Wrigley argues that with some exceptions in fantasy, and in accordance with social expectations concerning female bodily appearance, older women in science fiction are usually relegated to supporting roles of 'fairy godmothers, wise crones, and evil witches' (2019: 586). However, she still expresses hope that science fiction novels might explore what it means to be human by presenting alternative worlds. As an author and scholar, Spruck Wrigley has made it her mission to collect and document 'witty female elders' in sci-fi novels and has so far found many in supporting roles, few as major characters. No wonder that Spruck Wrigley raises questions about the role of cultural representation and its relationship to – in her terms – 'the real world' and demands that literature should 'counter bias' (2019: 586) and 'explore new roles for female elders as multifaceted beings' to 'completely change the landscape' (2019: 587). Despite pointing to the fact that the few older female characters are often presented as asexual, threatening or uninteresting, she does use the term 'grandma' – an ageist way to speak about old women in general, as it reinforces the patriarchal notion of positioning women only in family relational terms – to petition that we collectively, the real and the sci-fi world, should 'focus on the strengths of older people and foster healthspan as well as lifespan' (Spruck Wrigley 2019: 587).

Literary and cultural scholarship had been hesitant to incorporate the aspect of age into its considerations, and an understanding of the quality of a 'narrative presence' of age and ageing as cultural constructions was possible only through feminist theory and an understanding of the interconnectedness of gender and age. Science fiction more than any other genre has always presented – through what the literary critic Darko Suvin has referred to as 'cognitive estrangement' (1979) – a stepping out of time and space by offering expressions of human 'narrative presence' in order to strongly critique the here and now. Within the imagined worlds in science fiction and fantasy, time in terms of the past, present and future is always a central concern and a matter of interpretation. Social, political, economic and cultural aspects are integrated in the telling of a good story, in creating an attractive 'narrative presence', which, in addition, provides a metalevel to discuss in more abstract terms social and cultural constructions. Representations of science fiction universes may question in radical ways our assumptions, our daily used 'narrative presence' as a cultural discourse, such as cultural constructions of gender and age, and make readers aware of any form of essentialism.

When Ursula Le Guin was announced as the recipient of the Medal for Distinguished Contribution to American Letters in 2014, the National Book Foundation in America based this decision on the fact that for 'more than 40 years, Le Guin has defied conventions of narrative, language, character, and genre, as well as transcended the boundaries between fantasy and realism to forge new paths for literary fiction' (National Book Foundation 2014). The organization emphasized the power of science and fiction 'to challenge readers to consider profound philosophical and existential questions about gender, race, the environment, and society' (National Book Foundation 2014). Given the fact that age/ing has been defined by Le Guin as an existential condition of human life, it is surprising that the category of age is omitted when listing the focus of her work as gender, race, the environment and society, as Le Guin was one of the few who used science fiction as a medium to explore and critique all aspects of female experience and, in more general terms, an essential understanding of the world. Therefore, with the help of the theoretical lens of anocriticism as 'a method to trace the aspect of female aging … in order to generate an understanding for what it means – in Margaret Morganroth Gullette's definition – to be "aged by culture"' (Maierhofer 2004: 322; see Gullette 2004), I will analyse some of Le Guin's non-fictional statements concerning age/ing and gender as a critique of the assumed 'reality' of these terms – or more specifically as a recognition of their 'narrative presence'. The term 'presence' describes the specificity by which the 'reality' of the human condition, such as gender or age, occurs: generated by humans – narrated, measured or acknowledged – 'reality' is enforced by social actuality – as a dominant expression – and thus consciously presented as historically changeable. As we cannot define 'reality' essentially, we can, however, recognize what we can understand by interpreting this 'reality' through a feminist theoretical lens. By focusing on two texts by Ursula Le Guin, the short non-fiction text 'Introducing Myself' (1992) and the earlier text 'The Space Crone' (1976), which was reprinted in the essay collection *Dancing at the Edge of the World* (1992), Le Guin's development of an approach to an understanding of 'reality' can be observed and interpreted as a commitment to the speculative definition of human conditions from a feminist perspective. This is central to what she describes as imagining the world differently:

> Oh, intellectual energy and curiosity, I suppose. An inborn interest in various and alternative ways of doing things and thinking about them. That could be part of what led me to write more about possible worlds than about the actual one. And, in a deeper sense, what led me to write fiction, maybe. A novelist is always 'trying on' other people. (Le Guin in Wray 2013)

In terms of an anocritical approach, knowing one's possibilities as well as one's limitations is a political act of resistance. However, this is not the only impact of the 'narrative presence' displayed by Le Guin, as her oeuvre, in form and content, both defies and reaffirms narrative conventions of fantasy and realism, thus forging 'new paths for literary fiction', as the National Book Foundation expressed it in its acknowledgement. Playing with the possibilities of texts, meanings, comments and processes, Le Guin communicates the human condition to create and establish, explore and criticize the 'narrative presence' of the *conditio humana*. The old woman in her essay 'The Space Crone' would – as the author who created her intended – no longer imitate, but narrate her life, and thus embody human possibilities by using a feminist and literary approach. Anocriticism offers a way to explore the interconnectedness of gender and age as expressed and experienced; cultural and social representations emphasize the importance of studying gender and age/ing in conjunction to understand them both as aspects of this 'narrative presence'.

Originally developed in the context of American culture, especially in terms of diverse and multi-ethnic texts and multifaceted portrayals of old women in literature (Maierhofer 2003: 33; 2007: 121), anocriticism offers a tool for exploring the wide-ranging literary representations of female ageing as part of the evident 'narrative presence', encouraging a more diverse imaginary of older women in general (2007: 121). In addition, there is an emphasis on the individual as a cultural narrative in American culture and its literary representations (2003: 33), which supports a 'narrative presence' of transgressions of the social status quo (2007: 121) and, thus, transgressions of established modes of interpretation. In the context of 'narrative presence', multidimensionality – here defined as the interconnectedness of usually separated aspects of 'narratives', such as facts, interpretations, analysis, statements or other text formats – is crucial.

Thus, to conduct an anocritical analysis of any form of text means to consider the influence of cultural representations – consisting of narrated possible human conditions – in the process of constituting 'presence' and of interpretation. Therefore, Le Guin's approach to exploring (rather than explaining) age/ing and gender and her playful and speculative method are the main focus of this chapter. In both her fiction and her non-fiction, her understanding of writing as a narrative testing and expanding of 'presence' becomes apparent. Thus, this creative process realizes the speculative status of human conditions.

Second-wave science fiction as a feminist trying on of other existences

In her book *How to Suppress Women's Writing* (1983), Joanna Russ describes the mechanisms of devaluing work by women and attacking gains made by the women's movement as a challenge that writers of science fiction, in particular, have been confronted with, regardless of whether they position themselves openly as feminists or not. Throughout her prolific career, Ursula Le Guin has declared herself in many instances a feminist, thus offering a lasting legacy of a writer where theory and practice are intertwined. Defining herself as a feminist writer in the wider sense – and not as a feminist science fiction writer – she performed transgressions of boundaries on different levels: occupying a self-confident political position with a demand for social change, on the one hand, and a self-confident cultural position as a writer not restricting herself to the genre of writing science fiction and refusing to be defined by a particular genre, on the other:

> But where I can get prickly and combative is if I'm just called a sci-fi writer. I'm not. I'm a novelist and poet. Don't shove me into your damn pigeonhole, where I don't fit, because I'm all over. My tentacles are coming out of the pigeonhole in all directions. (Le Guin in Wray 2013)

In her statements concerning her position as a writer, Le Guin has continuously emphasized the fundamental relevance of process versus results, not only in terms of writing itself but also as the possibility of opening up new ways of understanding and awareness that evolve from the putting down of thoughts and perceptions in writing. By stressing process over product, Le Guin extends the potential of creativity and declares the relevance of 'fiction' as a specifically and uniquely human enterprise and narrating as a form of exploration: 'Fiction is something that only human beings do, and only in certain circumstances. We don't know exactly for what purposes. But one of the things it does is lead you to recognize what you did not know before' (Le Guin 2019: xix). This broader anthropological understanding of 'fiction' includes also texts traditionally defined as non-fiction, which are all part of the interpretative analysis and creative construction of 'narrative presence'. Ursula Le Guin, therefore, not only was a prolific writer of fantasy and science fiction texts but also produced a number of non-fiction publications: short essays on different topics, interviews, book reviews and reports on reading events. These – often very short – texts are not systematic or carefully crafted statements about her approach to writing but can be interpreted as texts that connect her narrating process and create this aforementioned narrated presence. Therefore, published journal or blog entries have often been revised with the changes made visible to the readers and then published in different contexts as a collection of her thoughts.

The critic Lisa Hammond Rashley acknowledges Ursula Le Guin's non-fictional writing as 'revisioning gender' and interprets Le Guin's text 'Introducing Myself' as a pivotal feminist text determining feminist discourse. By acknowledging 'her ongoing effort to reconceptualize gender' (Rashley 2017: 22), interpreting her as performing 'affirmative action' and referencing Adrienne Rich's concept of revisioning (Le Guin 1993: 12), Le Guin is thus being defined as a political writer who challenges writing conventions and normative 'narrative presence' by continuously searching for new possibilities of human existence. Yet, even a critic as sympathetic and appreciative of Le Guin's work as Rashley does not avoid oscillating between interpreting Le Guin's reconsiderations of previously stated positions as 'an ongoing process of redefinition' (Rashley 2017: 22) and as 'changing attitudes' and 'former beliefs' (2017: 25). Lefanu in her analysis of feminism and science fiction, however, explains such contradictions as part of the flexibility of the genre, evident in Le Guin's fictional as well as non-fictional work, which establishes a more open writing style and format, allowing more freedom of expression:

> What I hope to show overall is that the plasticity of science fiction and its openness to other literary genres allow an apparent contradiction, but one

that is potentially of enormous importance to contemporary women writers: it makes possible, and encourages (despite its colonisation by male writers), the inscription of women as subjects free from the constraints of mundane fiction; and it also offers the possibility of interrogating that very inscription, questioning the basis of gendered subjectivity. (Lefanu 1989: 10)

What has been defined as an ongoing process of redefinition and reconsidering of Le Guin's position (Rashley 2017: 22) can be seen as an arrangement of 'narrative presence' throughout her oeuvre, a conscious process of contextualizing and arranging values anew in the light of new experiences and knowledge. It is not so much about a change of opinion from one text to another but a continuous development of awareness from text to text, which ends up in different texts, a process that creates transparency or makes the hidden seen, enabled by the format of the science fiction genre. By exploring different text formats, fiction and non-fiction, Le Guin explores the possibility of getting closer to 'reality'. A focus on the individual leads to an understanding of social and cultural contexts as structures enforcing discrimination and exclusion concerning female experience. By narratively exploring discovery, alternative models of the known and world-building, thus inviting readers 'to revise presumptions of plausibility' (Seed 2005: 4), 'fiction of science' highlights the complex status of human expression. According to Seed, reading science fiction is a comparative exercise establishing cross-relations of the familiar and the 'strangely new', and it is exactly this activity of comparing that is an implicit part of reading Le Guin's work over time (2005: 4).

In her book *Feminism and Science Fiction*, Lefanu has suggested that there is a specific conjunction between feminism and science fiction, and despite a strong male bias, it offers a freedom to women writers in terms of both style and content and, as a pronounced intersectional form of science and fiction, the possibility of connecting political concerns with creativity and imagination (Lefanu 1989: 2). This is highlighted by the fact that – as for example with the work of Charlotte Perkins Gilman in the nineteenth century – an implied or stated critique of the dominant male social and political system is expressed in two ways: on the one hand, through the socialist-inspired pragmatic aspects of utopian writing with an emphasis on social structure and, on the other, through the interiorization of female experience (1989: 3). Informed by the feminist, socialist and radical politics that developed during the 1960s and 1970s, science fiction – following Lefanu's argument – was challenged by the development of second-wave feminism. Women science fiction writers of the time were able to subversively, satirically and iconoclastically exploit the characteristics of science fiction to oppose dominant ideology. As Lefanu points out, established conventions of science fiction, such as time travel, alternate worlds, entropy, relativism and the search for a unified field theory, are ideally suited – both metaphorically and metonymically – to investigate gender and sexuality as social and cultural constructs, as expressions of the human organization of existence, as 'narrative presence'. Lefanu reaches the conclusion that feminist science fiction embraces the freedom from the constraints of realism to explore in various ways what it means to be constructed as female. In terms of both content and form, science fiction with its fluidity of form offers women new ways of writing. In addition, the special bond between SF writers and their readers reaffirms a more open and less hierarchical relationship which enlightens – aside of the formal object character – the process character of any 'narrative presence'. Ideas, themes and characters are borrowed, elaborated and reworked by different people in different forms. Women, from the 1970s on, could thus develop a new language and way of writing and escape the male-dominated world of ordered discourse and the declared professionalism of the writing process.

Although science fiction writing by women in the 1970s was dismissed as a fad, as passé or as unoriginal, these writers established themselves firmly in the science fiction writing community (Lefanu 1989: 8). By exploring the subversive potentialities of science fiction, Lefanu raises the question whether science fiction can, or should, reflect the experiences of women in the 'mundane' – using a science fiction term – and positions this individual dimension in the broader discussion of the role of science fiction narratives, which allow the inscription of woman as subject (1989: 9). Much like cyberpunk, mundane science fiction is a form or subgenre of science fiction that is practised by a small – though growing – number of science fiction writers (Calvin 2009: 13). When the opening statement of 'The Mundane Manifesto' declares that the authors are 'pissed off and needing a tight girdle of discipline to restrain our sf imaginative silhouettes' and asserts that many of the familiar tropes, techniques and technologies of science fiction are unrealistic and, therefore, should be avoided, they not only position sci-fi literature as a strong political, social and cultural tool for change ('the most likely future is one in which we only have ourselves and this planet') but also reflect the demands of feminist science fiction writing (Ryman et al. 2004). Although 'mundane' is often taken to mean 'banal' or 'ordinary', it also denotes 'of the world' (2004). The Manifesto offers an 'imaginative challenge' to science fiction authors to work from the standpoint that 'Earth is all we have' (Calvin 2009: 13) and that narrative resistance is necessary. Combining different ways of writing evokes possibilities for more radical reflections on the human condition: to include and centre the notion of the individual. Building on the traditional 'what if?' of the genre, the focus shifts to the 'if only' and moves the narrative to expressions of desire, declarations of intentions and ('utopian') demands for change: 'l will return to woman as subject of her story, looking at the constitution of self and other and the expression of desire' (Lefanu 1989: 9f.).

Le Guin uses the science fiction genre to explore how the format is useful to answer existential questions concerning gender and age. Therefore, she is not only central for second-wave science fiction writing, as Lefanu has pointed out, but is also important in terms of her discursive and processual writing for engaging in more general philosophical questions concerning the meaning of life.

Gender and age/ing: Embodiment as a feminist concern

In 'The Space Crone' (1976), Ursula Le Guin suggests an old woman as 'an exemplary person' to explain to friendly aliens from the fourth planet of Altair the human condition as a constant form of transformation in order for them to understand 'the nature of the race' (Le Guin 1992: 5). To clarify the concept of transformation, Le Guin compares menopausal change with the transition from virginity to womanhood. While the 'first pregnancy', the sexualization of a woman, is a step from the sacred to the profane, menopausal change, 'the third pregnancy', offers women the possibility of attaining sacred qualities and becoming a crone. This view reclaims embodiment as a basic dimension of both lived reality and 'narrative presence'. According to Le Guin, virginity and menopause as possibilities of female self-assertion independent of male relationships have no value in a world dominated by men. On the level of embodiment, these self-assertions, however, demand an interpretation in order to be understood. Both forms of female being are merely accepted as a time of preparation, on the one hand, for child bearing and, on the other, for death. Pearson and Pope in their analysis of the female hero have linked the heroic quest to the moment of birth, or more precisely of rebirth:

> In fact, disorientation is an inherent part of any transition from the known to the unknown, and the heroic descent into the primal chaos is a necessary prerequisite to the moment of rebirth. Bereft of the conventional truths that have given life meaning and order, the hero descends to the primal chaos of unexplained reality which is followed by a rebirth in which she sees the world in a new way. (Pearson and Pope 1981: 82)

Le Guin's use of the metaphor of birth – very intentionally echoing the physical and embodied meaning and transplanting it into different phases of our lives – provides a more radical, provocative and also extraordinary image of what it means to age. By linking the process of ageing – a physical as well as spiritual process – to pregnancy, the abstract metaphor of 'rebirth' becomes sterile and immaterial. Although the term 'birth' has the potential to hold more violent physical images, which Pearson and Pope choose to ignore, Le Guin's term 'pregnancy' emphasizes the bodily aspect of change and as a metaphor expresses a powerful, painful and very physical experience and reminds us of the fact that a woman's body after pregnancy and birth is radically changed:

> The woman who is willing to make that change must become pregnant with herself, at last. She must bear herself, her third self, her old age, with travail and alone. ... That pregnancy is long, that labor is hard. Only one is harder, and that's the final one, the one that men also must suffer and perform. (Le Guin 1992: 5)

By 'becoming pregnant with oneself', the creative act of defining oneself develops into a procreative one – of creating a 'presence' – where the body becomes decisive. As Pearson and Pope's approach shows, birth can be harmonized only when ignoring the bodily aspects. A similar 'paradox' is central to age and ageing:

> Aging, like illness and death, reveals the most fundamental conflict of the human condition: the tension between infinite ambitions, dreams, and desires on the one hand, and vulnerable, limited, decaying physical existence on the other – between the self and the body. This paradox cannot be eradicated by the wonders of modern medicine or by positive attitudes toward growing old. (Cole 1986: 5)

Focusing on the fact that 'the labor is hard', Le Guin acknowledges the difficulties of the third pregnancy, as she recognizes the value of the embodied experience of ageing. Le Guin's metaphor overcomes this paradox, the tension between the self and the body, by insisting upon the embodied as well as the psychological and cultural experiences of ageing. Sontag's (1972) notion that gender and age can only be understood together as a narrative ('social judgement' and 'imagination') that restricts women resonates with Le Guin's emphasis on the female embodied experience of pregnancy as a metaphor for living a life over time. Prominent second-wave feminists have also used metaphors of sexuality, pregnancy and birth to express the associations young-male and old-woman of our embodied existence (Maierhofer 2003: 155ff.). Ursula Le Guin offers a new way of imagining the 'human condition' with its existential challenges of gender and age as 'the incredible realities of our existence' with the revolutionary potential to move beyond the patriarchal paradigm of human development. This potential emerges out of the 'incredible realities', which are 'incredible' because of their constitution as human-world-interconnectedness as a '(human) presence (reality)'. As Carolyn Heilbrun has pointed out in her book *Writing a Woman's Life*, 'It is perhaps only in old age … that women can stop being female impersonators, can grasp the opportunity to reverse their most cherished principles of "femininity"' (1988: 126).

From a feminist point of view, old age allows a recognition of the specificity of gendered aging, of what it means to be old and woman at the same time. Acknowledging these restrictions, ageing offers women the possibility to move beyond accepted social positions.

Embodied gender identity as 'narrative presence'

Within science fiction, the human body as such and the possibility of radical material transformation – in shape, size or any other form – have long been the site of cultural negotiations. Ursula Le Guin's playing with possibilities can be seen not only in the wealth of her fictional work but also very impressively in short theoretical essays such as 'Introducing Myself' (Le Guin 2004: 11–14) that – despite their brevity – not only help to interpret and understand her fictional writing but also allow for a comprehension of Le Guin's approach to the 'narrative presence' of gender and age. Le Guin's self-description evokes this power:

> I am a man. Now you may think I've made some kind of silly mistake about gender, or maybe that I'm trying to fool you, because my first name ends in a, and I own three bras, and I've been pregnant five times, and other things like that that you might have noticed, little details. But details don't matter. If we have anything to learn about politicians it's that details don't matter. I am a man, and I want you to believe and accept this as a fact, just as I did for many years. (Le Guin 2004: 3)

Her reflections on her own efforts to be a man to fulfil the socially dominant 'narrative presence' lead to a desperate conclusion:

> And it is all my own fault. I get born before they invented women, and I live and I live all these decades trying so hard to be a good man that I forget all about staying young, and so I didn't. And my tenses get all mixed up. I just am young

and then all of a sudden I was sixty. There must have been something that a real man could have done about it. Something short of guns, but more effective than Oil of Olay. But I failed. I did nothing. I absolutely failed to stay young. (Le Guin 2004: 4)

Whereas in her earlier essay 'The Space Crone,' Ursula Le Guin defines being a woman in terms of embodied change by describing the transition from virginity to womanhood as empowerment, she playfully refers to herself in 'Introducing Myself' as a man exploiting – in Nicholls's terms – 'linguistic possibilities' in the context of science fiction as 'the great modern literature of metaphor' (1976: 179–82). By the simple statement of 'I am a man' and toying with the incredulity of the audience, she uses a metaphor as a form of 'transport,' substituting terms, moving us readers to imaginary locations, creating new associations and combinations (Botting 2005: 112).

In her essay 'Rehearsing Age' (2016), Elinor Fuchs relates the experience of ageing – as an acknowledgement of its revolutionary potential – to Brecht's theory of estrangement (*Verfremdungseffekt*), when she views the human condition of old people as feeling estranged and excluded from the familiar:

> I considered: Was this what it meant to grow old? Do we become 'old' when the familiar world around us has changed beyond recognition, when people are gone and places have changed and social organization is transformed – and then we die? Was this Brecht's *Verfremdungseffekt* of life? Maybe the *V-effekt* was not just a theatrical method to awaken spectators to their true political situation, but a kind of socio-biological law of nature? (Fuchs 2016: 144)

Whereas Fuchs concentrates on a threatening reality of the here and now, both in her fictional and non-fictional work, Le Guin offers a playful interpretation of different categorizations of intersectionality by providing imaginative worlds that transcend the female/male and old/young dichotomy. Le Guin's use of speculative fiction provides a new way of thinking about a gendered life course and the possibilities of imagining living and growing old in creative ways which are advanced and arranged within the 'narrative presence' of her writing. Growing old can then be re-evaluated as an act of imagination, a telling of a different story, a constant negotiation between continuity and change that demands imaginative creativity and – to use Le Guin's term pretence (Le Guin 2004: 4). On the one hand, the concept of gender and the dichotomization of the sexes are challenged by age; on the other hand, we can recognize how strongly these concepts define our social roles and create boundaries and limitations. Dissolving gender, age and other polarities by interpreting narratives and texts can create an understanding (or should I say feeling) of existing material realities not as a given and stable, but as subject to time and space and explored as a varied 'narrative presence' of the human condition.

Conclusion

The discussion of identity is often a discussion of both the possibilities and the restrictions of the individual through social structures and the necessity to express this search for the self within the social context as a narrative of both success and failure. Ambivalence goes hand-in-hand with estrangement, as the discrepancies revealed lead to an awareness of the restrictions of the status quo. Playing with possibilities leads to an awareness and thus to an articulation of the 'narrative presence' of the human condition with the ageing process embedded, which Le Guin expresses as a radical thought by a simple statement: 'If I'm not good at pretending to be a man and not good at being young, I might just as well start pretending that I am an old woman. I am not sure that anybody has invented old women yet; but it might be worth trying' (Le Guin 2004: 4).

In more general terms, Le Guin's texts explore 'the incredible realities of our existence' as a 'narrative presence'. The imagining of different worlds allows us as readers to understand the matrix of time and experience in their interconnectedness as articulated interpretations of our own impermanence. Following Simone de Beauvoir's notion of old age as the 'unrealizable' (1972: 324) which can be understood only through an act of imaginative identification, feminist interpretations of science fiction, such as Le Guin's, are challenges to 'master narratives', creating new ways of negotiating the world and deconstructing conventional epistemologies. Science fiction and fantasy play with possibilities; the genres imagine possible 'narrative presence' by creating worlds not yet 'imagined' – sometimes reaffirming in different settings and contexts values of the status quo, sometimes as affirmations of subversion transcending the accepted and established understanding of the social, political and cultural order.

References

Botting, F. (2005), '"Monsters of the Imagination": Gothic, Science, Fiction', in D. Seed (ed.), *A Companion to Science Fiction*, Blackwell Companions to Literature and Culture, 111–26, Malden: Blackwell.

Calvin, R. (2009), 'Feature: 101: Mundane SF 101', *SFRA Review*, 289: 13–16.
Cole, T. R., and S. Gadow (1986), *What Does It Mean to Grow Old? Reflections from the Humanities*, Durham: Duke University Press.
De Beauvoir, S. (1972), *The Coming of Age*, New York: Putnam's Sons.
Fuchs, E. (2016), 'Rehearsing Age', *Modern Drama*, 59: 143–54.
Gullette, M. M. (2004), *Aged by Culture*, Chicago: University of Chicago Press.
Heilbrun, C. G. (1988), *Writing a Woman's Life*, New York: Norton.
Lefanu, S. (1989), *Feminism and Science Fiction*, Bloomington: Indiana University Press.
Le Guin, U. (1992), *Dancing at the Edge of the World. Thoughts on Words, Women, Places*, London: Paladin.
Le Guin, U. (1993), *Earthsea Revisioned*. Cambridge: Greenbay.
Le Guin, U. (2004), *The Wave in the Mind: Talks and Essays on the Writer, the Reader, and the Imagination*, Boston: Shambhala.
Le Guin, U. (2019), *The Last Interview and Other Conversations*, ed. D. Streitfeld, Brooklyn, London: Melville House.
Maierhofer, R. (2003), *Salty Old Women: Frauen, Alter und Identität in der amerikanischen Literatur*, Essen: Die Blaue Eule.
Maierhofer, R. (2004), 'The Old Woman as Prototypical American', in W. Hölbling and K. Rieser (eds), *What Is American? New Identities in U.S. Culture*, 319–36, Münster: LIT.
Maierhofer, R. (2007), 'BottinDer gefährliche Aufbruch zum Selbst: Frauen, Altern und Identität in der amerikanischen Kultur. Eine anokritische Einführung', in U. Pasero, G. M. Backes and K. R. Schroeter (eds), *Altern in Gesellschaft: Ageing – Diversity – Inclusion*, 111–27, Wiesbaden: VS Verlag für Sozialwissenschaften.
National Book Foundation (2014), 'Ursula K. Le Guin Accepts a Lifetime Achievement Award from National Book Foundation'. Available online: https://www.nationalbook.org/videos/ursula-k-le-guin-receives-the-medal-for-distinguished-contribution-to-american-letters-from-neil-gaiman-at-the-2014-national-book-awards/ (accessed 28 January 2022).
Nicholls, P. (1976), 'Science Fiction: The Monsters and the Critics', in P. Nicholls (ed.), *Science Fiction at Large*, 159–83, London: Gollancz.
Pearson, C., and K. Pope (1981), *The Female Hero in American and British Literature*, New York: Bowker.
Rashley, L. (2007), 'Revisioning Gender: Inventing Women in Ursula K. Le Guin's Nonfiction', *Biography*, 30(1): 22–47. Available online: http://www.jstor.org/stable/23540596 (accessed 28 January 2022).
Rich, A. (1972), 'When We Dead Awaken: Writing as Re-vision', *College English*, 34(1): 18–30. doi:10.2307/375215.
Russ, J. (1983), *How to Suppress Women's Writing*, Austin: University of Texas Press.
Ryman, G., et al. (2004), 'The Mundane Manifesto', *SFGenics: Notes on Science, Fiction, and Science Fiction* (4 July 2013). Available online: https://sfgenics.wordpr

ess.com/2013/07/04/geoff-ryman-et-al-the-mundane-manifesto/ (accessed 28 January 2022).

Seed, D. (2005), 'Introduction: Approaching Science Fiction', in D. Seed (ed.), *A Companion to Science Fiction*, Blackwell Companions to Literature and Culture, 1–7, Malden: Blackwell.

Sontag, S. (1972), 'The Double Standard of Aging', *Saturday Review of the Society*, September 23, 29–38.

Spruck Wrigley, S. (2019), 'Space Ageing: Where Are the Galactic Grandmas? The Lack of Older Women in Sci-fi Novels Reflects and Reifies Ageism and Sexism', *Nature*, 575: 586–7.

Suvin D. (1979), *Metamorphoses of Science Fiction: On the Poetics and History of a Literary Genre*, Ralahine Utopian Studies, Oxford: Peter Lang.

Woodward, K. M. (1999), 'Introduction', in K. M. Woodward (ed.), *Figuring Age. Women, Bodies, Generations*, ix–xxix, Bloomington: Indiana University Press.

Wray, J. (2013), 'Ursula K. Le Guin, the Art of Fiction 221', *Paris Review*, 206. Available online: https://www.theparisreview.org/interviews/6253/the-art-of-fiction-no-221-ursula-k-le-guin (accessed 28 January 2022).

Index

Note: endnotes are indicated by the page number followed by 'n.' and the endnote number, e.g. 20 n.1 refers to endnote 1 on page 20.

Achenbaum, W.A. 191 n.2
Adiseshiah, S. 2
Agamben, Giorgio 5, 82
ageing 87, 195
   age and 6, 30, 221
   and age-based extinction 115
   anachronism 199–201
   anxieties about 23
   in children 37
   in contemporary European dystopian literature 93
   cure for 173
   and de-ageing 30–2, 41
   and death 11–12, 15
   and gaze 197
   and gender 58
   human 2
   living and 29
   in narratives of longevity 54–6
   nonhuman 2
   photographing 17
   politics of 75
   progress and 137
   rapid population 38, 94, 95, 101, 109
   reverse 39, 41
   in science fiction 35
   studies 2, 6
   and youthing 29, 40
ageism
   definition of 110 n.1
   demographic change and 94–6
The Agony of Power (book) 190
Aldiss, Brian 140
Allen, Paul 142
Almereyda, Michael 160, 170 n.2
Altered Carbon (TV series) 38, 88 n.5
anachronism 4, 195, 199–201
   generational disorder and 58–64

Andrews, G. 2
anocriticism 214–15
anti-ageing techniques 2, 13, 54
antihumanism 135
   absence of queer ecology 149–152
   nature and culture 146–9
anti-transhumanist campaign 19
Arc of a Scythe series 49
Ariés, Philippe 189
Aristotle 118
As You Like It (play) 38
Asimov, Isaac 115, 137
Atwood, Margaret 3, 104, 109, 195, 197, 199, 201, 202, 203
Avicenna 11
Ayalon, L. 95

'baby boomers' 52, 108, 119, 124–5, 128, 129
Bacon, Francis 11, 24 n.4
Banerjee, M. 31
Barad, Karen 31
Barber, Marilyn 206
Basting, Anne Davis 160
Battlestar Galactica (TV series) 44 n.6
Baudrillard, Jean 190
Bauman, Zygmunt 10, 82
Berenger, King 10
Bernard Williams's hypothesis 16, 20
Bessant, Walter 13, 15
'Bio-Actuarial Dyna-Metric Age Predicator (BADMAP)' 130
biocapitalism 71–3, 74, 78, 87
biodystopias 73, 79, 84, 87
bioexploitation dystopia 84
biological slaves 71
biopolitics 6, 72–3, 87, 115–19, 123, 131, 132, 177
   negotiations of power 72

biopower 4, 5, 72, 73, 87, 117
Black Mirror series 6, 38, 174
Black, Russell 25 n.14
Blackford, R. 20
Blade Runner (Dir. Ridley Scott) 37
Blaikie, A. 186
body 72–3, 75–6, 100, 179, 180,
    198, 221–2
  cloning and nanotechnology 15, 20
  enhancement 14
  and mind dualism 54, 57, 144, 149
  swapping 30
Bonnard, Pierre 203
Boomsday (book) 5, 115, 116, 132 n.1
  and 'voluntary transitioning' 123–131
The Book of Joan (book) 6, 135, 141, 149
Bostrom, Nick 12, 24 n.6, 141
Botelho, Teresa 5, 10, 12, 16, 20
Botting, F. 223
Bould, Mark 3
Bradbury, Ray 157
Brand, Mark R. 2, 54, 55
Brantley, Ben 158
Brewster, Shelby 159, 160, 167
Bristow, Jennie 52, 53
Britannula 110 n.3, 117
Brogden, Mike 97
Brooker, C. 187, 188
Buckley, Christopher 5, 123–131
Butler, Judith 5, 74, 82
Butler, Octavia E. 74, 82, 138
Butler, Robert 110 n.1

Calvin, R. 219
Campanella, T. 102
Čapek, Karel 165
Caprica (TV series) 38
care 6, 30, 107, 130, 157, 163, 175–9, 180
  and ageing 177–8
  and generationalism 4
Carlson, Marvin 155
  'ghosting' 155
Carnes, Bruce A. 10, 11, 24 n.3
Cave, Stephen 10
Charise, Andrea 97, 116–17
Charlwood, C. 81
Chen, T. 17
Child's Play (Dir. Tom Holland) 197
Childhood's End (book) 137, 140, 145
The Children of Men (book) 151

Chivers, Sally 44 n.6, 178, 195
Christian, Brian 157, 158, 166
Christie, Agatha 108
Chu, Seo-Young 139
Chuckies 196–7, 199, 201, 206, 209
CIEL 135, 143–5, 151
Clark, S.R.L. 4, 12, 13, 14
Clarke, Arthur C. 137, 140, 145
Cocoon (Dir. Ron Howard) 40
Coeckelbergh, Mark 168
Coggan, D. 202
Cohen, S. 80
Cole, Sara 139
Cooper, M. 88 n.2
Crawford, Richard 208
'creative euthanasia' 108
'crisis of care' 173
  and silvering screen 175–9
Crossley, Robert 140
Cuddy, Amy J.C. 95
cure for ageing 15, 38, 60, 61, 173
A Cure for Wellness (Dir. Verbinski, Gore) 173

D'Eramo, Luce 94, 101
Dante's *Inferno* (poem) 110 n.6
Daraiseh, I. 174, 186, 187
Davis, Mackenzie 188
DeFalco, A. 156, 162, 164
Degnen, C. 99
Delany, Samuel R. 138
Demerjian, MacKay 93
dementia 155–160
demodystopia 2, 5, 98, 110 n.2, 195
Dick, Philip K. 137
digital cloning 173–189
Dinerstein, Joel 14
'discardable bodies' 4, 5
  in dystopia 71–87
diversity 3, 95, 168
Doctor Who series 33
Doctorow, Cory 15, 17, 20, 24
Dolan, Josephine 32, 33, 43 n.3, 44 n.6
Domingo, Andreu 2, 94, 110 n.2, 195
Domingo, Colman 162
Down and Out in the Magic Kingdom (book) 15, 20, 23
Drage, E. 174, 183, 188
Duff, C. 2
Dunford, Christine Mary 162, 163

dystopia 3, 5, 54–8, 63, 93, 103, 109, 123, 131–2, 173–4, 187–8, 195
  ageing studies in 93–109, 195, 197–9
  anachronism 199–201
  anti-human and anti-social grounding 19
  bioexploitation 84
  conservatism 67
  demographic change and ageism 94–6
  discardable bodies in 71–83
  European literature 93–106
  film adaptation 204–9
  geronticide 96–8
  Harvest (play) 75
  intertexts 201–4
  literature 66
  longevity and 65
  narratives 195–7
  novels 93–4, 98, 116, 139, 151
  perception in 195
  science fiction 3
  speculative narratives of 59
  The Unit (book) 83–8, 103–6
  about value of human life 103–6
  see also utopia

ecology 135, 149–153
Edelman, Lee 53, 60, 63–4, 151, 200
Edmunds, June 52
Ehlers, N. 88 n.1
Ehrlich, Paul R. 110 n.2
The Electric Grandmother (Television movie) 157
Emanuel, Ezekiel 191 n.3
end-of-life care
  in 'San Junipero' 173–7, 182
Erickson, Steve 170 n.2
Erll, Astrid 51, 52
Esposito, Roberto 5, 82
Eternity Express (book) 94, 98, 106, 108, 115
euthanasia 42, 56, 97–8, 108, 122, 125
  as digital cloning 179–185
Evander, Duke 118
The Expanse (TV series) 34

Falcus, Sarah 2, 3, 58, 98, 109, 200
familial generations 53, 59, 60, 61
fantasy 3, 9, 17, 18, 44 n.5, 75, 77, 105, 183, 213, 224

Farrell, John 56, 57, 59, 60–1, 65
'fascist transhumanism' 19
fatalistic approach 11, 13
The Father (Dir. Zeller, Florian) 173
feminism 35, 217, 218
Ferreira, Aline 5
fertility 103, 195
Fiske, Susan T. 95
The Fixed Period (book) 98, 115, 116, 118–19, 120, 128
Flynn, K.M. 88 n.5
Follows, Stephen 34
Foucault, Michel 72, 84, 88 n.6, 132 n.3, 173
Fraser, Nancy 173, 175
Freeman, Elizabeth 151, 152
Freud, Sigmund 155–6, 158, 167
From the Land of the Moon (Dir. Nicole Garcia) 191 n.1
Frow, J. 3, 75
Fuchs, Elinor 160, 223
Fuller, S. 17
Futurama series 38

gender 2, 5, 6, 31, 33–5, 72, 104, 150–2, 176, 185, 197–8, 202, 204, 213–14
  and age/ing 220
  embodiment as feminist concern 220-2
  identity as 'narrative presence' 222–4
generation 1, 2, 35, 49, 94, 100, 101, 107–8, 119, 124, 128, 188, 200
  disorder and anachronism 58–64
  time and identity 51–3
generational order 61–2, 63, 67
'generationalism' 4, 6, 35, 51, 53, 60, 64, 66–8
generationality 52, 68
  and collectivity 64–7
  and generational identity 52
George, M. 157, 170
geronticide 5, 84, 96–8, 106, 109, 115, 117–18
Gershwin, George 207–8
Gibson, William 138
Gilhooly, M. 99
Gilleard, Chris 35, 36, 95, 178, 179, 185, 188–9
Gillespie, K.A. 73
Gillis, W. 20
Gilman, Charlotte Perkins 218
Giroux, H.A. 73

The Giver (Dir. Lowry, Lois) 115
Gli Scaduti (short story) 94, 98, 101, 108
Goggin, Peter 5
Goldman, Marlene 156, 160, 195, 204
Gone with the Wind (book) 201–3
Gordin, M.D. 185
Gray, John 141, 144
Grenier, Amanda 36, 170 n.5
de Grey, A. 25 n.19
Gruner, O.C. 11
Gullette, Margaret Morganroth 2, 10, 39, 53, 54, 59, 89 n.14, 96, 195, 214
Gulliver's Travels (book) 11, 49, 126

Hall, G. Stanley 97
The Handmaid's Tale (book) 65, 104
Harari, Yuval Noah 94, 142
Harrison, Jordan 6, 156–7, 158, 159, 161, 163, 164, 165, 166, 167, 168, 169, 170
Hartung, H. 2, 97
Harvest (play) 5, 71, 75–9, 83, 86
Hassler, D.M. 9
Hayles, Katherine 143, 150
Heilbrun, Carolyn 222
Heterotopias 186
Heywood, Thomas 117, 118
Hickey, T. 110 n.7
Higgs, Paul 35, 36, 95, 185, 188–9
historicity and formalism 3, 152
Holmqvist, Ninni 5, 71, 76, 84, 85–6, 94, 106
Holy Fire (book) 15, 17
Hooper, Michael 6
Hotel Splendide (Dir. Terence Gross) 191 n.1
Hughes, James 17, 20
Hutchinson–Gilford syndrome 37
Huters, T. 4

I Care a Lot (Dir. J. Blakeson) 173
I, Daniel Blake (Dir. Ken Loach) 173
immortality 1, 2, 5, 9, 10, 11, 14–23, 38, 55, 71, 78, 151, 180, 201
In Time (Dir. Niccol, Andrew) 49, 56, 57, 62, 64, 67
The Inner House (book) 12, 15
Intertexts 57, 201–3
Inventing Tomorrow: H. G. Wells and the Twentieth Century (book) 138–9
Ionesco, Eugene 10

The Irishman (Dir. Martin Scorsese) 41–2
Isaacson, N. 4
Ishiguro, Kazuo 5, 71, 76, 79–83, 85, 86, 89 n.9, 104, 166
Istvan, Zoltan 17, 18, 25 n.11, 142, 145

James, P.D. 151
Jameson, Frederic 50, 51, 56, 136, 143, 187
Johnson, George Clayton 5, 98, 115–19, 123
Jones, A. 187, 188

Kant, Immanuel 140
Karasik, R.J. 40
Karmakar, M. 83
Kasun, J. 132–3 n.6
Katz, Stephen 2, 55, 57
Kauffman, A. 157, 158, 166
Kelly, R.T. 78
Knowles, E. 208
Kriebernegg, Ulla 2, 5, 195, 202
Krupar, S. 88 n.1
Księżopolska, I. 3
Kubrick, Stanley 37, 141

Laslett, Peter 35
Last and First Men (book) 140, 145
Le Guin, Ursula K. 6, 138, 213–224
Lebow, Richard 50, 54
Leeming, D. 201
Lefanu, S. 218–19, 220
Levin, Ira 115
Liddy, S. 189
life course 2, 5, 49, 51, 55, 59, 79, 195, 200, 209
Logan's Run (Dir. Michael Anderson) 5, 38, 42, 98, 115, 116
  population and age-based extinction in 119–123
Lonergan, Kenneth 163
longevity 1, 4, 5, 11, 12, 13–14, 31, 50–1, 54, 61, 62, 65
  age and ageing in 54–8
  ageing and generation in 49
  and immortality 15, 19, 24, 31
  and rejuvenation 23
Looper (Dir. Rian Johnson) 37
Lopez, P.J. 73
Lovelock, J. 141
Lowell 139

Lowry, Lois 115
Luckhurst, R. 3

Magary, Drew 49, 50, 60
Maierhofer, Roberta 6, 214, 215, 221
de Man, Jean 135–6, 144–6, 149, 151, 152
Mangum, Teresa 1, 2, 16–17, 49, 51, 54, 56, 78
Mann, Thomas 174
Mannheim, Karl 51–2
Mantegazza, P. 108
Marjorie Prime (play) 6, 165–9
  dementia 155–160
  haunted mind 6, 160–4
  nonhuman in 155–160
Marshall, Barbara 2, 55, 57
Marshall, Leni 2
Marvel series 32
Mason, P. 141
Massinger, Philip 115–16
Masten, Jeffrey 132 n.4
Matthews, S. 81
McDaniel, Hattie 202
McEwan, Ian 3, 166
McKee, Philip 204, 209
McLean, Helen 164, 170 n.4
McNulty, Charles 158
McQueen, S. 72
memory 13, 25 n.17, 38, 119, 155–7, 159, 163–4, 167, 169, 170, 198
'memory technics' 167
Metamorphoses (poem by Ovid) 10
'Methuselah Syndrome' 37
Middleton, Thomas 94, 98, 115, 117, 118, 127, 131, 132 n.4
Mills, C. 179, 180, 191 n.4
Mirren, Helen 33
Mitchell, Margaret 168, 201, 202
A Modern Utopia (book) 138, 140, 145
Moni, S. 75
Moon, Chaney 122
Moore, Hugh 120
Moore, S. 132 n.6
More, Thomas 191 n.3
Mori, Masahiro 156, 166
'The Mortal Immortal' (short story) 12
mortality 9, 14, 15, 38, 40, 50, 61, 64, 81, 142
'mortality paradox' 10
Morton, Timothy 148, 150

Moylan, Tom 103, 109, 138
Musa, M. 110 n.6

'narrative presence' of gender and age 6, 213–224
Nayar, P.K. 89 n.12
Neilson, B. 74, 88 n.8
Nelson, T.D. 95
Never Let Me Go (book) 5, 71, 74, 76, 79, 81–6, 104
Niccol, Andrew 49, 56
Noble, L. 83
Nolan, William F. 98, 115–122, 131
Noys, Benjamin 188
Nussbaum, Martha 10

O'Connell, Mark 142, 144
Ojakangas, Mika 117, 118
old age 2, 5, 15, 23, 30, 33, 35, 37–8, 41, 72, 81, 87, 95, 100, 116, 122, 131–2, 173, 179, 186, 196, 198, 200
Olshansky, S. Jay 10, 11, 24 n.3
Orczy, Baroness 203
organ donation 81–2, 85, 87, 104, 105
Oró-Piqueras, M. 3
Orquiola, John 43
Orwell, George 102
Owram, Doug 119
Oziewicz, M. 44 n.5

Padmanabhan, Manjula 5, 71
Parker, Alan 191 n.1
Parui, A. 83
Paul, N.W. 31
Payne, Gideon 128–9, 131
Pearson, C. 220, 221
Penny, Laurie 49, 55, 62, 67
Phiddian, R. 133 n.10
Phillips, Susan B. 173
Picard series 29, 30, 42
Picard, Jean-Luc 29, 42
Piercy, Marge 138
Pilcher, Jane 52
'planetary subjectivity' 139, 140, 142
Plato 116, 118
Pogońska-Baranowska, Aleksandra 5
Pope, K. 220, 221
population ageing 74, 87, 94, 95, 97, 109
populism and literary value 3
Porgy and Bess (opera) 207, 208–9

Port, Cynthia 2, 152
Posner, R.A. 97
Post, S.G. 97
The Postmortal (book) 49, 56, 57, 59, 60, 65, 67
posthuman ageing 2
posthumanism 137, 150
post-scarcity economics 25 n.10
Prisco, G. 25 n.14
prolongevity 11
promethean curse 38–42

queer ecology 135, 149–153
queer utopia, spaces of 185–9

Ranisch, R. 74
Rao, Mohan 132 n.4
Rashley, Lisa Hammond 217
Ravera, Lidia 94, 98–9, 100, 101, 102
Red Dwarf (TV series) 38
Reeves, Nancee 98
rejuvenation 2, 4, 10, 12, 15, 23, 71
    and immortality 2
    narratives 1, 10
'rejuvenescence narratives' 54, 78
Renzi, Matteo 100
'reproductive futurism' 151, 200, 206
Rich, Adrienne 217
Rizzini, Marianna 101
The Road to Wellville (Dir. Parker, Alan) 191 n.1
Roberts, A. 3
Robinson, Kim Stanley 138, 140
Roduit, Johann A.R. 56
Rogers, J. 88 n.5
Rogue One (Dir. Gareth Edwards) 32
Rose, N. 74, 86
Rowley, William 117, 118
RUR (play) 165
Russ, Joanna 138, 216
Russell, E. 89 n.10
Russo, Mary 59, 200
Ryman, G. 219

'San Junipero'
    episode of *Black Mirror* 173–189
'Sanctuary' 123, 133 n.7
Savran, D. 169
The Scarlet Pimpernel (book) 202–3
Scheper-Hughes, N. 75, 78, 81

Schotland, Sara D. 2, 84, 98
Schwarzbaum 12, 15
science fiction (SF) 1, 3–5, 9, 14, 23, 29, 30–2, 35, 43, 116, 118, 136, 159, 213–14, 216–220
    age and gender in 33
    and imaginary of 'fourth age' 35–8
    progress and ageing 137–141
    rhetorical view of 30–1, 97, 144
Scythe series 49
Searle, R. 17, 19
Seed, D. 218
Seeger, Sean 3, 6, 135
Selig, S. 110 n.7
Selznik, David O. 202
Shakespeare, W. 38
Sharkey, Noel 170 n.5
Shaw, George Bernard 97
Sheldon, R. 53
Shelley, Mary 9, 12
Shteyngart, Gary 49, 55, 57, 65, 67
Shusterman, Neal 49, 89 n.9
Silverberg, R. 88 n.5
The Simpsons (TV series) 43 n.2
Snaith, H. 2, 198, 201
Solo (Dir. Ron Howard) 32, 33
Song, M. 4
Sontag, S. 104, 160, 221
Sorgner, Lorenz 74
Sorrentino, Paolo 173
Spackman, B. 173
speculative fiction 1, 3, 17, 32, 44 n.4, 98, 125, 132 n.1, 195, 223
Spielberg, Steven 205
Stapledon, Olaf 137, 139–140, 145
Star Trek (TV series) 30, 32, 34, 35, 38, 43 n.2
Star Wars series 31–3, 44 n.6
Stargate SG1 (TV series) 37, 40
Sterling, Bruce 15
Still Alice (book) 162, 163
Stoic philosophy 11
Stone Mattress (book) 195, 201
Stross, Charles 15
subgenre 3, 6, 32, 44 n.5, 49
Sunder Rajan 73
Suparno, B. 4
Super Sad True Love Story (book) 49, 55, 57, 61–2, 65–6
Supernova (Dir. Harry Macqueen) 191 n.5

Suvin, Darko 3, 49, 57, 214
Sweeting, H. 99
Swift, Jonathan 11, 126, 133 n.9

Taoist philosophy 11
'technological fetishism' 18
technological utopianism 5
Theis, Mary E. 122
Thiel, Peter 142
Thomas, P.L. 3
Thornber, K.L. 191 n.3
Tolan, F. 209, 210 n.1
Tomlinson, T. 110 n.7
Torching the Dusties (Dir. M. Goldman and P. McKee) 195, 198, 204
transhumanism 18, 19, 24 n.6, 74, 135, 150, 183
  materiality and stagnation 141–6
The Transhumanist Wager (book) 17
Three Laws of Transhumanism 18
Trollope, Anthony 94, 98, 115–16, 118–19, 124
Truong, Jean-Michel 94, 106, 107, 108, 115
Turkle, Sherry 165
Turner, Bryan S. 52
2001: A Space Odyssey (Dir. Kubrick, Stanley) 37, 137, 141

The Unit (book) 5, 71, 74, 83–6, 94, 98, 103–6
Unwind (book) 89 n.9
Ureczky, Ezster 6, 191 n.1
utopia 3, 15, 19, 20, 54–5, 71, 102, 137, 173, 185–9
  ageing 14, 19, 21, 55, 71, 102, 140, 185–9
  see also dystopia
Utopia (book) 3, 102, 191 n.3

Vermeulen, N. 89 n.15
Vernon, J.A. 33–4
Vincent, John A. 54
Vint, Sherryl 3, 23
'voluntary transitioning' 124–132
Vora, K. 88 n.3

Wagner, E. 196
Wagner, R. 208
Walkaway (book) 17, 20
'war generation' 51
Wasson, S. 88 n.7, 89 n.11
Watkins, Susan 6, 200
The Waverly Gallery (play) 163
Wells, H.G. 77, 138, 141
Westfahl, Gary 139
Wilde, Oscar 57
Williams, B. 16, 20
Willmetts, Simon 55
Wittkowsky, G. 133 n.10
Wolfe, Cary 143, 150
women action heroes 33–4
Woodward, Kathleen 29, 198
Wrigley, Sylvia Spruck 213
Wyndham, John 197

Yeung, V. 81
Yoke, C.B. 9, 49
Youth (Dir. Paolo Sorrentino) 173
youthing 29, 31, 35
  and immortality 38
Yuknavitch, Lidia 6
  The Book of Joan 135–148

Zamyatin, Y. 102

www.ingramcontent.com/pod-product-compliance
Lightning Source LLC
Chambersburg PA
CBHW062143300426
44115CB00012BA/2023